Masters of Men

Rory McIlroy, Ken Venturi ... and Their Epic Journey from Augusta to Bethesda

LIAM HAYES

First published in Great Britain in 2013 by Arena Sport,
an imprint of Birlinn Ltd
West Newington House
10 Newington Road
Edinburgh
EH9 1QS

www.arenasportbooks.co.uk

ISBN: 978 1 909715 09 7
eBook ISBN: 9780 85790 693 9

British Library Cataloguing-in-Publication Data
A catalogue record for this book is available on request from the British Library

Typeset by FMG using Atomik ePublisher from Easypress
Printed in Sweden by ScandBook

Contents

PROLOGUE

Greg: and other grown men who have choked over a three-footer

'Choking is surreal to observe because it often involves a world-class performer, someone who has spent a lifetime honing his skills and touch, suddenly looking like a novice, his highly refined technique is replaced by a curious mixture of twitching and lethargy; his demeanour is overhauled with confusion; his complex motor skills, built up over thousands of hours of practice, seem to vanish into the ether.'

– **Matthew Syed,** *Bounce: The Myth of Talent and the Power of Practice*

Arnold Palmer needed only a par on the 72nd hole at Augusta National to win the 1961 Masters title. He had already struck what seemed a perfect approach shot and, briefly, Palmer suitably responded to the cheers of the crowd as he walked the final fairway to the 18th green. However, when finding his ball in a greenside bunker, everything changed for quite possibly the greatest bare-knuckled golfer in the rich history of the game. Arnie would overshoot the green from the sand. As it happened, he would eventually record a double bogey for the tournament's 72nd hole. And Arnold

Palmer would hand over the green jacket to the tidiest competitor in the world, South Africa's Gary Player, by one shot.

Augusta National, more than any other golf course ever built, has encouraged a great many outstanding men to flounder on a Sunday afternoon, and helplessly find their tightly packaged golf games come undone. Some of them have been true greats of the game. Some have choked spectacularly and without much warning, some more dramatically than Arnie, whilst others have been just plain sad in their hasty demise in East Georgia.

In 1979, Ed Sneed reached the 16th with a three-shot lead, but bogeyed the hole, also dropped shots at the 17th and 18th, and handed his ticket to glory over to Fuzzy Zoeller. In the 1980 Masters, Tom Weiskopf tried five times, from the same spot, to clear the water at the 12th hole with a seven-iron, before finally holing out for a 13. In 1985, Curtis Strange had the competition in the palm of his hand, but on the two par-fives, the 13th and 15th, which offer such hope on the back nine, he twice sought the green in two shots and twice ended up in water. In 1989, Scott Hoch blew putts from four feet and three feet, on the 17th and on the second play-off hole, and allowed Nick Faldo to slip through and win the green jacket. In 2003, Jeff Maggert was the leader after 54 holes and he played exceedingly well on the final day, carding five birdies and 11 pars, but he triple-bogeyed the par-four third hole, and took eight shots on that now notorious par-three 12th, forfeiting his chance of winning a first major. In 2009, Kenny Perry needed only to par the last two holes for victory, but bogeyed each and lost his play-off to Angel Cabrera.

But nobody, absolutely nobody, has ever imploded at Augusta National as spectacularly as the Great White Shark, Australia's blond, blue-eyed, big-shouldered hero, Greg Norman, who literally fell to his knees on the 15th hole as he closed out his final round in 1996 and offered up his putter to apparently vengeful gods, as he lost a six-shot overnight lead and the Masters title to Nick Faldo, shooting a preposterous 78 on the final day to the eventual champion's 67.

In *Bounce*, Matthew Syed writes how a lifetime of practice allows sportsmen and women of all gifts and crafts to '*automate*' their stroke-making. 'Many hours of practice have enabled him to code the stroke in implicit rather than explicit memory,' writes Syed. 'Russell Poldrack, a neuroscientist at the University of California at Los Angeles, has conducted a number of brain-imaging experiments to trace the transition from explicit to implicit monitoring that occurs over many hours' practice. He has discovered that the prefrontal cortex is activated when a novice is learning a skill, but that control of the stroke switches over time to areas such as the basal ganglia, which is partly responsible for touch and feel.

'This migration from the explicit to the implicit system of the brain has two advantages. First, it enables the expert player to integrate the various parts of a complex skill into one fluent whole,' continues Syed, further explaining, 'something that would be impossible at a conscious level because there are too many inter-connecting variables for the conscious mind to handle. And second, it frees up attention to focus on higher-level aspects of the skill such as tactics and strategy.' Syed asks us to understand the transition by thinking how we all initially learned the many different hand, foot and eye skills necessary to drive a car, and how these many different skills are ultimately performed by us all with perfect calm, and without any conscious control. Syed also introduces his readers to the workings of Sian Beilock, a psychologist at the University of Chicago.

'Once [a motor skill] is de-chunked, each unit must be activated and run separately. Not only does this process slow performance,' states Beilock, 'but it also creates an opportunity for error at each transition between units that was not present in the integrated control structure.'

Choking, therefore, and alas, is a neural glitch to which every single sportsman and woman is potentially vulnerable.

'It is not the pressure in a pressure situation that distracts us into performing poorly,' Beilock further explains. 'The pressure makes us worry and want to control our actions too much. And you cannot think your way through a routine, practiced action, like making a three-foot putt. Compare it to quickly shuffling down a flight of stairs. You could do that without thought.

'But if I asked you to do it, and at the same time think about how much you bend your knee each time or what part of your foot is touching the stair, you would probably fall on your face.

'That's what happens when people choke. They try to think their way through the action.'

That first week of April in Augusta, Georgia, in 1996 was of the glorious kind, and Greg Norman had marched for three days, in complete control, half godlike, half John Wayne strutting his way down the main street of a hushed, utterly respectful town.

On the Saturday, Norman had gone head-to-head with Britain's calm, plodding champ, Faldo, and heroically increased his lead from four shots to six by the end of the 18 holes. After that, Norman relaxed a while in the semi-darkness of the first-floor locker room at Augusta National, the room reserved for the non-champions who turn up each year.

The locker room for champions is on the second floor of the clubhouse, with a sign on the door insisting '*Masters Club Room – Private*'. A guard stands sentry during the week of the tournament.

The honour of entering the room is accentuated by the fact that it holds only 28 oak lockers, each with the brass name plate of a past Masters champion, and each containing the green jacket belonging to that champion. With new champions having to share lockers with some of the past winners who no longer play or who have passed, the exclusivity of the room is immediately apparent, with its distinguished, old-world charm further enhanced by the three card tables in the centre of the room, all containing bridge scorepads, and reminding everybody who enters of the club's age and history.

Norman had been last off the course that Saturday evening in 1996. The attendant had turned the lights off in the locker room for non-champions and gone home. Norman was unable to switch them back on, so he sat there.

'Your last night in this locker room!' a friend had happily informed him.

'Damn... I hope so!' Norman replied.

Then, Peter Dobereiner, the distinguished but ailing English golf writer who had always championed Norman, grabbed him by his shoulders and gushed: 'Greg, old boy... there's no way you can fuck this up now!' His rounds of 63, 69 and 71 had him at 13 under par, six ahead of Faldo and seven ahead of a 25-year-old Phil Mickelson.

Norman was famed for living his life in a larger-than-life manner, for hunting sharks, and flying air force jets. 'He stroked bull sharks sleeping in underwater caves; drove at 190 miles per hour in Lamborghini Diablos on desert highways; hugged the wall at 180 miles per hour in Roger Penske Indy cars; and ran out of oxygen eighty-eight feet below the sea and rose to the surface no faster than his own bubbles, suffering from only a mild case of the bends,' recounted Lauren St John in *Shark: The Biography of Greg Norman.*

Norman was also a distinguished businessman, signing off deals valued at tens of millions of dollars at a time. Very early in his career, he had taken to arriving at tournaments in his Rolls-Royce. He had 73 victories to his name on golf courses all over the world, though he had also finished second 52 times in his illustrious career. He knew what it took to win.

He also knew what had gone wrong when he nearly won!

Ten years earlier, Greg Norman also led the Masters going into the final round, when he shot a 70. He knew full well that a pushed approach shot on the 72nd hole had left him with a bogey and a missed chance of bringing Jack Nicklaus into a play-off. The evening before the final round in 1986, in the press room, Norman as the tournament leader had told everyone gathered around him to be respectful, and not just expectant.

'You still have to respect the old girl. When the pressure's on... you still have to be careful,' Norman stressed.

The first time he played Augusta National, in 1981, five years after turning pro, Norman had the honour of standing on the first tee with Nicklaus, the Golden Bear of golf. Norman felt quite ill, a completely different response to how he had been earlier in the week when he had felt energised by his first impressions of the place.

'I'll never forget how I was struck by Augusta that first year,' he recalled in *Golf Digest* magazine. 'This was what golf was meant to be, pure golf. This was the purest form of golf tournament.

'That drive up Magnolia Lane... with the clubhouse ahead... the practice ranges on either side... it just gets you in the perfect frame of mind for a golf tournament.'

But that energy had quickly drained out of his body as he stood on the first tee in 1981. He felt stiff, and even his practice swing was forced and wooden. He somehow got his drive away and walked with his head down towards the hill in front of him. Just then, Nicklaus put his arm around his young partner's shoulders.

'I don't know about you,' said Nicklaus, 'but by the time we reach the top of the hill, my feet will just about be back on the ground. I'm so nervous.'

Nicklaus's first piece of advice to Norman was to take the deepest breath he could possibly take. Norman did exactly that, and when the round had ended he was tied for the lead, on 69, with Johnny Miller, Keith Fergus, Lon Hinkle and Curtis Strange. By the end of his first week in Augusta, Norman, flushed with happiness, asked his first wife, Laura, to marry him.

Norman had finished fourth in his debut appearance, with excellent scores of 69, 70, 72 and 72, but when he returned the next year he shot 73, 75, 73 and 79 to tie for 36th place. In 1983, another final round of 79 left him again positioned in the 30s. In 1984 he was 25th at the end of the tournament, but in '85 he fell back to 47th after finishing with 75 and 78. Then came his first fateful week in Augusta, in 1986, and his loss to Nicklaus.

'From the last day of the 1986 tournament, when I hit that second shot and missed that putt for par, from that very moment, and for the next year, 24 hours a day, I thought about the Masters,' Norman would admit. 'Every day it was in my mind.

'More than anything else in my life, I wanted to win that one.'

In 1987, however, Norman once more left empty-handed, despite displaying as much courage as any golfer may ever have summoned up at Augusta. His first two rounds were forgettable enough, but then on the Saturday he put down a round of 66. On the Sunday he went out in 37, bogeyed the 10th, and double-bogeyed the 11th. But he sank a 35-foot putt on the 17th to recover a dropped shot on the 16th hole.

Norman was level with Seve Ballesteros and Larry Mize going to the 18th and needed a birdie for outright victory, but his 22-footer gently slid just past the hole. Seve lost out on the first play-off hole, and Norman and Mize strode to the 11th to sort out the tournament between them.

Mize hit his five-iron second shot to the right, finishing 140 feet away from the flagstick on a small hill near the 12th tee. Norman, meanwhile, was on the green in two and, watching Mize mess with his second shot, he had turned to his caddie, Pete Bender.

'Pete... I think if we just cosy this little son down to within two feet of the hole, we'll have a two-footer to win the golf tournament.'

Mize, however, would snatch the title with his next shot, his ball from far out bouncing, then skipping towards the hole, and diving in.

In 14 Masters appearances, Norman had twice finished second and twice finished third. But he had it all figured out, as best as anyone on a golf course could figure out the damndest game man had invented.

'I'm going to enjoy tomorrow,' the 41-year-old world No.1 confirmed for those listening, and for himself, before his final round in 1996.

'Irrespective of what happens… I'm going to enjoy every step I take. I've been there before and there is no better feeling than having a chance of winning a major championship.

'I'm going to enjoy the moment. I'm going to go to the first tee as relaxed and comfortable as I have been since the first day.'

The complete destruction of Norman's final round at Augusta National that year started on the fairway of the ninth hole, when he still held a three-shot lead. But, watching on a television screen in Bali, where he was doing a corporate day, fellow Aussie pro Rodger Davis knew that Norman was in big trouble. 'There are not many things that I feel sorry for Norman about,' Davis admitted, 'because he's made so much money and all this, but when it came on TV, and I saw his face, I thought, "I don't believe this." He was on the eighth and he was still four in front but you could see it in his face… and his expression didn't change all day.'

Norman's great big beautiful swing had broken down ever so slightly, such a tiny breakdown that nobody would have noticed, had not his ball rolled back off the ninth green and reversed 30 yards down the hill.

On the 10th hole he hooked the ball off the tee, subsequently missed his seventh green of the day, hit a weak chip to 10 feet, and dropped another shot. On the 11th, the choke tightened. He hit his approach to within 15 feet of the pin and it looked like he could pull a shot back. But he knocked his putt three feet past the hole and then, quite panicked by what had just happened, he missed the one coming back.

He shook his head. His brain swirled with confusion. His walk had slowed appreciably.

On the 12th tee he second-guessed his swing, and the club head was short on acceleration. His ball landed on the front of the green and then slowly rolled back towards Rae's Creek. He took a double bogey to Faldo's par.

Norman's big handsome face was now frozen in a look of astonishment and complete anguish. He drove into the pines on the 13th.

Norman's ball would be in the water, again, on the par-three 16th, where a double bogey left him four strokes behind. Faldo would win his third Masters title by five shots and, as he holed his final putt, the Englishman turned to Norman and told him he didn't know what to say.

'I just want to give you a hug,' Faldo told his opponent.

On the eve of the final round at Augusta National, a four-shot lead has been held by only 13 golfers in the history of the Masters tournament. Nine of those golfers won and helped themselves into one of the club's immaculate green jackets.

Four would be destined to fail.

Those four were Ken Venturi, who led by four shots in 1956; Ed Sneed, who led by five in 1979; Greg Norman, who led by six in 1996; and Rory McIlroy, who also led by four in 2011.

Fifty-five years separated Venturi and McIlroy as they stood on the first tee at Augusta National, ready to defend their four shots, ready to fight for their first major title.

Both men struck the ball nicely down the middle of the opening fairway. As they handed their clubs back to their caddies, and took off on a determined walk, however, Venturi and McIlroy shared a common destiny.

The golf game of each man, within minutes, would start choking itself to death.

And there was no escape.

PART ONE

The Masters

CHAPTER ONE

Augusta National

He delighted in being three-quarters of an asshole, and more or less his whole adult life he had also been a consummate bully. Quite rightly, Clifford Roberts was sadly missed by only a chosen few upon blowing his brains out with a Smith & Wesson .38 on the par-three course at Augusta National Golf Club, beside the pond he had insisted should be specially built for his friend, President Dwight D. Eisenhower. It was shortly after 8 a.m. on September 29, 1977, when Roberts was discovered.

His body had rolled partly into the water.

Entering the water, really, was the only mistake Roberts, or Mr Cliff as he was called by his hand-picked employees, had made upon deciding to take his own life. He liked things to be neat and tidy in his club, and he liked people to remain in their appointed place at all times. More than anything else, upon deciding to end the wretchedness that a stroke had brought to his life, while also making certain that terminal cancer would not have its way with him, Roberts was aware that he was breaking all his own rules at his own precious Augusta National Golf Club.

That morning the grounds of the club were as quiet as ever in the early hours. Roberts had always liked his people to retire generally at a respectful hour, and usually so before midnight. It was his club after all. He had co-founded Augusta National with the impossibly handsome Bobby Jones, an amateur player with the hands and the nerves of a professional craftsman and who was, perhaps, the greatest golfer the world had ever known when the club opened for members' play in December of 1932.

Roberts had been chairman of Augusta National from that time, and Jones had been club president until his death in 1971. Theirs had been the supremely masterful double act. Members were always encouraged to call Clifford Roberts 'Mr Roberts', never Cliff, and they never called Jones 'Bobby'. It was always, officially, 'Bob'. The personable and usually kindly Jones brought folk to East Georgia, and into the magnificent home of Augusta National, and there they quickly enough found 'Mr Roberts'.

It would become his club more than Jones's. His trademark stare could manacle a man to the nearest wall, and beneath his imposing, sloping eyebrows, those dark eyes nearly always remained exceptionally unforgiving, and naturally suspicious, most especially when he patrolled the clubhouse at Augusta National and observed those who had decided to spend some of their time there. A great many of the greatest golfers in the history of the game were not spared from that look. Most knew him to be cold-blooded one day, madly tyrannical the next.

All of them knew to be prepared for Mr Roberts. 'Cliff was a tough bastard,' Sam Snead, who won the first of his three Masters titles in 1949, remarked after Roberts' death. 'But you have to be to run that place.'

That September morning, the skies were partly cloudy. The air still held longingly to the heat of the day before.

It was 65 degrees Fahrenheit when Roberts left his apartment. At 2.27 a.m. one of the security guards thought it very surprising that Roberts should be in his golf cart at such a late hour. He was wearing a trench coat and trousers over his pyjamas. The guard took a long look to make sure that the 84-year-old was safely making his way to wherever he was heading at that ungodly hour, and he then headed back to where he needed to be, and where Mr Roberts would expect him to be.

Earlier that Wednesday night, the Yankees had won their 99th game of the season. It's unlikely that Roberts, who had made his fortune as a New York-based stockbroker in the years before he built Augusta National, had kept an eye on the television. There were other things to be done, papers to leave in order. Roberts, who disliked children as a rule and firmly believed that over-population would be the ruin of society, had decided to leave most of his fortune to the organisation Planned Parenthood, which would become the largest provider of reproductive health services in the United States.

He had written a note of apology to his third wife, Betty, and pinned it to his doctor's prognosis. He had done some other tidying. Earlier still, he had called in one of the guards who was operating the club switchboard and, after producing a gun, he asked the startled man how such a gun should be properly used. Roberts explained that he had heard some unusual noises outside his window.

In the late afternoon, the club barber was summoned to Roberts' apartment, and after a 'tight back and sides' the two men talked for almost an hour, until 6 p.m., when Roberts made a call to his wife, who was staying at the couple's home in California, in Beverly Hills. He asked her to come down to Augusta.

Betty said she would, in a day or two.

The par-three course at Augusta National, comprising just the nine holes and measuring 1,060 yards, was designed by George Cobb, a Georgia native and Korean War veteran who built more than 100 courses throughout the South, and who had Roberts as his unofficial and argumentative assistant for the task at hand. When President Eisenhower suggested a fishing pond might be of some use, the chairman stepped in to oblige a man he held as dearly as he had once held Bobby Jones.

Only on one occasion, during all of Ike's visits to Augusta National, had Roberts not shown up at the airport in his formal green jacket to greet him, and that was in 1958 when he was on honeymoon in Europe with his second wife, Letitia. Ike returned the compliment, and during the eight years of his presidency staff in the White House would often refer to the Red Room as 'Mr Roberts' bedroom'. A pair of pyjamas and a toothbrush, the property of Clifford Roberts, remained in the room through both of Ike's two terms.

The journey from the clubhouse to the pond was downhill, and Roberts took it very slowly. All journeys, even short walks, had become difficult and tiresome since his stroke. He had felt especially weary for some days. He had stopped taking his medication. He could not sleep, and could not remember his last good night's sleep.

Years earlier, he had watched Bobby Jones being robbed of his good health at such a young age and left a broken man for so long, sorrowfully isolated and neglected by so many, including Roberts himself.

He would avoid such an ending to his own life.

He would not remain locked away, day after day, unable to gently amble even the little distance to his office, almost formally condemned to the life of a prisoner in his own magnificent club.

A floodlight measured the pathway leading to the pond.

Roberts walked without a cane. He wore galoshes. They had been easier to fit on than his shoes. He soon arrived close to the water's edge.

It was private there.

He knew his own people would find his body, not some damned stranger! Emergency vehicles could easily get to the spot. It would be a place of least disturbance to the daily life of Augusta National

Golf Club. That he also knew, just as he knew so intimately every square foot of the 365 acres on which Augusta National stood; every rise, every slope, every offering of sand, every watery grave for those who swung their clubs too gingerly or far too contemptuously for their own good. He also knew enough about the gun in his hand to know that he would not leave a complete mess for his staff who would have to remove his body. A Smith & Wesson .38 was up to doing the job that Roberts wanted done, but it would not leave his face unrecognisable or in smithereens.

It was indeed a tidy job. And, by lunchtime the same day, Augusta National Golf Club dealt with the tragic ending of its founder with a businesslike, and extremely efficient, choice of words.

'It is with great regret that the Augusta National Golf Club announces that its chairman, Clifford Roberts, died during the night. Death was caused by a self-inflicted wound. Mr Roberts had been in ill health for several months. Funeral services will be private. No flowers are requested.'

No mention of family, and no fanciful dalliance to entertain perfect strangers. To the point. Mr Roberts would have worded it just so himself.

Neither might Mr Roberts have privately felt disrespected, or at all furious, at the very first person – who was quickly followed by so many others when told about Mr Roberts' death and who had known or long heard about the chairman's unquenchable thirst for law and order – to state that Clifford Roberts controlled every single thing at Augusta National... right down to 'the last shot'.

****

Cliff Roberts had not been invited to the funeral of Bobby Jones six years earlier. It was family only. The Jones family had remained absolutely furious since the chairman took the decision to remove his lifelong friend from the Masters post-tournament ceremony, when the club's famous rye green jacket is presented to the champion by his winning predecessor in the basement of the Butler Cabin. Jones, after the 1968 Masters tournament, was never asked to participate in the ceremony again.

The tradition of slipping the jacket on to the winner of the Masters, thereby symbolising his entry into the exclusive club of Masters champions, had begun in 1949 when Sam Snead tried one on for size, and for 20 years the presence of the great Bobby Jones had always been the central focus of attention, often rivalling the first words from the mouth of the delighted new champion. Roberts, however, first handed out green jackets to his members 12 years earlier, before the tournament, so that visitors would know who to ask for help. Members hadn't liked them at first. They thought them too warm, and far too garish, but soon enough the jacket became the most famous club membership card in the history of sport.

The classic three-button style jacket, single-breasted, centre-vented, is now known simply and best as 'Masters Green' by golf fans. Originally made by the Brooks Uniform Company in New York, the contract was won in 1967 by the Hamilton Tailoring Company of Cincinnati, who still ensure the fabric is 55 per cent wool and 45 per cent polyester, that the coats are fully lined with rayon and silk, with the colour of the green lining matching that of the outside. The three brass buttons on the front and the two buttons on each sleeve are embossed with the club logo, a map of Georgia with only a golf flag planted in the bottom right-hand corner, which also appears on the left breast pocket. Only members and Masters champions get to wear them. And none is allowed to be worn outside of the club's grounds, with the one exception. The reigning Masters champion is given a custom-made jacket to take with him around the world for one year, but after 12 months it must be returned to the club. When Gary Player told Cliff Roberts, upon returning to Augusta in April 1962 to defend his title, that he had left his jacket at home in South Africa there were, naturally, some strong words. Jackets remain in the Augusta National clubhouse at all times for all of their owners. The name of each owner is stitched into the lining.

When Bobby Jones was first informed that he would be excluded from the jacket ceremony, Roberts pointed one of his longish bony fingers in the direction of CBS. He explained that the blame for the sharpish exit of the wheelchair-stricken Jones from the most watched presentation in the long history of the ancient game lay solely with the damned television executives.

Everyone knew that to be untrue, including the once immaculate Robert Tyre Jones Jr, the golfer with the matinee idol face and physique, whom Roberts had once felt blessed to have as his business partner. In 1968, however, Roberts and others agreed that the presence of a disfigured Bobby Jones, who had aged beyond recognition owing to too much smoking, too much pain and too much whiskey, and far too much codeine and cortisone, was unnecessarily distracting, and a little unsightly for such a marvellous occasion.

Bobby Jones is the only sportsman to have received two ticker-tape parades through the streets of Cliff Roberts' home town, New York. The second came after he became the only man to win the 'Grand Slam', all four major championships in the one calendar year, in 1930, when he was simply too good for all the world's amateurs and professionals, winning the US Open, the Open Championship, the British Amateur Championship and, finally, the US Amateur Championship on the 11th green at Merion Golf Club near Philadelphia when he defeated a hapless gentleman named Gene Homans 8 and 7.

Two months later, at 28 years of age, Bobby Jones quit the game he sometimes loved and so often resented. For Jones, there had been no money in amateur golf, and the only large cheque he ever received for swinging a club came the year after he retired, when Warner Brothers produced 18 instructional films of Bobby giving golf tips to Hollywood stars. That deal earned him the princely sum of $250,000.

Jones had earned his living primarily as a lawyer. After studying mechanical engineering at Georgia Tech and English literature at Harvard he had decided to spend 12 months studying law at Emory University. He was admitted to the Georgia Bar in 1928, but he was not a wealthy man by any stretch of the imagination when he made his decision to step away from the game. He had no home of his own and, although married, and the father of one child, Robert Tyre Jones III, he still lived in his parents' house in his home town of Atlanta.

From 1922 to 1930 Jones had placed first or second in 11 of 13 US and British Open Championships, winning seven times and losing twice in play-offs, and never once in his life had he submitted himself to a golf lesson, or asked an elder statesman of the game to observe his swing. But, upon announcing his retirement, he had a life to restart and important decisions to make.

At that time Bobby Jones was celebrated for his modesty and his sense of humour, as well as his brilliance on a golf course. 'As a young man, he was able to stand up to just about the best that life can offer, which is not easy, and later he stood up with equal grace to just about the worst,' wrote *The New Yorker*'s Herbert Warren Wind. Bobby had been a sickly child. He could not eat solid food until he was five years old and he remained troubled by life when he entered his teenage years, during which he richly earned a reputation as a precocious youth and a distastefully consistent hot-head.

With those perfect blue eyes and thinned-out blond hair, Jones looked charming from a distance. Up close, however, he was easily disliked, and the game of golf and his quest for perfection from tee to green were distrustful bedfellows. 'I wish that I could say here that a strange thrill shot through my skinny bosom when I swung at a golf ball for the first time,' Jones wrote in his 1927 autobiography

Down the Fairway, 'but it wouldn't be truthful.' At six, Bobby was swinging a few sawed-off golf clubs. At seven, he was mimicking the swing of Stewart Maiden, the club pro at East Lake Country Club where, on the old course at 11 years of age, Bobby shot his first 80. A year later, on the same course, he shot 70 and won two club championships.

Between the ages of 14, when he became the youngest player to enter a US Amateur Championship, and 21, Jones felt that the game was his enemy. During those disheartening seven years of searching for whatever it was Jones believed he could find within himself, there were countless breakdowns, including one occasion when Jones's putter, nicknamed Calamity Jane, was thrown over the heads of a large gallery and into a clutch of trees beyond the green. 'I was full of pie, ice cream and inexperience,' admitted Jones in his latter years. 'To me, golf was just a game to beat someone. I didn't know that someone was me.'

The lowest point for Jones in this tortured journey was at the 1921 Open Championship at St Andrews where, on the 11th green, after already accumulating 50 shots on his card for the day, he committed the sin of all sins and picked up his ball and stomped off the Old Course.

The next seven-year passage in Jones's life, however, brought peace. They brought the true character of the man out into the open, but only after Jones had conquered his first major title. Jones's demons were locked away for good after the 1923 US Open at Inwood Country Club in New York.

That day Jones finished his final round with bogey, bogey, double bogey. 'I didn't finish like a champion,' he told reporters afterwards, 'I finished like a yellow dog.' But, after opening the door to Bobby Cruickshank for an 18-hole play-off, Jones never let those cursed demons have their way with him. Jones and Cruickshank were still tied going into the par-four 18th hole at Inwood in that play-off, and both men drove into the rough.

Cruickshank laid up; Jones took his time.

Jones's ball was 190 yards from the green, but it was resting in loose dirt at the edge of the rough and a watery grave was in his sights as he examined the green in the distance.

Throughout his career, Jones liked to refer to a shot that only a golfer with nerves of steel could pull off as a shot that needed 'sheer delicatessen'. Now, as he stood over his ball preparing to play his second shot to the green, Jones knew in his heart that he needed such a shot. It had to be 'sheer delicatessen'.

And it was just so, as he lifted his ball over the water and to within eight feet of the pin. Two putts later he had won his first major.

Bobby Jones's life changed when he met Cliff Roberts, when the businessman came south with his East Coast friends, booked into the Bon Air Venderbilt and played their golf at Forest Hills and Augusta Country Club. It was local hotelier Walt Marshall who introduced the two men, in 1925. And some years later the lives of both men changed for ever when they summoned Dr Alister MacKenzie M.D. and invited the physician, who had been the consulting architect at the Old Course at St Andrews, to build them a golf course close to Augusta, on an abandoned 365-acre plant nursery where peaches once predominated called Fruitland.

There, Augusta National Golf Club would be born.

Bobby Jones would see the course grow and mature through its early and teenage years, survive dire financial straits and, slowly at first and then spectacularly, unveil the Masters tournament. The invitational tournament was named by Roberts, and it was a name forever frowned upon by Jones, but despite its high-handed title the Masters would become the most-loved competition in the world of golf.

By then Jones was already in a bad way. His physical condition deteriorated after 1948, the year when he played his last 18 holes of golf, when doctors noted a difficulty in the use of his right hand and a stubbing of his right foot. His was a rare neurological disorder called syringomyelia. Messages from his brain to his arms and legs were intermittent or short-circuited. During those years, from the diagnosis until his death in 1971, he fought to live a normal life. At first he used a cane. Later he decided upon a leg brace. There was soon the need for a second brace. But there was no escape and by the mid-1950s he accepted that a wheelchair would have to be brought into his home.

His sanctuary was his cabin at Augusta National, and the classical music that filled his private rooms and allowed him to close his eyes, and move adventurously and athletically, and play golf shots that other men might only dream about playing, but which Jones had known to be relatively straightforward in their delivery.

Bobby Jones died in Atlanta on December 18, 1971.

His wife, Mary Malone, and his three children were at his bedside. He weighed less than 90 pounds. One week earlier, in his bed at his home after suffering an aneurysm, he had converted to Catholicism and invited the attending priest, Monsignor John Stapleton, pastor of the Jones family church, the Cathedral of Christ the King in Atlanta, to have a drink of alcohol with him afterwards.

Jones admitted to the pastor: 'If I knew how happy (becoming a Catholic) was going to make Mary, I would have done it years ago.'

****

Clifford Roberts and Robert Tyre Jones Jr were opposites in every way. Jones was cerebral and graceful, and extremely well educated, whereas Roberts' formal education came to a halt when he exited his small town high school in Texas. But they found one another when they needed one another in life. They then founded Augusta National Golf Club in 1932. They started their own invitational tournament in 1934. And they further bedded their relationship in a company called Joroberts Inc., which they formed in order to bottle Coca-Cola in South America.

Until Roberts met General Dwight D. Eisenhower in 1948, the same year in which Jones was diagnosed with syringomyelia, the pair were inseparable. However, within months of that meeting, the hero of the Second World War had joined Augusta National, and had told Roberts to 'call me Ike'.

Cliff Roberts had met his new best friend, who would become the President of the United States of America five years later. The friendship was profitable for the President. Representing Reynolds and Company, a New York investment banking firm in which he owned a substantial stake, Roberts found a safe home for President Eisenhower's money, and his portfolio increased four times in value over the next 15 years. Ike also put some cash into Joroberts.

Building a new golf course in Augusta was Cliff Roberts' idea. He was advised that an old nursery, owned by the Berckmanses and called Fruitland, might be worth a look, and he subsequently called Jones to tell him of his potential find. They wished for a place that would be private and exclusive. Jones especially clung to the dream of absolute privacy, which would leave his competitive golf career far behind him and, to all intents and purposes, abandoned. He didn't just want the course for himself. He wanted it for wealthy and influential men from all over the country.

As Georgia's second oldest, and second largest, city, Augusta had profited from its location on the Savannah River, as abundant water power helped industry to prosper. The city had taken its name from the tragic Princess Augusta of Saxe-Gotha, the Princess of Wales, whose husband Frederick predeceased her by nine years in the late 1700s. Rumoured to have had an affair with the tutor of her son, the future King, the Princess suffered widespread hostility from the public and when she died of cancer of the throat, at the age of 52, her funeral procession attracted a rabble and insults were hurled as her coffin was lowered into the ground.

As Augusta National was about to become a reality for Roberts and Jones, the Great Depression was still fixing itself with intent upon the lives of the great majority of people living in the United States. Georgia in particular had been upended by the financial ruin of most of its inhabitants, as well as the near suffocation of the cotton industry, which had incurred nature's wrath a decade earlier. The boll weevil, a member of the beetle family, was first recognised to be a problem in Georgia in the early 1900s, but from 1915 it wreaked havoc on the state's precious cotton industry. Small farmers were left without any hope of making a living. Those forced off their land became sharecroppers, having to accept grim terms dictated by large landowners. On the eve of the stock market collapse in the United States in 1929, about two-thirds of the farmland in the state of Georgia was already operated by sharecroppers. The majority of these farmers were poor whites who lived on an annual income of some $200 or less, but the situation was far more brutalising for black families. By 1935, as Augusta National was in its infancy, only 12 per cent of blacks owned the land they worked.

Yield losses across the entire state associated with the scourge of the boll weevil had reduced cotton acreage from a high of 5.2 million acres in 1914 to 2.6 million acres by 1923. Insecticides provided only temporary relief for the industry and the decline continued at rampant levels, with planted acreage tumbling to a low of 115,000 acres by 1983. By the time the bell tolled for the Great Depression, Georgia's land and its economy, and the lives of the majority of its people, were already in tatters.

The US stock market spectacularly crashed in October 1929 but, over the next two years, Cliff Roberts found the money to build Augusta National, just about, with the help of his close business acquaintances and others on the East Coast. The depression hit the South harder than most other parts of the country, and it did not fully recede in states such as Georgia until the country entered the

Second World War. As a result of the hard times for all, land came cheap to the likes of Cliff Roberts.

Once the required parcel of land was purchased for $70,000, a further $100,000 was put together for the construction of the course. Cliff and Bobby knew that it would be tight, very tight. Walt Marshall had put up $25,000 for Cliff. So too did Alfred Severin Bourne, whose family owned Singer Sewing Machine Inc., while assorted others handed over sums of $5,000 per man. Augusta National Golf Club, therefore, with money so tight, was built fast. The construction started at the end of November 1931 and the course was finished early the following year, on May 27, 1932.

So furiously was it built, in fact, that Augusta National Golf Club came in $15,000 under budget. One of the reasons Dr Alister MacKenzie was chosen to design the course was his capacity for offering instruction at speed and seldom second-guessing his own instinct. It also helped that he was not a great believer in bunkers, either from a strategic point of view or for visual effect, and he included a third fewer sand traps than an average golf course in his plans for Augusta National; a total of 29 bunkers in total.

MacKenzie was the choice of Bobby Jones. They had been friends since 1929 when Jones was sensationally beaten in the first round of the US Amateur at Pebble Beach and, with the pressure of competition abated and his lodgings booked for the full week, he decided to play a round at a new course nearby, and also overlooking the Pacific. It was called Cypress Point. It was a MacKenzie course.

MacKenzie had announced in 1914 that he was giving up medicine to pursue golf architecture full-time. However, it was not very long before he was back to his former career. At 47, he rejoined the British Army to serve as a front-line surgeon in the First World War. Eight years after the war's end, he decided to make his way to America for good and make his living building outstanding golf courses. He was then 55 years old, but threw himself into his first love and thrived, nowhere more so than on the Monterey Peninsula.

MacKenzie would die of a heart attack on January 7, 1934, at his small home bordering the sixth fairway at Pasatiempo Golf Club, one of his own personal favourite pieces of work, in California. He was 63 years of age and he never saw his immaculate work at Augusta in all its glory. Nor would he see all of the money he had been promised for working on it. Just over a week before he died, he had sent a series of desperate telegrams on New Year's Eve to Roberts, begging for the last instalment of his agreed commission. Augusta National was indeed MacKenzie's finest work, but his ashes would be scattered over the fairways at Pasatiempo.

It was hard labour from the very beginning for those employed in digging up the Augusta earth and moving it around. This back-breaking task was spearheaded by Prosper Berckmans, whose grandfather had started Fruitland Nurseries over 70 years earlier, and who now faced the extermination of his family's once great dream, clearing and grubbing the land. Berckmans and his men moved in front of another crew, who swung axes and mattocks, and they transplanted more than 4,000 small trees, moving them from the future fairways and placing them to MacKenzie's instructions. Having being born on the property, it was entirely appropriate that Prosper Berckmans would be appointed the club's first manager.

It was not just the architect of Augusta National Golf Club who found great difficulty in getting his brilliant hands on sufficient money to pay his way. The lives of so many who helped build Augusta National lay close to ruin. Bank failures were common throughout the state. Opportunities for loans had dried up. Small businesses were being pummelled into the ground, as less money in circulation meant fewer paying customers. In 1930 and 1931 the state then experienced the worst drought in its history.

The people thought there was no escape. A typical Georgia family had no electricity in their home, no running water, and no toilet facilities. Diets were inadequate, consisting mostly of molasses, fatback and cornbread, and for those who fell by the wayside, there were few if any rural clinics or hospitals. Healthcare workers were never to be found, and tuberculosis and malaria were commonplace. The people were indeed impoverished. They were also close to defeat.

The African-American population within the state were already quite defeated, as the income of rural blacks had been half that of rural whites to begin with. In the whole state of Georgia there were only four black insurance companies, one bank and one wholly-owned newspaper for blacks. According to the US census of 1930, there were 10,110 black professionals in Georgia, the majority of them clergymen and teachers, out of a population of 1,071,125. Hospitals for blacks existed only in the largest cities. The literary critic and essayist H. L. Mencken, when seeking to identify the country's 'worst American state', ranked Georgia close to the very bottom of the barrel in terms of wealth, education, health and public security (which was a polite way of saying lynching).

With so many willing hands available throughout Augusta, and neighbouring counties and towns, there was really no shortage of man-hours that could have been worked every day at Augusta National. Human mules were more than willing to work for 10 cents an hour, for as many hours as God and their bosses allowed them. Six days every week, for men and mules, and tractors. A dime an hour was almost twice as much as a man or woman might get on a local farm picking cotton, though the work was punishingly hard, especially on the 12th and 13th holes.

An old swamp at the bottom of the property, which was to be the 12th green, had eight mules and two tractors stuck in the deepest mud one particularly long day under the hottest sun.

Dr MacKenzie was hand-building a course with Bobby Jones, and with Jones's long drives and high hooks in mind. Augusta National was completed with a high number of dog-leg left holes that suited a long hitter of the ball, especially so on each of the par-fives.

The labouring done, the ground was layered with Scott's Bermuda seed, before the 90 acres of brown fairways were watered, unfiltered, from the Savannah River. The grass grew quickly and perfectly. Seeded on May 27, the course was mowed on June 10, and the men with the mowers were then paid 15 cents an hour to encourage them to take that little bit of additional care in their work. On August 26, 1932, Jones and some of his friends played Augusta National for the first time. Bobby was happy as he shot an even-par 72.

The next January, Cliff Roberts was the man in the middle at the grand opening of Augusta National Golf Club, and the celebrations began with an 18-hour railway journey from New York to Augusta. A total of 80 men had joined the club prior to its opening, and 60 of them were Roberts' New Yorkers – lawyers, investment bankers, and assorted do-wellers – who enjoyed a plentiful supply of whiskey on their journey down south even though prohibition still had a further month of life. Also aboard the Pullman carriage was the sportswriter Grantland Rice, who proposed to members that same week in Augusta that their new club should be run 'without the hindrance of meetings'. Augusta National would, therefore, be left in the hands of just two men. Bobby Jones, and mostly Clifford Roberts.

Bobby and Cliff soon told disappointed members that Augusta National could never host the US Open, which is traditionally held in June and July, as the course was to be closed during the fiercest heat of the southern summer. Members, instead, were informed that Augusta National would hold a tournament of its own. Roberts wanted it called the Masters, and he wanted Jones to come out of retirement, once every year, to play in his own invitational tournament. Jones did not like that idea, and he greatly disliked such a potentially offensive name.

The first Augusta National Invitational tournament was held in 1934, when Bobby Jones did indeed temporarily, for one week, end his retirement. It was decided that April was a suitable month for the tournament, a month that had the advantage of catching the nation's sportswriters as they returned north from baseball's spring training camps in Florida.

Jones finished the tournament in 13th place. It was won by Horton Smith, from Springfield, Missouri, who was known among his fellow golfers as 'The Joplin Ghost', with rounds of 70, 72, 70 and 72, for a four-round total of 284 and a one-shot victory. Smith would reappear to regain the Masters title two years later, shooting 74, 71, 68 and 72, for a total of 285, which once again gave him the tournament by a single stroke.

****

The cheeky little American shot-maker, Gene Sarazen, had become the world's No.1 golfer upon the retirement of Bobby Jones. He won eight tournaments in 1930, the year Jones bid the game adieu, and within the next three years he had added the US Open twice, the PGA Championship three times, and also the Open Championship, but when an invitation to play at Augusta landed in Sarazen's home he took one look at it and dismissively tossed it to one side. The envelope bore Cliff Roberts' name and Sarazen thought it was a promotion at selling some real estate or stocks. Instead, Sarazen kept to his schedule, which had him, the same week of the Augusta National Invitational tournament, participating in an exhibition tour with the trick-shot artist Joe Kirkwood.

The next year, the same invitation from Augusta had Bobby Jones's name on the envelope. Sarazen travelled to Augusta and won the title in 1935. When Sarazen finally finished his week's play, which included a 36-hole play-off on the Monday in front of 400 spectators or so who found the time to turn up for the day, he accepted a $50 bonus cheque from Cliff Roberts for his exceptional efforts in his 108-hole victory.

Attendances at the tournament were continually poor through that first decade, and Roberts had to add zeros to every day's numbers for the sake of his club's good name. For too many of those years, Roberts had to repeatedly lean on Jones to attract a decent level of curiosity in what was slowly developing at Augusta National, and while Jones never enjoyed the role of host, he did take to the course he had made and, thanks to MacKenzie's favourable design, he was able to shoot a course record of 65 in 1934, and break that record with a 64 one year later, though neither was in tournament play. During tournament week, Jones played like a gentleman from an older, forgotten era, and in 11 tournaments between 1934 and 1948 he never managed to break par for 18 holes. By then, the tournament bore the proud name of the Masters, though Jones never felt it appropriate and, even many years later, in the 1960s, he formally made mention of the 'so-called Masters'.

By that time, the Masters had grown into one of the foremost golf events in the world, thanks mainly to the stubborn qualities of Cliff Roberts, and the support of his close friend President Eisenhower.

It was also helped enormously by the arrival of television sets into the homes of middle-class America (the Masters, in 1956, was the first tournament to be televised live by the network giant, CBS) and finally, and most significantly, by the appearance of three golfing giants in quick succession, Ben Hogan, Arnold Palmer and Jack Nicklaus. All three enriched their early stature by thrilling fans and fellow professionals alike on the manicured fairways and lightning-fast greens of Augusta National, between them winning the tournament on 12 occasions.

Augusta National, and its prized home tournament, had become a jewel in the crown of golf in the United States, though with this rising stature a storm was brewing at the club's gates, off Washington Road, the thoroughfare that had become an eyesore-lined strip of cheap restaurants and bargain stores, but which had one sign very simply bearing the instruction 'Augusta National Golf Club Members Only'.

In the guardhouse at the entrance off Washington Road security personnel knew members by their faces, and any guests showing up had to remain in place until a member appeared to sign them in. Even then, members were allowed only four guests at any one time. Not welcome at Augusta National were members of the black community, not unless they were there to serve and caddie, and generally make themselves useful. The club's exclusivity, and the barely concealed racist utterances of Cliff Roberts at the best of times, had become a real problem, both for those gentlemen who were allowed to drive their large cars through the gates and travel the 330 yards down Magnolia Lane, with its 61 magnolia trees standing guard on either side, before arriving at the magnificent clubhouse, and also for those people who cared never to go within 100 miles of Augusta National.

Cliff Roberts had a very clear judgement of people based on the colour of their skin. Having travelled through South America on Joroberts business, he thought whites, blacks and mixed race should be accepted in that order in life. But, in his own words, he definitely thought of mixed race as 'the most worthless of all in every respect'.

An African-American player did not receive an invitation to the Masters until 1975, when Lee Elder was asked to play. That was four years after the Dallas-born Elder had received a personal invitation from Gary Player to participate in the South African PGA Championship in Johannesburg, marking the first integrated tournament in the country's troubled history of apartheid, though the American golfer agreed to travel only after he had received confirmation that the South African government would not subject him or tournament spectators to the normal segregation requirements.

Back home in the United States, Elder made his way to Augusta National by winning his first PGA Tour title, the Monsanto Open, in 1974. Not surprisingly, after a barrage of hate mail and several threatening phone calls, Elder was not at his best in East Georgia and shot a 74 on day one, followed by a 78 on the Friday, which left him out of the tournament and on his way home.

Throughout his time in Augusta, Elder was advised by his manager to rent two houses in the city and keep moving between them, and to always have friends around him when he went out to eat. An important piece of history had been made, nevertheless, though on the club's membership list things did not change at all and the first African-American member, Ron Townsend, the president of a CBS affiliate in Washington DC, was not asked to join Augusta National until 1991, a long and wearying 14 years since the club's deeply ignorant chairman had decided to blow his own brains out.

With giants of the game walking the magnificent fairways at Augusta National in the 1950s and 60s, and their images pouring into homes all over the country, the club quickly prospered, and never looked back. The Masters was on its way to becoming the most tempting tournament for every single professional wandering the United States and looking to scratch out a more than decent living.

And, then, there was always the President.

Dwight D. Eisenhower is recorded as having played 800 rounds of golf during his two terms in the White House, but only in Augusta National did he have a house next to Bobby Jones. There, also, he had a friend in the club chairman, Cliff Roberts, who would move heaven and earth for the President, and who most helpfully moved the President's handicap upwards on occasions. And only in the grounds of Augusta National did Ike have his very own fish pond.

Tickets to the Masters, by the late 1960s, had become scarce and hard to find even for those who deserved to attend the event. So in 1972 the club started a waiting list. Six years later the same list was put away for good when it became unmanageable and impossibly long.

Everything had changed since Augusta National had held its first tournament in 1934. The course had changed, evolving into perhaps the most wonderful parcel of colourful and exciting land anywhere on the planet, and some holes were hardly recognisable any more to those members who had first paid their dues. Trees had grown into magnificent specimens; greens had changed shape; more bunkers were added, others deleted, and the sand in those bunkers was bleached to look just about perfect for anybody to visit such a place with a golf ball.

By the 1970s, when colour television sets had arrived in most homes in the United States, Augusta National seemed like an almost impossibly beautiful place. But it had reached out to seek this perfection at quite a price.

Trees and grass have never lived happily side by side, and with the Augusta National chairman demanding, ever since he opened his course in 1932, that not one inch of his personal kingdom should ever appear browned or burned, that precious grass was fed abundant quantities of water, and extremely rich supplies of feeds and chemicals. The spectacular pine trees, in particular the loblollies, with their lower branches self-pruned up to 100 feet, which dissect the course and leave visitors in awe at their majesty and wonder, have also been drinking from the same water table, and too much enriched water leaves pines diseased and dying.

The golfing home of Bobby Jones and Cliff Roberts had become unnaturally beautiful, and nature, ultimately, never allows humans to have their way for good.

****

Cliff Roberts was something of an insomniac and he often drove his cart around the course in the early hours of the morning, by which time his guests had long since turned in. Before the club reopened for its members at the end of the summer of 1977, Roberts made his usual early visit to inspect the grounds and its people. His body was quickly breaking down. Almost all of his friends were dead. It was quite natural for him to return to Augusta National to die.

He would end his life, suddenly and violently, as his mother had, and also his father. Rebecca Roberts celebrated her 44th birthday on July 31, 1913, and eight days later she turned a shotgun on herself next to the garage of her home, and that is where her husband, Charles, found her at five o'clock the next morning. The blast did not awaken her husband or her five sleeping children, each of whom, according to the local newspaper, the *Palacios Beacon*, was left a note from their mother expressing an 'affectionate farewell'.

Cliff's father, Charles de Clifford Roberts Sr, threw himself in front of a Gulf Coast Lines passenger train in October 1921. The wheels of the train severed the body in two.

In 1977, when Cliff Roberts decided that his time had come, he wanted nobody to be left in any doubt about his state of mind or his immediate wishes. His will insisted on no funeral service. Instead he asked that his body be cremated and that his ashes be 'buried at an unmarked spot on or scattered to the winds over the grounds of the Augusta National Golf Club'.

It remains a mystery as to what happened next.

The ashes may have been scattered over the course, though members with more local knowledge like to think that Roberts' remains are in three possible locations: in Ike's pond on the par-three course; in the fairway bunker on the 10th hole; or in the pond in front of the 15th.

The gun used by Cliff Roberts to end his life has had less intrigue attached to its whereabouts, unfortunately. It turned up in 1990, in an auction house catalogue in Japan.

Its morbid value was appraised at $15,000.

CHAPTER TWO

Ken

When Ken Venturi was five years old, his parents decided he should switch from being left-handed to right-handed. This determination by Fred and Ethyl Venturi left their only child with a speech impediment for the remainder of his life.

Ken developed a stammer, which he fought against and sought to control until his early teens, but by then his parents were told that his difficulty was incurable and that their son would have to suffer, and live with, his impediment.

When he was 13, Ken told his mother that he was going to take up the 'loneliest sport I can play… I'm going to be a golfer.' Like so many other young Italian-American kids living on the West Coast, Venturi worshipped Joe DiMaggio, and he was a pretty decent baseball player himself. But, that same summer, he had also started caddying at the San Francisco Golf Club, making 50 cents, sometimes even a dollar, per bag, and out there on the course he could see that it was easy to keep conversation to a minimum.

He could keep out of people's way.

He could keep conversations short and to the point.

He would forsake baseball and become a golfer.

The game, and its beautiful surroundings, captured Ken's head and heart. He'd wander down to the 16th at Cypress Point, take in all of its magnificence, and read his golf magazines while he waited for his father to complete his sales calls for the day, at the canneries in Monterey. His father would pick him up and they'd head back up the highway together.

It might be six, seven o'clock in the evening. 'I'd be sitting on the steps, waiting for him. Sometimes we'd drive all the way home, and he'd barely say a word,' Venturi would fondly recall.

'In those days, I had a terrible stammer and it was hard for me to get a full sentence out. When my father spoke, it was to say something meaningful.'

Frederico 'Fred' Venturi, whose father came to the United States with tens of thousands of other Italians to make a better way of life for his family at the turn of the century, worked for 30 years as a ship chandler, selling nets and twine on Fisherman's Wharf in San Francisco and up and down the California coast, before retiring and becoming manager of Harding Park Municipal Golf Course in San Francisco. His wife, Ethyl, who sold real estate, had family back in Ireland. Their only child was born on May 15, 1931, in the black heart of the Great Depression.

Fred and Ethyl lived in the Mission District, which was a heavily populated Italian corner of San Francisco. The Venturis would honour their family tradition every Sunday afternoon when the threesome sat around a large round table for an Italian feast, and some years later, when in college, Ken would have his friends knocking on his bedroom door when they smelled the leftover lasagne, or ravioli, which he had brought back with him from his weekend home.

Unlike many of their neighbours, Fred and Ethyl were also keen golfers. They welcomed their son's new-found interest in the game, but at 13 years of age Ken's speech was often uncontrolled and difficult, resulting in fights in the school yard and also in the classroom whenever anyone mocked his efforts.

Anyone who dared mimic him would have to answer for their cruelty immediately. One one occasion, one young boy was clubbed with Ken's chair, though most often it was Ken who would come off the worse for wear after such altercations, with a busted nose or lip. The stammer would remain with Ken Venturi all his life, but he did gain some control over it, learning to compose himself and adapt different techniques that would be sufficient to allow him to make speeches in public, and also complete a 35-year career in the second half of his adult life as an eloquent and hugely respected commentator for CBS.

Venturi, though, never came to rule completely over his speech defect. Nor, as a younger man and a touring pro, was he ever able to convince people that his reluctance to say very much on a golf course, or before and after his round, was a naturally defensive, self-protective trait that had been ingrained in his character in order to avoid awkward situations and embarrassment. Some people thought Venturi simply full of his own importance. Others considered him indifferent to making a decent effort at being even half friendly.

Compared to his great friend, Mike Souchak, who was born on the East Coast and was always talkative and warm towards people, in the clubhouse and out on the practice tee, Venturi was a cold wall of silence most of the time.

'People like Mike relax when they have someone to talk to,' explained Venturi, 'or when they pick out someone in the gallery and say hello.

'I just can't do that.

'If I see someone in the gallery and just barely nod to them, people think I'm being stand-offish or something, but actually a slight nod from me is like Mike going over to them and giving them a big slap on the back.'

Venturi's first official score on a golf course was 172 shots, after he played a round at his father's Harding Park with a golf bag that contained two hickory-shafted woods and two hickory-shafted irons. He was proud of his bag, certainly much more so than his efforts on the course, though Venturi would one day, as a hardened professional, complete another 18 holes at Harding Park in 59 shots. By the time he had finished with the course, later in his life, he had eagled every par-five, made a two on every par-four, and aced three of the course's four par-threes.

But, as a kid, when he walked with a bag on his shoulder Venturi saw himself as one golfer, and one golfer only – the greatest golfer in the world in Ken Venturi's eyes, Byron Nelson.

In 1945, Nelson would win 11 tournaments in a row on tour, a feat that most likely will never be equalled. The next year, at 34 years of age, Nelson retired from playing the game competitively. In his all too brief but brilliant PGA Tour career, Nelson won 52 tournaments, finishing with 18 victories alone the year before his retirement. He was Masters champion in 1937 and 1942, a US Open winner in 1939, and in 1940 and 1945 he claimed the PGA Championship.

'In one US Open during Byron's prime he hit the flagstick six times in 72 holes,' Venturi wrote in *Golf Digest* magazine in 2000. 'Byron's divots all looked the same. And he is the only guy whose natural ball flight was a straight shot. He could hook and fade it easily, but Byron could hit the ball dead straight on demand. That's the hardest thing to do in golf.'

Nelson would teach Venturi so much about the game of golf. And he also would teach him about life. Venturi always most fondly remembered their decade spent together in the 1950s, when the dazzling young talent and the graceful older champion had the opportunity of playing countless exhibition matches together all over the country. Repeatedly, as the pair of them arrived on the first tee, Ken would hear his friend ask a local member what was the course record, and who held it. After almost 12 months of such questioning of locals, Ken asked why was this information always so important at the beginning of a round?

'As long as you play with me, Ken... remember one thing,' replied Nelson. 'You never break the course record if it is owned by the host pro. He lives there... you're only visiting!'

Despite frequent opportunities of taking course records after that, Venturi always made sure on occasions to avoid doing so. More than 20 years later, when Venturi was enjoying himself during a relaxed round at the Westchester Country Club, he began scoring, and scoring well, going eagle, par, birdie, eagle, birdie. When he soon landed a hole-in-one he knew that he could break the course record with a par at the last hole. Remembering Nelson's advice, Venturi intentionally hit a double-bogey seven on the 18th.

Byron Nelson was the son of second-generation cotton farmers. He was Texan, through and through. As was his once great friend, who later became his bitterest oppponent, Ben Hogan.

Both men had young lives that could never be termed easy, though for a while, Hogan's was filled with as much love and kindness as Nelson's. That all ended for young Ben when his father took his own life. Ben was nine years old.

Hogan had watched his mother and father argue over the family's dwindling blacksmiths business and, by all accounts, Ben chased after his father into an adjoining room in their home and witnessed Chester Hogan shoot himself in the chest with his revolver. His father had been treated in a local sanatorium for a mental illness, most likely bipolar disorder, or manic depression. He was 37 years old. Ben Hogan would never speak of what happened in the family home that day, and neither would his mother, Clara.

Nelson and Hogan, and one or two others, such as Sam Snead, who was the youngest of five brothers from a Virginian coal-mining community, were the first golfers America would come to know and truly respect as professional sportsmen. From the turn of the century, and through the 1920s and '30s, golfers who sought to earn some sort of meagre living as professionals were treated, and so often dismissed, as the hired help.

The amateur career was viewed as the purest way to play golf, and gentlemen who doubled as outstanding golfers, and who won major championships, such as the great Bobby Jones, were considered to be an exalted club of their own. Professionals a generation earlier were not allowed through the front door of a private members' clubhouse. They were considered strictly working class, and for their very best efforts on a golf course they were usually paid according to such a lowly status in society.

Nelson, Hogan and Snead, all born within six months of one another, were among the first group of golf professionals who did not have, as their primary consideration at the start of every week, the cost of a meal or the price of a roof over their heads. They could actually think of making themselves some money.

For Nelson, every cent spent, and every cent in winnings, was recorded in his 'little black book', which, one day, he believed would finally present him and his wife, Louise, with a princely sum that would afford them the ranch of their dreams back home in Texas.

Like most young men his age in Fort Worth, Nelson got out of school for good by tenth grade, and started scuffing out a living, beginning as a railroad clerk. He did other jobs too. And he played his golf, qualifying for the US Amateur Championship in 1931 when he was 19 years old. When he needed to hit the road and play some serious golf, he usually had to sell the cups or valuables he had already won. He still lived on the farm with his folks.

The next year Nelson turned pro. Hogan by then was already working his golf clubs for a living, having turned professional two years earlier. Together, they formed an immediate friendship, often bunking down in the same rented bedroom – three dollars for the night, between them, usually. It wasn't a good time to be travelling the country, looking to earn a living, as golf courses and golf tournaments had been shaken up and left the worse for wear in the immediate aftermath of the Great Depression. Hogan could tell Nelson what it was really like out there.

Hogan had come home once already with his tail between his legs, taking up a room once again in his mother's house, and looking for some work around Fort Worth, mopping floors, running errands, parking cars, whatever came his way.

Trying their luck in tournaments on the West Coast was a risky business. Both Hogan and Nelson would come home without a dollar's profit in their pockets on occasions. Nelson had spent all of his spare cash on a roadster, for him and his new bride, and to keep her warm in the unheated vehicle he would heat blocks in the stove of their motel room, wrap them in newspaper the next morning, and leave them on the floor of the passenger's side.

Nelson got his career up and running faster than his friend and rival Hogan, and won his first professional tournament, the New Jersey State Open, in 1935, which brought with it a first-place cheque for $400. His winnings and club work for the full year amounted to $5,146.40. His expenses were $3,946.40. Nelson's little black book showed a profit of $1,200.

For every pro golfer things slowly began to look more promising by the end of the decade, as a full nationwide 'Tour' was taking shape, with the professional golfing community playing their way through the West Coast, swinging south and playing some more in Florida.

Nelson won his first Masters in 1937, but had retired from the game by the middle of the next decade, and his historic 11 Tour wins on the trot in 1945 had him and Louise well on their way to being able to land their dream ranch, a 650-acre spread 20 miles north of Fort Worth, for one all-cash payment of $55,000. By 34, Nelson had had a stomachful of life as a professional golfer. In his previous 113 tournaments he had never failed to make a cut, not once. He had earned his early retirement, even if Byron and Louise had only $2,500 in savings left in their bank account.

Hogan was the same age in 1946. That summer he won his first major, the PGA, and he would win eight more. But Hogan never shook off the hardships and disappointments of his childhood and young adult life, nor his father's tragic death, nor the repeated humiliations of turning up in Forth Worth dead broke, and certainly not the breakdown of his great friendship with Byron Nelson.

Hogan knew what he wanted from life. He met his future wife, Valerie Fox, when he was 12 years old. His career as a champion golfer was not quite a story of love at first sight, however. It was bloody hard work, and work he never shirked. 'If you can't outplay 'em... outwork 'em,' as he liked to say.

By his 17th birthday, Ken Venturi had decided that golf should be receiving his undivided attention. At high school he arranged his classes so that he could finish as early as possible most afternoons. Then, school done for the day, Ken drove the 1931 Model A Ford that his father had bought for him for $125, to Harding Park and hit golf balls every afternoon and did not quit until 5.30 p.m.

He'd have his dinner at 6, before working from 7 to 10 p.m. in Shaw's Ice Cream Parlor, where he would also take care of his homework during every peaceful five minutes he could find. On Sunday mornings he mowed lawns, that was another $15 a month, and at the golf course he offered to wash cars in the parking lot for a few dollars more. His most important work, however, was saved for the golf course.

Out there, alone, he could concentrate on a particular shot he was looking to craft or a difficult green he sought to master, often spending between six and nine hours at a time on one or the other, developing calluses on both hands in the process.

Within three years, Venturi had won all of the junior titles in the city, and he had set his sights on the biggest title of all. He wanted the 1950 San Francisco City Championship, which regularly drew just under 3,000 entries, as golfers from all walks, and all ages, sought to be No.1 in San Francisco.

That year, in the first round of the City Championship, Venturi drew a man named Martin Stanovich – a 'Minnesota Fats of the fairways' as Venturi recalled. Stanovich was a fair enough player, but sharp-minded and tough to beat. Stanovich also had money in his pocket from his successful mattress company in the city. The match would attract a lot of bets. Venturi's friends raised more than $3,000 to place on Venturi's back. Stanovich liked that particular bet. He covered the $3,000 all by himself. Venturi won the match 3 and 2.

He had entered a man's golfing world. He also won the championship title, coming from three down with nine holes to play in the final and finally claiming the title after his match against Bob Silvestri went to two extra holes. It was that same evening that Ken Venturi met Eddie Lowery for the first time.

Eddie Lowery was already a multi-millionaire car dealer. Born and raised on the East Coast he was tough, resilient and, most of all, street-smart, and these qualities, in addition to a sense of humour ingrained in him through his Irish and Boston heritage, were with him on every step of his journey through life.

Lowery would quickly become young Ken Venturi's guiding hand, in his life and in his golfing career. At a time long before sports agents came into being as a species of business person, the likes of Lowery had important work to do influencing young men and helping them realise their dreams.

Eddie Lowery never did, through hard times or even on his best of days, think twice about greeting life's unexpected generosity with an accepting face.

As a 10-year-old kid Lowery had first begun balancing his own priorities in life, skipping school in the summer of 1913 and triumphantly turning up at the door of Francis Ouimet's home in Brookline, Massachusetts, which was situated directly across the road from the Country Club course that was to host that year's US Open. There, Eddie offered his caddying services to the teenage amateur Ouimet as he faced an emotionally charged week in which he would play against the greatest golfers on the planet. It would finish with victory for Ouimet in a play-off over the exalted British professional pairing of Harry Vardon and Ted Ray.

A magnificent photograph of the tall, gaunt Ouimet, and pudgy little Eddie, striding down the fairway at Brookline together, remains one of the iconic images in American golf history, the latter wearing a long tie but with the sleeves of his big white shirt rolled up to his elbows, and with Ouimet's large bag high on his back. The photo was best used as the logo for the US Golf Association's centennial celebrations. The book that perfectly immortalised that epic week in golf, Mark Frost's *The Greatest Game Ever Played*, was also made into a movie in 2005 and precisely captured the spirit and unquenchable belief of Eddie Lowery, the son of hard-working but usually penniless Irish immigrants, John Lowery and Maria Curran.

In the moments after Ouimet's victory in the US Open, the watching crowd gushed to offer him some money for his heroic efforts, but Ouimet, amateur to the core, declined the contents which soon filled little Eddie Lowery's hat. So Eddie kept the money for himself, a precious sum which totalled just over $125.

Eddie's father had died, in an industrial accident, the year before Ouimet's triumph at Brookline. His mother had nothing and Eddie, as the youngest of Maria's family of six children, knew as well as the others in the home that everyone needed to do their bit.

Lowery had been in the advertising business in Boston to begin with. His first wife had died shortly after his only son was born and by the mid-1930s he decided to head west, where he took up a portion of a car dealership in San Jose. Twenty years later, he had the most successful Lincoln-Mercury dealership in the United States.

While Lowery was an eager benefactor of precocious young talent, he could also play a bit himself, and had won the Massachusetts Amateur Championship while in his twenties. He would have backed himself to beat most opponents across America, but his car business, and the power-game of golf officialdom, quickly took up more of his time than he could devote to playing. In the early 1950s, he represented California on the USGA Executive Committee.

When his second wife, Mary Louise, died of cancer in 1954, golf became Lowery's whole life. He loved nothing better than the days before a big golf tournament, when the richest of businessmen got the opportunity to put their cash where their mouths were, and bid for players in an open auction before play got under way. Lowery, like everyone else, won, and lost, big time! But that was his life. Whether at golf tournaments or at the poker table in one of his many homes, Eddie Lowery simply liked to make life as interesting as possible, to the point where, at any moment, it might burst at the seams.

As well as Augusta National, Lowery was a member at several of the West Coast's outstanding clubs, including San Francisco Golf Club and the beautiful Cypress Point. He also had the best of golfing friends. Byron Nelson, Ben Hogan and a host of the game's greatest players talked with Lowery regularly, and Bing Crosby was in his circle of movers and shakers, as was the CBS talk-show host Ed Sullivan.

Having lost his only son in the Second World War, Lowery had a natural inclination to help young guys coming through the ranks. Here, he had a natural partner in Byron Nelson, who had no children. When he was 11 years old, and the family had settled in Fort Worth, Nelson lost almost half his body weight when he contracted typhoid fever and never recovered the necessary physical health to have a family of his own.

As *Sports Illustrated*'s Alfred Wright once wrote, Lowery liked to play golf 'where the scores were low and the stakes were high'.

It was in Lowery's company, not surprisingly, that Ken Venturi first learnt about pressure on a golf course. 'I got used to being where the money was riding,' Venturi remembered, 'and I didn't get scared off by it. I probably never had more than $10 or $20 of my own on a match, but for me that was blood, and I knew that Lowery was going with me for a lot more... sometimes $600 or $700.'

But with Lowery in his corner, Venturi was being well looked after. 'I remember once, one of our opponents shot a 65,' said Venturi, '...and lost every bet.'

There were times, though, when Lowery created some tricky situations for Venturi and others to extract themselves from, and none looked more remarkable or foolhardy than the fourball match, in the second week of 1956, to which Lowery challenged a fellow self-made multi-millionaire, George Coleman.

Lowery told Coleman that his two car salesmen, Ken Venturi and Harvie Ward, could beat any pairing that Coleman could put together. A couple of phone calls later, Coleman took up the challenge and Byron Nelson and Ben Hogan were summoned to the first tee, at a quiet and private Cypress Point, the next morning to take on the two amateurs.

The match was all-square after nine holes, with each pairing on six under par. They were still level when they came to the last, where Hogan made a birdie to win the match. In the process, Hogan equalled his own course record at Cypress Point, scoring 63. Venturi shot a 65 while Nelson and Ward posted 67s.

Nobody would ever find out how much money Lowery and Coleman wagered on the remarkable match, although some reports put the figure as high as $20,000. The golfers also had themselves a little side bet, agreeing to put up $100 for the result of the front nine, $100 for the back nine, and a further $100 for the match overall. It was a tastier 'Nassau' than either Venturi or Ward would have wished for, but, back in the clubhouse at Cypress Point after the match, when the four golfers finally sat down to gather themselves, Nelson and Hogan refused to take their $200 winnings from the two amateurs.

It was Lowery, who else, who had first properly introduced Ken Venturi to his hero, Byron Nelson. Venturi had just been beaten in his first match in the US Amateur Championship in 1952, in Seattle, and Lowery suggested that Ken come to the clubhouse to meet a friend of his.

Nelson invited Venturi out for a game of golf the next morning, but surprised his young fan by suggesting that they play back in San Francisco. Lowery and Nelson flew out of Seattle that evening.

For Ken there was an overnight haul in his 10-year-old Buick Roadster. At 3 a.m., on the road from Seattle to San Francisco, Venturi was changing a flat tyre with a flashlight. The tee time with Byron Nelson was fixed for 1 p.m.

The pair played 18 holes the next day and, as he had promised before they teed off, Nelson did not offer one word of advice, or criticism, to his young playing partner that morning at San Francisco Golf Club.

Afterwards, Venturi walked into the clubhouse feeling quite delighted with himself. He had just shot a 66 in front of his boyhood hero. Nelson, however, made no mention of the game as they both ordered tea and toast. As they finished their snack, however, Ken could not hold back any longer. He asked the great man what he thought of his game.

Nelson, ever so quietly, calmly told Ken that he would be staying three more days in San Francisco, and was prepared to meet him at the course at nine o'clock each morning. 'There are about seven or eight things we can fix up in your swing,' Nelson then informed him, 'which might make you a good player.'

The work then started on building the solid one-piece swing that Ken Venturi would trust for the rest of his life. Venturi was using his hands too much, according to Nelson. He needed to have his hands, shoulders and body moving in one fluid action. After that, he needed a swing that could withstand the fiercest competition. So that meant better positioning, smarter timing, finer balance, a different grip and a more even weight distribution.

He needed to do nearly everything a whole lot better.

Venturi had entered San Jose State University in 1949 with the intention of becoming a dentist. He thought that dentists had money, and had plenty of time to play golf. It was during his time at San Jose that he met Conni MacLean, a sophomore, who would become his wife.

Twelve months before they first met, Conni had informed her mother that she was going to marry Ken Venturi. She had travelled to Pebble Beach to watch her father compete in the California State Amateur in 1950, and had stayed to watch the winner, Venturi, up close at the presentation ceremony. Conni stayed calm, and mostly nonplussed, as the man she had set her heart on finally walked in her direction on campus one afternoon and stood before her.

Conni wanted to be an actress. She had already been accepted at the College of the Pacific to pursue her career on the stage but, late in the day, she decided to enroll at San Jose State because she knew that that was where Ken Venturi was studying. In San Jose she lived in a boarding house with 21 girls. All of her house-mates knew she wanted to marry Ken. They had seen the scrapbook that Conni kept to mark his career. But, on their first date, Conni remained serene.

At one point, as they began talking golf, Conni told Ken that her father played, and asked him did he play the game, too?

'What's your handicap?' wondered Conni, playfully.

Finally, when informed that Ken was playing off scratch, Conni advised him that he should try competing in a tournament some day.

Venturi graduated from San Jose in the summer of 1953. By then, his golf game under the tutelage of Byron Nelson was just about the complete package. By then, also, Conni MacLean had become his first serious girlfriend. One year later, in 1954, they would be married, the same year in which Ken Venturi competed in the Masters for the first time.

Eddie Lowery paid Venturi's expenses for the week in Augusta. Venturi had never seen a place, never mind a golf course, as beautiful as Augusta National was the first occasion he drove up Magnolia Lane.

Venturi played his first round in the 1954 Masters tournament with his pal, Harvie Ward, and shot a 76. In comparison to Ken, Harvie was quite at home at Augusta National already. He'd played his first Masters tournament six years earlier, when he tied for 51st, but the cocky young amateur made sure that he was not forgotten on his maiden drive up Magnolia Lane. He had borrrowed a pink Cadillac convertible and had a string of cans hanging from the rear. A hand-painted sign on the back of the car shouted 'Masters or Bust'. The club chairman, Clifford Roberts, heard all about the young man's effrontery, took one look at Harvie smiling and talking to everybody later that same afternoon and, surprisingly, decided to give him a 'pass' on his disrespectful, but peculiarly charming, entrance to the most invigorating party in golf.

On Thursday evening, after his first ever round at Augusta National, Venturi was having dinner with Eddie Lowery and Bill Danforth, a distinguished member at the club, when the pair asked him who he would like to play with the next day? Venturi, uncertain, replied 'Ben Hogan', but thought there was little chance of that happening. But, right there and then, Danforth turned around and called out to Roberts.

'Cliff,' he said, 'pair Ken with Ben Hogan tomorrow.'

The chairman was happy to do just that.

Venturi had followed Hogan for the last 36 holes the previous year, when Hogan won the US Open at Oakmont Country Club in western Pennsylvania. Now a private in the US Army and on temporary leave, Venturi was going to be playing with the great man himself, on the most magnificent course he had ever seen. It was a long night of fitful sleep for Venturi.

He was in awe of Hogan. Later in his career, Venturi would also wear the same kind of short-billed flat linen cap that Hogan favoured in competition. But, when the two men got chatting during the early holes of their first round together in Augusta, Hogan soon made a cheap remark about his playing partner's irons.

'What do you expect,' replied Venturi. 'I'm a private in the army making $72 a month.'

At the start of their round, Hogan had asked the young man to call him 'Ben... not Mr Hogan', but after their stiff few words Venturi retorted, 'You want me to call you Mr Hogan again?'

'No,' Hogan replied. 'But I want your address when we get in. I'm going to send you a decent set of clubs.'

Venturi finished his first Masters, in 1954, in a tie for 16th, eight shots back from the leading pairing, Hogan and Sam Snead, on 297. He had had rounds of 76, 74, 73 and 74. Harvie Ward also made the cut for the eighth time in nine visits. On the Monday, Hogan lost an 18-hole play-off to Snead by a single shot, 70 to 71.

Less than two weeks later, a magnificent new set of Ben Hogan irons arrived at Ken Venturi's home.

CHAPTER THREE

Rory

By the time he was just nine years old, Rory McIlroy's life had already reached an interesting place. Two very interesting golf courses, in fact. The plush beauty of Doral Golf Resort and Spa in Miami, and the brilliant ruggedness of Royal Portrush closer to his home.

At the first venue, he won the world championship for the nine-ten age group. At the second golf club McIlroy got to meet Darren Clarke for the first time when his father, Gerry, took him to play the links at Royal Portrush as a birthday present. McIlroy would meet his hero again, at the Darren Clarke Foundation, when he was 13.

Rory McIlroy, who had received his first proper clubs, a cut-down set of ladies' Mizuno irons when he was five years old, when he also began receiving coaching lessons from Michael Bannon, the pro at Holywood Golf Club near Belfast in Northern Ireland, had found a friend for life.

At 15 and 16 years of age McIlroy became the youngest winner of the West of Ireland Championship and the Irish Amateur Close Championship, and he was doing things on great golf courses all over Ireland that seemed ridiculously improbable for someone so young. At 16 also, on the Dunluce course at Royal Portrush, he shot a record 61, even though he had been only two-under after six holes. From the seventh tee, putts began to fall for him.

'I stood on the 16th tee and said, *Right, let's go for it! Even if I drop a couple of shots it'll be worth it,*' he remembered some years later. 'A six-iron to six feet at 16 set up another birdie. Seventeen was an easy birdie, downwind at the par-five. Then I knocked it into 15 feet at the last and, in trying to just two-putt, I holed for a closing birdie.'

McIlroy was moving fast up through the gears of his golfing career. He made his first appearance on the PGA European Tour when he was only 16, competing in the British Masters. By then he had left school, Sullivan Upper, after completing his GCSE exams, so that he could concentrate on golf full-time. At 17, he made the cut at a European Tour event for the first time, at the 2007 Dubai Desert Classic, where he had to pass up his earnings of €7,600 to protect his amateur status. One day in Dubai he borrowed a photographer's armband so that he could follow Tiger Woods around the course and watch him from close up.

McIlroy shot an opening-round, three-under-par 68 at the Open Championship at Carnoustie in 2007, his first major championship appearance, when he outplayed Ryder Cup stars Henrik Stenson and Miguel Angel Jimenez. He finished the Open at five over par and won the silver medal for the highest finishing amateur. His playing partner, Scott Verplank, a Ryder Cup veteran and someone with more than $20 million in career earnings, had been overpowered and was deeply impressed by the bushy-headed wonder, who reduced the 499-yard closing hole at Carnoustie to a drive and a seven-iron approach, which finished eight feet from the pin. McIlroy, naturally enough, rolled in the putt to sign off with another birdie.

'He's 18, looks 14, and plays like a 28-year-old,' was Verplank's verdict. McIlroy then watched as Padraig Harrington became the first Irishman in 60 years to win the Open Championship, prevailing after a dramatic four-hole play-off over the long-time leader, Spain's supremely talented but so often sorrowful Sergio Garcia.

By then, journalists from all over Ireland and Britain had been making the trip to the humble surroundings of Holywood Golf Club in County Down, on the north-east coast of Ireland, for many years. They had been seeking more information on Rory McIlroy, and some quickly sat down on the little bench overlooking the 18th green where there is a plaque in memory of Jimmy McIlroy, a long-time club member who passed away in 1992. Jimmy's son Gerry, once a scratch golfer, was bar manager in the clubhouse.

Out on the course, Jimmy's grandson, Rory, born on May 4, 1989, three years before his grandfather's death, had proved himself the most talented young golfer anyone in the club had ever seen. Rory and Gerry McIlroy have both been club champion, taking charge of those holes stretching from Hazel Wood, past Cherry Tree, to Nun's Walk, through the valley, over Irish Hill and by Holly Bush before reaching the 18th green, overlooked by that simple bench.

When enquiring journalists visited Holywood, close to the top of their list of questions was Rory McIlroy's religion?

In the troubled history of Northern Ireland, especially from the late 1960s, it was never very difficult to identify who was a Catholic, and who was a Protestant, but when McIlroy became a household name, in the homes of golfing fans at least, nobody was too sure on which side his family lineage resided. Most people presumed he was Catholic, and there was confirmation that he attended a Catholic primary school, St Patrick's, but there were peculiarities, like the fact this his website bore the flag of Northern Ireland, a definite Loyalist symbol that has the Red Hand of Ulster at its centre and is typically presented in public by anyone who is a Protestant and immensely proud of it.

McIlroy himself avoided any talk of religion, or passports, or flags for that matter. 'Everyone I knew could identify in an instant the religious affiliation of even the most apolitical people who had propelled themselves from Northern Ireland on to the bigger stage,' explained Niall Stanage, a journalist from Northern Ireland, in

The New York Times. 'Van Morrison was Protestant. Liam Neeson was Catholic. George Best, perhaps the finest soccer player of his generation, Protestant. Dennis Taylor, a snooker world champion, Catholic. And on and on.'

The Red Hand of Ulster was also centre-stage on the crest of the Ulster Volunteer Force, a paramilitary organisation that murdered Rory McIlroy's great uncle in 1972 at the height of The Troubles in Ireland.

Rory, his father and his management have never commented on the murder, the investigation of which was reopened by the Police Service of Northern Ireland in the summer of 2011. Joseph McIlroy was shot through his kitchen door on November 21, 1972, as he fixed a washing machine. The gunmen had hidden out that evening in the McIlroy family's back garden. The case is one of hundreds of cold-blooded killings still being re-examined by the police force.

A computer technician, Joseph was Jimmy McIlroy's brother, and he had moved with his wife Mary and their four daughters into the Sandhill Drive area of the North Road in East Belfast, when the housing development opened in 1968. They were one of only two Catholic families in the area, also known as Orangefield, which was overwhelmingly Protestant, and they were easy targets for either the UDA or the UVF, who had death squads that would randomly visit Catholics in their homes and workplaces.

Joseph, known to everybody as Joe, worked at the computer company ICL, and he was chatting to his wife moments before he was gunned down, while his daughters, Kathy, Maria, Geraldine and Helen, all slept upstairs. Mary heard five shots, before her husband staggered into their living-room and collapsed on to a couch.

'I put my arms around him and then I noticed my hands were covered in blood,' Mary McIlroy told the inquest into her husband's murder. 'I ran screaming into the street.'

Joe was shot several times in the stomach and was pronounced dead on arrival at hospital. He was the 74th person to be assassinated in Northern Ireland in four chilling months.

Rory McIlroy's grandfather, Jimmy, had worked repairing cranes in Belfast docks, where the *Titanic* was built and sent on its tragic way. 'In those days, while only Protestants were allowed to work in the shipyards actually building the ships, Catholics worked in the docks,' recounted Suzanne Breen, in the *Daily Mail*. 'But what made Jimmy McIlroy stand out was not his tradesmanship but his skills with a wedge. He picked up golf in his 30s and became a stalwart at Holywood Golf Club where ability outweighs all. He was considered the man to beat in the club, peerless from short range.' Jimmy McIlroy's love for golf was passed down to his sons, Gerry, Colm and Brian.

Gerry McIlroy married Rosaleen McDonald on January 13, 1988, in St Colmcille's Church, which had held his Uncle Joe's funeral mass in 1972, and where his son, Rory, would be christened 18 months later.

After primary school, Rory was sent to a religiously mixed grammar school, Sullivan Upper, which has as its school motto, and printed on pupils' blazers in the Irish language, '*Lamh Foisdineach An Uachtar*', meaning 'With the Gentle Hand Foremost'. Gerry and Rosie lived in a red-brick terraced house, where they brought up their only son and built him an artificial putting green in their tiny front yard, though Gerry also had Rory around his feet or close by practically any time he stood on a golf course.

As Rory's abilities blossomed and his young career began incurring heavier costs, Gerry took a second job working in a bar in Belfast in the evenings, after he had finished work at Holywood Golf Club. He also began working as a cleaner in the early mornings at a local rugby club, clocking up more than 90 hours' work some weeks. Rosie, meanwhile, worked in the local 3M factory packaging rolls of tape, and minded the home. All of their hard work bore fruit in providing their son with opportunities that were denied to most young golfers his age.

Rory McIlroy began to call himself 'Rory Nick Faldo McIlroy' and he liked to sign autographs at home or for club members with this full, confident signature.

McIlroy had to wait for more than a year for his first win as a European Tour professional. It came, finally, in February 2009, at the Dubai Desert Classic at the Emirates Golf Club and even then he was made to sweat. McIlroy enjoyed a six-shot lead at the start of the final round, but by the nailbiting climax that had been whittled down to just one stroke by England's Justin Rose. After watching Rose miss a 15-foot putt that would have forced a play-off, a relieved McIlroy was able to collect by far the largest cheque of his pro career to date, €323,514.99.

'You watch it on TV and you see guys coming down the stretch with a four or five-shot lead,' McIlroy quickly explained in the press room. 'And you think it's easy… but it's not.'

His first phone call after he completed that final round was to his girlfriend Holly. The second was to Holywood Golf Club, and he asked that a drink be bought for every member on the premises. The win moved him up to 14th in the world rankings, from a placing of 232nd at the end of 2007, and brought his prize money in the 16 months since he had turned professional to just over €1.5 million. McIlroy believed that his breakthrough win was due in no small measure to his caddie J. P. Fitzgerald, who had been on his bag for only six months, but who had already earned his master's complete trust.

On the 17th green, as his lead was tumbling, Fitzgerald had crouched down beside McIlroy.

'Big players love these situations,' Fitzgerald whispered. 'You're a big player… this is why we are here.'

The words immediately calmed McIlroy down and he was able to hold on for that precious first victory.

He had 2009's four majors sitting invitingly in front of him: Augusta, Bethpage, Turnberry and Hazeltine; four courses he had only ever seen before on his television set.

'He knows what he's doing, he's not living the dream,' his extravagantly loud and confident manager, Andrew 'Chubby' Chandler told an increasingly inquisitive media pack. 'He knows what's going on and where he's going.

'He's unbelievably impressive. His feet are on the ground, and his dad takes it all in his stride. It's unbelievable.'

Chandler was struck by the different generations of golfer that he had in his stable. His oldest client, Darren Clarke, liked to relax after a good round with a couple of glasses of red wine and a good cigar. McIlroy's choice was often a packet of crisps, washed down with a Mountain Dew.

McIlroy was ready for his first visit to Augusta National. He was preparing to be the first debutant to seize the tournament and win it since Fuzzy Zoeller had beaten Ed Sneed and Tom Watson in the event's first sudden-death play-off 30 years earlier. McIlroy would be 19 years, 11 months and eight days old on the final Sunday of the 2009 Masters tournament, whereas Tiger Woods was 21 years, three months and 14 days old when he won his first title in Augusta in 1997.

What some people were overlooking, however, as McIlroy was speeding towards the most perfect golf course in the whole world, was that on average each champion at Augusta National had taken six attempts before winning his first green jacket. Tiger Woods had only managed to halve that average, winning there on his third visit.

Woods was asked if he could see McIlroy as the world No.1 some day.

'There's no doubt... the guy's a talent. He's only 19... just give him some time, and I'm sure he'll be there.'

McIlroy wanted to get to Augusta early. He was excited, and nervous. In the previous month, playing in the US, he was amazed and flattered to find himself being recognised in the shopping malls. He had to pose for some photos with locals. He found it weird. His face would be on the cover of *Sports Illustrated* magazine on the week of his arrival. 'I think it's important to get to know the course a little bit so that when I get there on the Monday, I don't get lost,' he explained.

'I don't know where the locker room is, I don't know where to sign in, I don't know where the players' lounge is.

'It's just an opportunity to get to know where everything is and to make it easier for myself. It'll make it an awful lot less stressful for me.'

On the Monday at Augusta National, at the start of Masters week, McIlroy was met with cheers and roars of 'RORY! RORY! RORY!' from the fans behind the twine ropes, as he made the 50-yard walk from the rear of the Colonial-style clubhouse to the driving range.

He could smell the azaleas and breathing in the warm Georgia air put a smile on his face.

Like so many golfers, McIlroy had dreamed of this moment, of stepping out on to the vivid green acres of Augusta. He was finally in that dream, though it would contain a bump or two, especially during his second round when he charged from 36th position to sixth, with three holes still to play. He then four-putted the 16th for a double-bogey five and ran up a triple-bogey seven on the 18th, which left him with a disappointing 73 on his scorecard and a two-round total of 145. He had fallen back to 42nd spot in the space of three holes, and he had survived the halfway cut with nothing to spare at one over par.

Furthermore, he had also narrowly avoided being thrown out of his first Masters tournament, when officials called him back to the clubhouse on the Friday evening to review a tape showing his 'footwork' in the sand trap to one side of the 18th hole.

McIlroy shot a 71 on the Saturday and, after a potentially head-wrecking 39 on the front nine on the Sunday morning, he recovered for his lowest round of his first week at Augusta National, shooting a two-under-par 70 that included five birdies in an error-free back nine. It earned him a share of 20th place and a tidy cheque for $71,400. By the end of 2009, the *Sunday Times* Rich List had put McIlroy's career earnings since turning pro at €3.4 million, though the three-times major winner Padraig Harrington, from Dublin, had accrued 10 times that amount.

There may have been the small matter of €30 million separating the two players back then, but their performance statistics in the summer of 2009 showed that the balance of power was shifting in the younger man's favour. In Europe, Harrington ranked 188th in driving accuracy, 133rd in driving distance and 147th in hitting greens in regulation. McIlroy was lowly ranked as well in terms of driving accuracy, standing at 118th, but he was eighth in driving distance and, despite the occasional waywardness of his booming tee shots, he was still able to make it to third place in the important business of hitting greens in regulation.

McIlroy didn't win another tournament in 2009, but his earnings continued to spiral upwards thanks to consistently high finishes and a growing band of big-spending personal sponsors. He was 20 years old and he already held a position within the hierarchy of the game that brought with it respect and fear. Also, in 2009, McIlroy had the satisfaction of finding himself on the 'options menu' and being able to play as his own computer-generated figure on the *Tiger Woods PGA TOUR 10* edition of the popular PlayStation game.

'It's pretty cool,' McIlroy admitted. 'I've played the game quite a bit, for the past 10 years, and more often than not I'd play as Tiger.'

Before making his debut appearance at the Players Championship at the magnificent Sawgrass course in Florida, a tournament widely regarded as the game's 'fifth major', McIlroy played the course on his

PlayStation console and scored a fanciful 18-under-par 54. In real life, however, he found Sawgrass an entirely different proposition.

'You get up to holes like 11 on the computer,' he explained, 'and you can drive it up to the big tree on the right, which is like 150 from the green. I had a good drive yesterday and was still hitting a five-wood in.

'It is not like it is on the PlayStation.'

In his opening round at Sawgrass, McIlroy needed 20 more shots than he'd hit during his virtual round and signed, wearily, eventually, for a 74.

In June 2009, McIlroy made his debut at the US Open, taking place that year on the Black Course at the majestic Bethpage State Park on New York's Long Island. The young Northern Irishman was fancied by many to win the event. No player had triumphed in his first US Open since the amateur Francis Ouimet beat Harry Vardon and Ted Ray in the play-off at Brookline in 1913. McIlroy opened with a two-over-par 72 and finished what torrential rain turned into a fairly miserable weekend six shots behind the eventual winner, American Lucas Glover.

McIlroy's first appearance in the Open Championship as a professional came the next month on the Ailsa links at Turnberry on the rugged coast of the Firth of Clyde in south-west Scotland. There, on the beautiful course laid out on the former air base, McIlroy and the cream of the world's best golfers stood to attention and saluted the great Tom Watson, who, at the age of 59, made a dramatic return to the course on which he won his first Open Championship in 1977, after his famous 'Duel in the Sun' with Jack Nicklaus.

Thirty-two years after that memorable victory, Watson had a chance to lift the Claret Jug for a sixth time, equalling Harry Vardon's record, but failed to sink his putt for par on the 18th and he went on to lose a four-hole play-off to fellow American Stewart Cink. McIlroy's week was ruined by a third round of 74, and by his travails on the eighth hole, at which he dropped seven shots during his four rounds.

A month later, in his professional debut at America's PGA Championship, taking place on the Robert Trent Jones-designed Hazeltine course in Minnesota, McIlroy wanted to finish his first year of playing all four majors as a professional on a high note, or at least a higher one than he had managed so far. Tied for 20th at the Masters, tied for 10th at the US Open and tied for 47th at the Open Championship were not the sorts of results that would have been at all acceptable to a young and eager Tiger Woods in his early 20s.

At Hazeltine, it was Woods who made most of the running. He was chased down hard by Padraig Harrington for three days, but South Korea's Y. E. Yang emerged as the strongest of all and he became the first man to beat Woods in a major when the American had led after 54 holes. McIlroy finished tied for third place alongside England's Lee Westwood, five shots behind the winner at three under par for the week. McIlroy and Westwood were handed cheques for $435,000.

By the end of 2009, McIlroy's riches were beyond his dreams as a young boy. From the final tournament of the year, in Dubai, he took home to Belfast €1,071,570, comprising €323,963 for finishing third, and €747,607 in bonuses. That result meant that he finished second to Westwood in the European Order of Merit. In total, McIlroy had won €3,610,020 on the European Tour, a sum that placed him 10th in the world rankings.

The new year found McIlroy with a US PGA Tour card in his back pocket and a new list of targets in his head. As well as desperately wanting a second tournament victory, McIlroy also announced that he should win a major within four years, and certainly before his 25th birthday.

'I'm gaining experience every year and by the time I'm 24, 25 I will have played in 20, 25 majors,' he stated. 'So, hopefully by then, I should know how to finish them off.' McIlroy also started off the year by soliciting the help of the renowned sports psychologist, Dr Bob Rotella. 'I think this could make a couple of shots difference in tournaments,' said McIlroy, who was, privately at least, becoming exasperated by his record of having only one victory to show for the 14 top-10 finishes in his career.

He also got to talk to Jack Nicklaus for 90 minutes in March, when they had lunch at Palm Beach Gardens during the Honda Classic. Nicklaus explained to the ambitious cub across the table from him that calmness and patience were two of the virtues that helped him to amass 73 wins on the PGA Tour, as well as his record 18 major titles.

All of which did not help McIlroy much at the Masters in 2010. His winnings for the few days he spent in Augusta didn't even cover the cost of his lodgings, not that he cared a damn about the $10,000 cheque, as rounds of 74 and 77 left him standing on a seven-over-par total of 151 on Friday evening, well out of sight of the top 44 and ties, and far more than 10 shots off the lead. He missed the cut.

However, less than a month after the disappointment of Augusta, he won the second tournament of his professional career, and his first on the PGA Tour, setting a new course record at Quail Hollow, in Charlotte, North Carolina, by signing for a final-round 62 and a spectacular four-shot victory over second-placed Phil Mickelson in the Quail Hollow Championship. The 18th flag, which his caddie acquired on his behalf, was destined to be framed and placed on the wall of the downstairs toilet in his new home, where it was joined by congratulatory letters from Nicklaus, Arnold Palmer and Seve Ballesteros, thereby turning a bathroom into a unique trophy room.

The remainder of the summer, and into the autumn, continued to blow hot and cold for Rory McIlroy. In June, he watched his best friend on the tour, his fellow Northern Irishman Graeme McDowell, win his first major when he triumphed in the US Open at Pebble Beach. McIlroy had missed the cut again, with rounds of 75 and 77, and while his form looked decidedly patchy, and his head seemed to hold anything but a strong winning mentality, the media were still more than willing to talk up his chances of success at the 150th Open Championship, being held at St Andrews in July 2010. As many wrote, and many pointed out to McIlroy, victory would make him the youngest Open champion since 1893. In addition, McIlroy was repeatedly reminded that he had never shot worse than 69 on the Old Course.

On the Thursday morning at St Andrews, picture perfect and with barely a puff of wind, McIlroy put together a swashbuckling nine-under-par 63, which was the lowest opening round in the long history of the tournament, and gave him a two-shot lead over his stablemate at Chubby Chandler's International Sports Management agency, Louis Oosthuizen of South Africa. McIlroy covered the final 10 holes in eight under par.

Any thoughts of McIlroy becoming the youngest Open champion for 117 years, however, were blown all over the place the next day when, in 40 miles per hour gusts, he took an 80. Play during the second round was suspended for 65 minutes because the wind was moving balls on the greens. McIlroy did not finish his round until just before 9 p.m., by which time he was 11 shots behind Oosthuizen, who would continue on to win the tournament and lead the Chandler entourage on a celebratory dance back to The Jigger Inn.

Incredibly, McIlroy would fight back on the Saturday and Sunday, and finish the Open in a tie for third place. He eventually left St Andrews delighting in the fact that in 13 competitive rounds on the Old Course he had never once shot in the 70s, shooting 12 rounds in the 60s and one round of 80.

In August, at Whistling Straits in Wisconsin, McIlroy again tied for third place, this time in the US PGA. It was the third time in 12 months that he had finished joint third at the end of one of the big ones. Moreover, Whistling Straits was the first golf course on which McIlroy was truly in contention going out for his final round, and playing in the second to last group on the final day of a major was a place he had never been before, despite his hectic two and a half years as a professional golfer.

He felt it on the first tee. It was different to anything he had ever experienced before; he felt a pressure on his shoulders and down his arms.

But he coped. He had birdie chances on the 11th, 12th and 13th holes, from distances ranging from 10 to 20 feet, but had to wait until the 14th for one to fall. That putt put him into a share of the lead with Martin Kaymer. But McIlroy missed out on a play-off by just one stroke, as Germany's Kaymer instead claimed his first major title.

As 2010 finally came to a close, and 2011 stood temptingly in front of him, McIlroy was talking patience, and more patience. He felt that a major title was within his grasp. Hazeltine, St Andrews and Whistling Straits had left him with an inner belief that he was, finally, very close to achieving just that.

But was a major championship title really what McIlroy needed? He already had a beautiful, luxury mansion in Belfast, which he often shared with his girlfriend of five years, university student Holly Sweeney. He had all the money he needed, and if he never won another euro or pound or dollar for the rest of his life, he would be financially secure.

It has become too easy, in many ways, to make money as a professional golfer. 'In normal life, money is fine,' McIlroy said as he reviewed 2010. 'But in golf, especially, you can earn an awful lot of money by finishing second or third... and that can make you very complacent. The *I can finish fifth and still earn a hundred grand* kind of idea. It's a dangerous mentality.'

McIlroy had seen enough of others on tour to know that it was possible to be an outstandingly talented golfer, but still sidestep the pressurised, stomach-churning moments that separate the truly great players from the very good players.

'You hear of these, it is a terrible phrase, journeymen pros who maybe play 30 events a year and make their half a million and are very happy. And it is a great way to live. It is a great living.

'But,' McIlroy insisted, 'I want to be better than that.'

CHAPTER FOUR

April 1956

Ken Venturi, a car salesman of some note, led the Masters by four shots on the evening of Saturday, April 7, 1956 and was ready, and absolutely 100 per cent prepared, to become the first amateur to try on his very own green jacket at Augusta National the next day.

In truth, Ken Venturi was a great car salesman. At Van Etta Motors in San Francisco, the used car lot owned by his Lincoln-Mercury dealership boss and loving mentor, Eddie Lowery, the 25-year-old Venturi had moved 47 cars in the previous six months. His sales technique was as simple as it was roguishly direct. While Venturi did not have movie-star looks, he undoubtedly had a definite appeal and considerable charm. He stood six-foot tall and exuded confidence. As someone who would soon become a friend of Bing Crosby's, and would live for a period of time with Frank Sinatra, Venturi was always comfortable in exalted company.

But, on the car lot, he believed in getting his customers to the bottom line as quickly as possible. As he recalled in his second autobiography, *Getting Up and Down*, published in 2004, he'd then deal his matter-of-fact salvo to the young or old gentleman – age didn't matter – sitting on the other side of his desk.

'I'm not going to sit here and fool around because I've got to eat lunch at 12 o'clock and I tee off at 1,' he'd happily confide in his customer.

'So if you can beat that price, I'll buy one too.'

Venturi was making good money on the car lot – he would take home $30,000 in salary and commission in an average year – so he didn't really need to become a professional golfer. If he ever did he knew damn well that he would have to work his ass and his socks off all over the country to be sure of hitting that same total.

In 1955, the leading money-winner on the US Tour, Julius Boros, earned himself a total of $63,000 for his labours. And that was before Boros itemised the costs of his food and his hotel bills, not to mention all of that heart-breaking travel. Having worked as an accountant for several years, and delaying turning pro until he was 29 years old, Boros could add up those little and big costs accumulated by a tradesman golfer faster than anyone on the tour.

Boros, born in Connecticut in 1920 to Hungarian immigrants who knew the value of every single dollar in their home, won the US Open in 1952 when he defeated Ed 'Porky' Oliver by four strokes at the Northwood Country Club in Dallas. While he had indeed waited almost to his 30th birthday before making the daring plunge, his maiden Tour win was a big one. That US Open was the first of 18 Tour victories for Boros, and he would win two more major championships before retiring, including the 1968 PGA Championship when, at 48, he became the oldest player ever to win one of the four majors that decorated the second half of the 20th century.

Boros, although technically untouchable with a club in his hand and possessing a swing that appeared utterly strain-free, still found the professional life as hard as he expected it to be in every way.

'I was as apprehensive as the next guy in a tight situation,' he admitted about his life on the Tour. 'It felt like razor blades in my stomach.'

In addition, his personal life held real tragedy. Boros's first wife, Buttons, had died in childbirth the year before that first US Open triumph, and Boros would have seven children to feed and care for with his second wife, Armen. But he did so quite successfully, in his own inimitable manner.

In the latter part of his life, Boros suffered ill health. After suffering a fatal heart attack at 74 years of age, he was found by two fellow golfers, sitting in his golf cart, under a willow tree near the 16th hole at the Coral Ridge Country Club in Fort Lauderdale, Florida.

No doubt about it, professional golf was a gut-wrenching way to make a living in the 1950s and early 60s and, with a family to support and with no way of guessing what next month's winnings might amount to, it took real guts to walk away from a safe job as the US economy righted itself after the Second World War.

Walking the fairways as a professional golfer, at that time in the game's history, was a selfish, often brazen choice for a man to make.

Like so many other magnificently talented amateur golfers, Venturi saw no need to be in any hurry to play the game he loved for a living. After graduating from San Jose State, Ken had first joined Eddie Lowery's sales team in 1953. Lowery liked having great young golfers working in his lot. It helped attract sales from all over the Bay Area, and once they kept up their numbers on the sales charts, the boss was more than happy to cover the $500 membership fee at the nearby California Golf Club for his star workers.

Venturi's numbers were among the best in the dealership's sales staff of 24. And he was on the golf course just about every afternoon he cared to be out there. Lowery had no problem with that.

In fact, he liked the romance attached to a man's dual life.

As an adult and respected businessman, Lowery cultivated his private stable of talented young golfers. This included not just Ken

Venturi, whom Lowery supported emotionally and financially in his golf career, but also another young wannabe named Harvie Ward, and a future Open champion, Tony Lema.

****

On the Thursday morning of the 1956 Masters, a light drizzle started as Freddy McLeod and Jock Hutchison teed off at 10.12 a.m., commencing the tournament's play. The two old boys striking off on that first tee was an important tradition at Augusta National through the 1950s.

The great Georgia sky above them was as grey as it was grim. Jock, now 72 years old, had claimed the Open Championship 35 years earlier on his home course of St Andrews in Scotland. He also loved Augusta National, but in his long career in the US his best finish on the course came in 1941 when he was 43rd. Freddy, two years older than his great friend and born in North Berwick in Scotland, had won the US Open 48 years earlier at the Myopia Hunt Club in South Hamilton, Massachusetts, when he also won lifelong fame for being the shortest man, at five feet four inches, ever to win the title. His best placing in the Masters was even further back that his fellow countryman's, a tie for 50th in 1934. Freddy had left his homeland for the United States in 1903, following the tracks of so many other Scots at that period on discovering that the golf clubs that were quickly appearing all over the United States had no local professionals with any worthwhile experience on whom locals could call. Freddy's first place of employment was Rockford Country Club in Illinois, but he moved around the country finding golf clubs in places he never knew existed.

By that early April afternoon in 1956, Freddy McLeod made the turn in 42 shots, but a rack of sixes left him on a score of 90 after his 18 holes. Jock Hutchison had a more respectable 83.

'You know what I'm doing, Fred?' he asked midway through his round, demonstrating his still competitive instinct. 'I'm not turning enough going back.'

The old Scottish players knew they might have done better. The continual light rain had made the normally lightning fast greens very approachable, and puttable, too. It was going to be a day for good scoring at Augusta National Golf Club.

In the early afternoon, Doug Ford, who would win the Masters 12 months later when he holed out from a plugged lie in a bunker on the 18th hole to win by three shots from Sam Snead, posted a two-under-par 70. Shelley Mayfield, who hailed from the town of Liberty, Texas, soon bettered him by two shots with a 68. There were four other sub-par rounds by the close of the first day's play: Oklahoma's quick-tempered Tommy Bolt also posted a 68; Ben Hogan shot a 69; and defending Masters champion Cary Middlecoff, who had chucked in his practice as a dentist to join the PGA Tour and would always be known as 'Doc' to those in the locker room, was on 67.

But the best round of the opening day's action belonged to Ken Venturi, who became the first amateur to hold the undisputed lead in the Masters after the opening 18 holes.

Venturi shot a 66, and really put the seal on his day's work at the marvellous 13th hole. This was a 470-yard dog-leg left, leading into a green that possesses an enchanting hillside backdrop of red and pink azaleas. Winding its way across in front of the green is Rae's Creek, named after John Rae, the 18th-century Irish mill owner who offered his home to local residents during attacks by Native Americans. Rae's house was the furthest fortress up the Savannah River from Fort Augusta, but the creek in his name, which works its way through the most prized land in all of the state of Augusta, offers nothing but danger to those who now come upon it.

After only a fairish drive, Venturi decided to try to carry the creek with his second shot. He smashed his three-wood on to the green, leaving himself with an awkward uphill 20-foot putt for an eagle. His playing partner, Billy Joe Patton, was 35 feet from the hole after a superbly struck four-iron. Two eagle putts were on offer to the two players to finish off the most tempting and most notorious three holes on the course, which had yet to be labelled 'Amen Corner'. It was two years later, in 1958, that the *Sports Illustrated* writer Herbert Warren Wind borrowed a couple of words from an old jazz recording called *Shouting at Amen Corner*, and so christened the three holes that were characterised by plentiful azaleas and white dogwoods, soaring pines and continuously chirping birds.

Venturi was classified as an amateur competitor, but he had long since thought like a pro, and he approached every contest with a desire to win that was greater than many seasoned, but weathered, professionals'. In addition, he had as an occasional tutor the five-times major winner, and the man most often credited as being the father of the modern golf swing, Byron Nelson. He was regularly to be found in Venturi's corner.

Those who had decided to follow Venturi and Patton for the first day's play, however, were mostly expecting the latter, the southern boy from Morganton, North Carolina, to beat up the course.

But on the first hole it was Venturi who saw the line of the green perfectly and birdied from 20 feet. On the second hole he birdied again, this time from six feet. A 12-footer on the third hole resulted in another birdie and, on the 170-yard par-three fourth, he hit a four-iron to 12 inches from the hole. With four birdies on the opening four holes, the smallish amount of spectators following Venturi and Patton was growing into an expectant crowd of people. Venturi kept his composure for the remainder of the front nine and was out in 32 shots.

After the turn, he parred the 10th, 11th and 12th holes. On the 13th green, he was 20 feet from the hole.

Venturi's putter had cooled slightly during the previous hour's play, and he waited as Patton stood over his putt a little longer than normal. Billy Joe then knocked his ball straight into the hole for a breathtaking eagle.

Venturi had waited much longer than he would have wished as Patton had carefully sized up his putt, so when Billy Joe extended his celebrations and appeared to do a little dance step or two, Ken felt obliged to move him along.

'Just step aside, Billy Joe, and I'll knock mine right in on top of yours,' he said.

And he did exactly that, to make it two eagles to be admired by the growing gallery, including the cameras of CBS, which was allowed into Augusta National to televise the tournament for the first time and which covered 15 of the 18 holes in its national broadcast.

Venturi sailed home from the 13th hole for a 34 and a round of 66, to finish four shots better off than Patton, who shot a fine 70 himself.

In his first round Venturi had hit 16 greens in regulation. He had one-putted eight of those greens. In the press room at Augusta National, shortly after his round, he was engulfed by the largest group of journalists he had ever seen in his life, from newspapers strung all across the United States. Venturi had so much to contain within his usually calm and organised head as he sat there, but he answered the questions that were thrown in his direction from all corners of the room. The preceding two years of his life had been a blisteringly speedy ride, and now, all of a sudden, he was leading the Masters tournament.

****

He had been, he thought, in the form of his life back at the start of 1954, when he was inducted into the US Army. That was on January 27. Venturi did his basic training at Fort Ord in California.

Early that same year he became engaged to his girlfriend, Conni, a keen student of the stage. Conni had the same striking features as actress Natalie Wood, whose career was about to take off with the help of the film *Rebel Without a Cause*, in which she starred with James Dean. In April, Venturi obtained leave to take up an invite to compete in his first Masters tournament, where he finished eight shots behind the leaders in a tie for 16th place with Julius Boros, among others. But when Venturi returned to Fort Ord, he duly found himself in the middle of a much-publicised investigation into athletes getting a soft, inside track during their military service, and by the middle of the summer an order was issued that quickly shipped overseas any athlete with 15 months still to serve.

Conni and Ken decided to get married immediately. The next 17 months were spent in Salzburg, Austria, where Ken occasionally tried to find some practice time for his golf career, even if it meant painting balls red and green so that he could find them more easily in the snow. Conni had joined him for 12 months of his European tour, but when she became pregnant she immediately headed home to the United States. Venturi followed not long after that.

By the time he got home to the West Coast in October 1955, his wife had bought their new one-storey, two-bedroom house in Westlake, a suburb of San Francisco, thanks to the generosity of her grandparents. Eddie Lowery, of course, had kept a sales job on his lot in the city open for the returning soldier.

Ken Venturi's first son, Matthew, was born one month before he found himself once again arriving at Magnolia Lane, in April 1956, on an invite from the former Masters champions. Ken and Harvie Ward spent four days in Florida one week before the tournament to warm up, and tune in, and the Sunday before the first round Venturi and Ward arrived at the house in Augusta that Eddie Lowery had decided to rent out for the three of them for the week.

Venturi followed his first-round 66 with a 69 on day two. The evening between the two rounds, the telephone in the rented house rang and rang and rang. Lowery, as normal, was the most animated and talkative of the three men.

In the second round, Venturi was paired with the 46-year-old three-times Masters champion Jimmy Demaret, but at the top of the leaderboard for everyone to see was the name of Ken Venturi, the 25-year-old amateur. The wind had picked up overnight after the first day's play and the greens were beginning to dry out under the sun now high in the Georgia sky. By the end of day two, the greens at Augusta National would be hard and ice-like.

'Don't let it get to you, Ken,' Demaret advised before they teed off for the first time together. Demaret was one of the gang of Texans, alongside Byron Nelson and Ben Hogan, who had so dominated the game through the 40s.

'If I can win this thing three times, anybody can win it,' Demaret said reassuringly.

'Keep your chin up,' he continued. 'And keep your swing loose and easy.'

On the second hole, Venturi left his drive behind a tree and he settled for a bogey, but the huge numbers following the pairing, keeping their eyes on the amateur and awaiting his inevitable struggle and panic, were left to think again when, on the long uphill eighth, the tournament leader hit a six-iron to the green and heard the crowds roar his ball into the cup for an eagle three.

It had started out as anything but a likely eagle as Venturi whacked his drive far to the right and his ball was heading deep into a grove of pines when it hit a tree trunk and ricocheted back on to the fairway. He then hit a mighty three-wood up to the right-hand apron of the punchbowl green. He was 45 yards from the pin, which could be found beyond, and below, the crest of an awkward ridge. Venturi had a seven-iron in his hand. He switched to a six before playing his shot and watched his ball make its way slowly to the top of the ridge before making its turn and trickling down the far side and into the cup. Venturi had gone out in 34 shots, two under par.

He quickly gave those two shots from the eighth back to the course, bogeying the 11th and 12th holes, which brought him back to even-par for his round. Any thoughts the gallery and TV audience had that he might buckle were banished by Venturi's play over the closing six holes. He finished birdie, par, birdie, par, par, birdie for a 69, and a two-round total of 135, which left him four shots ahead of second-placed Middlecoff, who had managed only a 72.

Others fared poorly on the hardening greens. Ben Hogan shot a 78, Sam Snead a 76 and, halfway through the tournament that they had made their own in the previous decade, Snead and Hogan were 14 and 12 strokes respectively behind the Masters' leader.

The day at Augusta National ended for Venturi with another long and exhausting press conference, before yet another evening of heightened anticipation in Eddie Lowery's rented house. The phone was already ringing when Venturi walked through the front door.

****

On the morning of day three, the players awoke to a wind gusting at up to 50 miles per hour. The tournament was back in the lap of the gods, and nature was about to have its say before a green jacket was to be neatly fitted over anyone's shoulders on the Sunday evening.

The tiredness from two long days and nights, and the impending pressure of having to go out at the head of the field on the Sunday against the greatest cast of characters in the game, worked against Venturi. It wasn't just the golf course that was about to trouble him during his third round. His own head was about to play tricks on him, too. He took 40 shots on the front nine.

His putting was truculent and inconsistent, and he missed at least three holeable putts, most notably on the ninth hole when he lost sight of a simple 18-inch tap-in. Four over par for the round at the turn, he quickly found himself five over when he bogeyed the 11th hole.

Cary Middlecoff, looking to hold on to his Masters title, was three twosomes behind Venturi and had been chasing him down all day, dropping two 15-foot putts on the front nine for an outward 35, compared to Venturi's hard-fought 40. At that stage Middlecoff had not only caught Venturi, but passed him, and was leading the tournament by one stroke.

Pressure was mounting all around him, so it was time for Venturi to steady himself, and quickly at that. He duly birdied the 13th, 14th and 15th holes and walked off the 18th green with a 75 at his back.

Good, sound judgement had brought Venturi home to the clubhouse safely. At the 13th, with the pin set in the far right-hand corner of the green, he shrewdly decided to play his second shot short of the creek. He then pitched to within five feet of the cup and holed the putt for his first birdie of the day. This stiffened his confidence and, on the 420-yard 14th, he holed from six feet after a brilliant seven-iron to the green ran over the edge of the hole. The wind was in his face on the long 15th. He decided again to be cautious, playing his second shot short of the pond before the green. His wedge then brought him to within five feet of the hole, and he duly sealed a hat-trick of birdies.

Meanwhile, as Venturi finished his third round with par, bogey and par, Middlecoff was looking to get off the course as quickly and securely as possible having lost shots on the 10th, 12th and 14th holes. On the tempting uphill 18th, the defending champ knew that a par-four would clinch a 73 and a fine day's work in the treacherous conditions, leaving him two shots behind Venturi. His second shot landed in the bunker to the right of the green, but he made a splendid recovery, leaving his ball five feet from the hole, but resting above the cup. Middlecoff missed his putt, and then, clumsily, also his two-footer coming back. Instead of a par-four for a 73, Middlecoff had a six for a hugely disheartening 75.

In the clubhouse, with Eddie Lowery at his side, Venturi, who had decided not to keep an eye on the leaderboard at any stage after day one, quickly discovered that all was not lost. Actually, nothing at all had been lost on day three. The best score by any competitor had been a 72, with Boros and Snead among the three who had managed a par score.

Nobody had made a run on his four-shot overnight lead. His playing partner, Jackie Burke Jr, had, like Venturi, struggled home for a 75 and remained eight shots back. It was 75s all round for Venturi, Middlecoff and Burke, and so Venturi's four-shot lead in the tournament was still perfectly intact that Saturday evening. 'The day ended much as it had started,' Warren Wind told *Sports Illustrated* readers. 'The tournament had apparently resolved itself to a two-man competition.'

It was between Venturi and 'Doc' Middlecoff, almost everyone reckoned. They were wrong. Cary Middlecoff would manage only a 77 in his final round and finish three shots behind the eventual winner of the 1956 Masters tournament.

The tradition at that time at Augusta National dictated that the great Byron Nelson should play the final round with the tournament leader. Up until Saturday evening, Venturi had not really given any thought to the fact that his great friend, and brilliant tutor, would perhaps be there to talk him through those last 18 holes. After meeting the press, Venturi was asked to come and see Cliff Roberts and Bobby Jones.

They told him they had a problem. They didn't think it would be appropriate to pair him with Nelson the next day. Jones told him that he believed he was about to become the first amateur to win the tournament, and that he didn't want anyone to be able to say that their mutual friend had talked Ken through the final round, hole by hole.

'We don't want anything to interfere with your great victory,' said Jones.

Cliff Roberts agreed. The chairman seemed just as pleased as Jones about Venturi's impending victory and that, at last, an amateur was about to wear the green jacket for the first time.

'You can pick anybody you wish, anybody in the whole field,' offered Roberts. The name of Jackie Burke crossed Venturi's mind, fleetingly. And he also thought about his good friend Mike Souchak, who was so damn talented. Mike had represented Duke University at golf and football, but would never win a major despite finishing in the top 10 at championships on 11 occasions.

'I've played and walked with Hogan, Nelson... the best,' replied Venturi, flatly.

'I'd like to play with Sam Snead.'

Slammin' Sam Snead!

With his strong, powerful swing, Snead had already won seven major championships, including three Masters, and by the end of his career it was agreed that he had won more golf tournaments all over the world than anyone else in the history of the great game.

'Keep close count of your nickels and dimes,' Snead liked to tell young golfers, in his folksy, disarming manner, adding for good measure, '...and stay away from whiskey, and never concede a putt.'

Venturi said he was certain that it would be a great honour to play with such an outstanding golfer and individual, and there and then, the final day's pairing for the 1956 Masters tournament had been decided. Sam Snead's name was next to Venturi's when the pairings were posted, on the Sunday morning, on the large white sheet that was displayed over the mantelpiece in the Augusta National clubhouse.

Once again, back at Eddie Lowery's rented house on the Saturday evening, the phone began to ring and ring but, on the eve of the biggest day in Ken Venturi's whole golfing career, Lowery made the decision to take it off its hook quickly enough.

That was a good decision it seemed, at least initially. Eventually, in the silence of the house for the remainder of the night, Venturi and Ward, and even Lowery, began to think too long and too hard about what the next day would hold in its fragile hands.

After dinner, all talk among the three men had dried up.

Venturi began to believe that he would be Masters champion in less than 24 hours' time and, over the next few hours, much longer than it would actually take him to complete his final round of the 1956 Masters tournament, he started to play every single hole that stood between him and his impending victory the next day.

CHAPTER FIVE

April 2011

Rory McIlroy arrived at the elegant, upmarket house in Augusta that his manager Chubby Chandler had booked for him and his three best mates from home, Ricky McCormick, Mitchell Tweedie, and Harry Diamond.

He didn't have his father, Gerry, with him. Or the man who had coached him since he had measured somewhere between three and four feet tall, his local golf club pro Michael Bannon. It had been decided that both men would stay at home, in Northern Ireland, during the week of the 2011 Masters tournament. Twenty-one-year-old McIlroy and his friends were on their own.

They ate burgers and fried chicken from the barbecue at the rented house most evenings, though they didn't have to worry about the cooking themselves, as Chandler had laid on a chef for McIlroy's needs for the full week. They sat in front of the giant-screen TV together, flicking through the sports channels. They drank a few beers and settled in for a movie one night. During the day they chilled out, with McIlroy enjoying driving his friends around in the gleaming silver, open-topped Mercedes that Chandler had rented for the hottest young prospect on his books. They visited some local malls, and got some shopping done. Each day they took an

American football around with them in the car. They spiralled it through the air to one another, clumsily, as best they could, the ball quivering madly.

It was a fun, relaxed few days. It was even more so for McIlroy's friends, who visited one or two local nightspots on a couple of evenings, and didn't get home until 3 a.m. on one of those nights. Their week was captured in an informal photograph taken in the players' car park at Augusta National at the beginning of the week. McIlroy's caddie, J. P. Fitzgerald, also stood in for the snap, on the right-hand side of the shot, wearing his green cap, white jumpsuit and white trainers, as dictated by Augusta National tradition, after chairman Clifford Roberts insisted that all the club's caddies should be African-American, but that they needed to have their shabby clothes covered from head to toe.

Ricky McCormick and Mitchell Tweedie stood on the left of the photo, arms by their sides, with McCormick wide-shouldered and strong-chested, slightly taller than the others. Harry Diamond, arms folded, behind McIlroy's left shoulder, is the most handsome member of the party. Diamond, who managed his father's nightspot, Cafe Ceol, in his home town of Bangor high up on the east coast of Ireland, was to caddie for McIlroy in the par-three contest at the start of the week. He had spent 10 days practising with McIlroy, and other professionals Luke Donald, Dustin Johnson and Camilo Villegas, in West Palm Beach in Florida before arriving in Augusta.

'It was fantastic,' said Diamond, who plays off scratch himself, upon arriving in Augusta. 'Rory was shooting 63s and 64s. He was giving me six shots. I was shooting level par and still getting beat.'

In the photograph, McIlroy's three friends appear good-looking, confident young men, enjoying one of the best weeks of their lives. McIlroy himself stands one pace in front of the others, holding his golf bag and presenting the biggest smile of all. He's the smallest of the four friends, at five feet nine inches, and the lightest, weighing about 11 and a half stone. Despite his brown eyes, he's also the least interesting-looking of the foursome by some distance, his bushy hair escaping from each side of his cap, his pinched nose as usual pointing slightly skywards on his still chubby, still teenage-looking face.

If the four mates were four other friends on any other golf course, McIlroy would probably be mistaken for the joker in the pack, the youngest member, the one who usually tries hardest to lock down his place in the group by being the noisiest, the most talkative, and always needing to be the centre of attention.

Rory McIlroy had played Augusta National on the Thursday and Friday of the previous week. He felt ready for the first major of the golf year after that, and was happy to limit himself to nine holes only on the Tuesday and Wednesday of the week of the Masters tournament. He had been the last player on the 2011 list to register at the start of the tournament week, which meant that when he drove up Magnolia Lane and parked in the players' car park on the morning of Thursday, April 7, for the opening round of the Masters, he had badge number 099 fixed to his cap.

'It's a good omen,' suggested McIlroy.

'Last to register and last to leave on Sunday night... well, hopefully!' Three days later, on the evening of Saturday, April 9, Rory McIlroy would lead the 2011 Masters tournament by four shots.

****

Chubby Chandler, by the end of the 2011 golfing year, would have the Masters champion, the US Open champion, and the Open champion on his books at his International Sports Management agency.

Chandler, a former journeyman pro who was born in Bolton, near Manchester, in 1953, would almost have it all as a golfing boss. He had played his first tournament on the European Tour in 1974, when he teed up in the Italian Open, the same day on which an eager, flamboyant Spaniard called Seve Ballesteros also made his European Tour debut. But Chandler gained entry to only one major through that decade and a half of toil and trouble on the fairways, and that was the Open Championship at Turnberry in 1986, when Greg Norman had five shots to spare over the field. Chandler tied for 65th place, which helped him to 44th on the Order of Merit that year. In fact, in his 15 years of playing for pay, Chandler won only one tournament, the Sao Paulo International in Brazil in 1985.

'The first golfer I had to sell was myself,' admitted Chandler, who looked back with regret and some amusement at his own performances, and mostly his failings, as a professional golfer.

'I always had little deals going on. But I was a lunatic. I'd play practice rounds with people like Greg Norman for £50. My bravado was way ahead of my ability.

'Looking back, I wish I'd had me as I am now managing me,' he confessed to *The Independent.*

Chandler believed that in the right hands he could have been a 20 per cent better golfer. However, in that period of time, he was well-liked by other professionals. They didn't keep their distance from one of the lowly members in their ranks. That was because Chubby Chandler was always larger than life, and welcoming in his appearance, and on top of all that he was so bloody helpful all of the time with bits and pieces of information.

'I became known on the Tour as the man to go to to find a bargain hotel, or even the best route to the next tournament,' admitted Chandler when his career was all over.

Upon retiring as a professional golfer in 1989, Andrew Chandler decided quickly to reinvent himself. With a £10,000 bank overdraft and with £8,000 set to one side for a PA, he set up ISM in a back room of Mere Golf Club in Cheshire. The business cards were the easy part, as was telling his friends and acquaintances that he would take 25% of whatever sponsorshp he brought in for them.

He was known as Chubby to everybody. He was gregarious, and not overly ambitious, and people liked that about him from the very beginning. Chandler started his company seven years before Hollywood's biggest acting name Tom Cruise made sports agents a cool breed of working man with the release of the movie *Jerry Maguire*, and perhaps the coolest and most endearing part of Chandler's personality through his ISM days is that he has always agreed to work for his clients after shaking hands on the deal. He always preferred not to ask anyone on his books to sign a contract.

Mark McCormack, the American founder of the gigantic International Management Group, had started out in the business with a handshake agreement with his first client, Arnold Palmer. Chandler, therefore, decided to kick-start ISM with a similarly trusting beginning, with the hugely talented amateur from Dungannon, in Northern Ireland, Darren Clarke. But Chandler never set his sights on ISM growing into a corporate monster like IMG, which had hundreds of employees inside its headquarters in Cleveland, Ohio, and located in cities all over the world.

Chandler wanted his business to remain personal. 'Chubby's cologne is on the contract of every endorsement deal he negotiates, and he doesn't want it any other way,' explained *Sports Illustrated*'s Michael Bamberger.

The cologne in question is called *Jo Malone*. Chandler likes to slap it on in the mornings, 'about three times the usual dose', he once happily admitted.

In 2010, at the Open Championship at St Andrews, Louis Oosthuizen from South Africa, who was ranked 54th in the world and had made only one cut in his eight previous major championship appearances, became the first ISM golfer to claim one of the big ones, which, from Chandler's mouth, is pronounced as a 'may-ja'.

As if anticipating Oosthuizen's victory, but in truth in typically Chubby style, Chandler had rented out the local Jigger Inn pub, less than 100 yards from the 17th tee at the Old Course, for the week. All of the ISM family – golfers and their wives and girlfriends, caddies, parents and anyone else helping out around the place for ISM – were welcome in the old pub for the week, where the food and drink was on Chandler. Nobody could enter the place, however, without the required password, usually the name of one of the game's legendary figures, which was changed daily.

'The Jigger Inn was sort of a one-off,' explained Chandler to *Sports Illustrated*. 'And it got a lot of attention because it was a public place. But what we did at Turnberry in 2009 was even more special. I rented out a big house and brought in three chefs, who during the week put on an Italian evening, Indian evening and Chinese evening. We had 16 players in the championship that year and at one point all 16 players and their families were there. I wasn't trying to create a family situation, but in effect that's what happened. It brought us together. It was magical.'

Since ISM caters for the needs of its players and their families, Chandler felt as close to Gerry McIlroy, Rory's father, as he did to Rory himself. He had first met and advised Gerry when Rory was in his mid-teens and weighing up a college scholarship offer in the United States, having signed a letter of intent to play at East Tennessee State University. Chandler advised Rory not to waste his time playing college golf. Instead he guided him into the professional ranks in 2007.

By the week of the 2011 Masters, even though he had won only two tournaments in his fledgling professional career, Rory McIlroy had had top-three finishes in three of his last five majors and the world No.9 was one of Chubby Chandler's best shots at a second major for his ISM stable. Chandler's company handled, among others: Oosthuizen; his fellow South African and three-times major winner Ernie Els; Clarke, who had piled on the pounds and lounged on the professional circuit since losing his wife Heather to cancer at the age of 39 in 2006; England's very own tubby, high-earning underachiever Lee Westwood, a runner-up at Augusta National in 2010 and ranked No.2 in the world; and another South African by the name of Charl Schwartzel.

****

Winning only twice, once in Europe and once in the United States, in more than 100 tournament starts as a professional was not good at all by Rory McIlroy's private standards. 'In the next 100, I would like to win 10 of them at least,' he said 24 hours before the start of the 2011 Masters tournament.

He was excited to be back at Augusta National. It was his third time to play in the Masters. It helped, of course, that he had his three best mates with him for company. 'Each morning is like waking up on Christmas morning,' he cheerily remarked.

In 2009, as a 19-year-old he had ended up with a 10-way share of 20th place on 286. However, 12 months later, McIlroy was packing his bags at Augusta on the Friday evening after missing the tournament cut with rounds of 74 and 77.

At 9.42 a.m. on Thursday, McIlroy teed off for his opening round in the 2011 and 75th edition of the Masters tournament with fellow twenty-somethings Rickie Fowler from California and the Australian Jason Day. He was ready to do some damage to the famed course, but not everybody was convinced. The coach and commentator Butch Harmon, whose father Claude was the last club professional to win the Masters title, when he owned the 1948 tournament, winning by five shots and earning himself $2,500, felt that McIlroy's short game was not of sufficient quality to last through the four punishing days that lay ahead.

'Rory hits the ball from right to left, so that's the good news,' explained Harmon, who usually convinced viewers that he knew what he was talking about since he was coach to the reigning champion, Phil Mickelson, and had also helped the four-time winner Tiger Woods to shape his game to meet the peculiarities and challenges of Augusta National.

At the end of his first round, McIlroy described his performance in shooting a 65 as 'more solid than spectacular'. Maybe the excellence of his 18 holes had not quite impacted on him, as he had spent regular intervals on the course talking cars and boats with Fowler and Day, thereby maintaining a relaxed mood between the threesome.

McIlroy had reached the turn in 32 shots after birdies at the second, third, fourth and ninth holes, and helped himself to three more on his way home, at the 11th, 14th and 15th. The course record of 63, set by Nick Price in 1986 and repeated by Greg Norman before his calamitous week's ending at Augusta in 1996, was in McIlroy's sights as he gave himself birdie opportunities at the 17th and 18th holes as well. The final two birdies didn't fall.

However, alongside the 28-year-old Spaniard Alvaro Quiros, McIlroy still led the tournament at the end of his first round by two clear shots from the South Korean Y. E. Yang, and three ahead of American Matt Kuchar. 'It was good, it was very good,' conceded McIlroy some time later, adding: 'The thing to remember round here is, once you pick your target you have to be aggressive with that target.'

With barely a breath of wind throughout the day, and with the greens more benign than any player had remembered them in half a dozen years, the 21-year-old was of a mind to keep his foot firmly down on the neck of a receptive Augusta National. Lift his foot for a minute, and he knew that the tables could be turned very quickly indeed, with dire consequences for the aggressor. In addition to the simmering threat from the course itself, McIlroy had the previous summer's Open Championship at St Andrews also providing regular reminders. After treating the most famed links in all of golf with complete disdain in 2010 by shooting an opening round of 63, he was dispatched into reverse gear on day two and limped home with a shocking 80.

'I think what happened [at St Andrews] will be a massive help to me,' reasoned McIlroy. 'Looking back, it was a valuable lesson in my development. It's possible I can go out and shoot another 65, but… at the same time… I know it's also very likely that I'm not going to do that.'

****

Back at Augusta on the Friday, a 69 would leave McIlroy at 10 under par. His playing partner Day had the best round of the tournament, shooting 64, leaving him two shots further back from McIlroy at the halfway mark, but what separated McIlroy and Day in their second rounds was the use of the putter. McIlroy's lead was also threatened by Y. E. Yang, and then his fellow South Korean K.J. Choi, but each lost some momentum on the back nine and finished on five under and seven under respectively. Tiger Woods, on the road to redemption after his private life imploded when a giant chest of sexual indiscretions was cranked open in 2009, looked troubled early on during his second round and at one point he dropped back to 36th position, and far too close to missing the cut.

But Woods got his game face on, and a total of nine birdies had him finish his day on seven under for the tournament, and just three shots behind McIlroy, who had impertinently, and a little too loudly, remarked one month earlier that the greatest participant in the modern era of the game was walking the fairways like an 'ordinary golfer'. Rounds of 70 and 72 left Mickelson on two under, with his chance of successfully defending his title fast disappearing. Also passed by in the greater rush on day two was McIlroy's co-leader Quiros, who dropped back to joint fifth after a troubling 73.

The key to McIlroy's round was his iron play. He was exquisite over the front nine and frequently left himself with great scoring opportunities before reaching the turn in 33, with birdies at the second, fifth and ninth holes. The second nine was more disappointing and included his first bogey of the week when he was unable to get up and down from the sand at the 12th hole, but McIlroy happily informed the waiting press afterwards that his game was in excellent shape with two rounds over and two more to go.

At the end of the working day, most journalists were talking about Tiger Woods, however, and asking the question as to whether the 14-times major and four-time Masters winner was ready to add another title to those big numbers? McIlroy replied that he had no intention of looking over his shoulder at anyone, before conceding that it would be great for the tournament if Tiger was 'up there'.

At that, the leader headed out on to the putting green to sharpen up the one part of his game that had creaked on the back nine. Not that he was worried. He insisted that golf would be the last thing in the world on his mind when he got back to his rented house, and to his friends.

'I think it's a big help having the guys with me, especially in the position I'm in,' he emphasised. 'Because I can switch off. I'd rather talk about anything but golf when I leave this place.'

Chubby Chandler's chef also had all the ingredients bought for a tasty Indian meal for the Friday night.

****

The McIlroy house rose a little late on the Saturday morning. It was nine o'clock before the first of the housemates called the others for breakfast. There was a busy morning ahead in the house, as the satellite channels on the giant television had McIlroy's favourite football team, Manchester United, in action live, while at the same time the most popular horse race in Britain, the Grand National from Aintree in Liverpool, was also running.

McIlroy watched United defeat the lowly London Premiership club Fulham 2-0 at their home ground of Old Trafford and move a whopping 10 points clear of second-placed Arsenal in the table. However, McIlroy and his friends also joined 600 million television viewers around the world in watching two horses die in the Aintree race, which had the added horror of runners diverting around the fences where the fatalities had occurred in order to avoid the bodies of the victims that had been covered by green tarpaulins.

During his busy morning, McIlroy took the opportunity to tweet his 188,000 or so followers some pictures of the football action on his giant TV screen. That done, and for the third day running, McIlroy and Jason Day met up with one another on the first tee.

The sun was shining and presenting Augusta National in all of its glory, and everyone on the leaderboard, it seemed, wanted a part of it, none more so than the happy, relaxed Aussie who was actually spending his week in a camper van across the road from Augusta National Golf Club, and who would move ahead of McIlroy by the fifth hole, recording a birdie as his playing partner bogeyed.

On the tournament's traditional 'moving day', the crusty looking Argentinian, Angel Cabrera, who won the green jacket in 2009, looked every bit as intent as the younger men. By the end of the round, however, McIlroy, somehow, inexplicably, would be four shots clear of the challengers crowding behind him, with Cabrera, Choi, Day and Charl Schwartzel, the last named being steadiness personified with rounds of 69, 71 and 68, all sharing second place on eight under par.

McIlroy had finished off his round majestically, making three birdies over the last six holes for a 70, and a 12-under-par 54-hole total of 204. His strong run to the finishing hole had been kick-started at the par-five 13th, which he reached in two, before two-putting for his birdie. On the 13th tee, McIlroy and Day had been level with one another but, as the Aussie stumbled to a bogey, and McIlroy grabbed his birdie, suddenly, a gap opened between the two young men.

McIlroy made sure of another birdie on the par-five 15th, but he still had the shot of his round in his back pocket.

That was finally produced on the 17th hole where, after pulling his drive left into the trees, he duly hit a wedge over more trees to 33 feet beyond the pin. He sank the birdie putt. McIlroy and his caddie, J. P. Fitzgerald, had held their round together under the mounting pressure that so often makes the leader of the pack imitate a jibbering wreck on the Saturday of the Masters.

McIlroy considered J. P. Fitzgerald more than an employee; he had become one of his closest friends since he had joined the fast-paced, man's world of the European Tour four years earlier. There was a calm, knowing quality to Fitzgerald, a worldliness that is common to so many of the outstanding bag men in the game of golf.

Before being introduced to McIlroy, Fitzgerald had been on the bag of Ireland's Ryder Cup stars Paul McGinley and Darren Clarke. He had also spent some time at the side of England's Greg Owen, but his greatest career landmark as a caddie was teaming up with Ernie Els. All the players he caddied for found him to be a man with a serious disposition when he was working, but someone who also had the capacity to stand back and see that the glass was half-full, rather than half-empty, when a round seemed to be heading for trouble.

Fitzgerald was a Dubliner, but during his own playing days he became more associated with County Louth Golf Club as his family kept a mobile home at Baltray on the east coast, just an hour south of Belfast. Fitzgerald was a very good amateur golfer, and one of his best days on the course came in 1987, in the semi-final of the Irish Close Championship, when he produced the right game on the day to defeat one of his future bosses, Darren Clarke. He reached two Irish Close finals in his time, losing in 1987 and again two years later, and among the fellow competitors with whom he struck up a great friendship was Paul McGinley.

Just over 10 years later Fitzgerald was on McGinley's bag when his fellow Dubliner sank his 10-foot putt on the 18th hole at The Belfry to clinch Europe's victory over the United States in the 2002 Ryder Cup.

'I had reminded Paul that we had the same putt two years previously during the Benson and Hedges International and it didn't break as much as we thought,' Fitzgerald explained after that emotional win that resulted in McGinley taking a swim in the lake alongside the 18th green, after his team-mates chucked him into the water. 'He had hit it left lip and it had stayed there. I told him this one was only barely on the left lip.'

His job done, Fitzgerald then prayed for McGinley's putt to drop. The 2002 Ryder Cup had been delayed for 12 months because of the terrorist attacks in New York on September 11, 2001. When the competition got back on track in 2002, Europe wrestled it out of American hands with McGinley's half-point against Jim Furyk, leaving the home team out of sight and on their way to a final score of 15½ to 12½.

McIlroy loved seeing Fitzgerald, for the first time, in his white Masters jumpsuit. It confirmed for him that they had indeed arrived in the big time, playing in the incredible tournament that McIlroy had watched on television at home in Belfast every single year; each year looking more fascinating than the last. He was as happy for Fitzgerald as he was for himself. So, too, was Chubby Chandler, who came to the defence of Fitzgerald when it was insinuated through 2009 and 2010 by commentators that McIlroy needed the best caddie that money could buy.

'J. P. is the perfect minder for Rory, as he is a very protective individual,' explained Chandler. 'He gets a bit of stick, but an awful lot goes on around Rory McIlroy that a normal caddie wouldn't meet.

'If you take the bits that he does very well, it may make up for the fact that J. P. is not the best caddie in the world. But he is certainly one of the better caddies in the world. And, for Rory, he is definitely the best caddie in the world.' It was a bit of a Chubby mouthful, but Chandler had made his point.

As a youngster, McIlroy had had no idea why the caddies at Augusta all wore their baggy white suits. He didn't know that Clifford Roberts had once, typically, insufferably, ordained it so. 'As long as I'm alive… golfers will be white and caddies will be black,' said Roberts.

But the chairman of Augusta National wanted his black caddies to wear white from head to toe in order to impress his members and guests. The tradition stuck fast, even if the rule that dictated that only Augusta National could provide caddies for golfers was subsequently relaxed. As the 75th Masters wound itself to a close in 2011, a piece of history was being made by one of the men who joined J. P. Fitzgerald in the ranks of the white jumpsuits. His name was Carl Jackson and he was a 64-year-old African-American member of the family of caddies, who was working Augusta National for the 50th time in his life.

But Carl Jackson was no ordinary caddie. Each year, he received as many requests for autographs as he walked to the first tee as some of the young, dashing competitors. Nobody has participated in as many Masters as Jackson, who was only 14 when he carried his first bag at the tournament, walking the fairway side-by-side with Billy Burke in 1961. 'He's as much a part of this place as the green jacket or Magnolia Lane,' insisted one local newspaper that celebrated Jackson's achievement.

'I keep thinking back to the old days,' said an emotional Jackson. 'Pappy Stokes, Iron Man… those guys are just on my mind right now.'

Jackson was also thinking of Stovepipe, Cemetery, Burnt Biscuits, Skillet, Skinny, and Marble Eye, all of them caddies who became part of the legend of Augusta National. The man they called Cemetery carried the bag of President Eisenhower. Arnold Palmer's wife, Winnie, once overpaid Iron Man, giving him a cheque for $14,000 rather than $1,400, which the flabbergasted caddie duly sought to cash at the clubhouse. For Jackson's part, he was always best remembered for emotionally embracing Ben Crenshaw on the 18th green at the end of the 1995 tournament. Crenshaw, who first had Jackson as a caddie in 1976, was still mourning the death of his mentor and friend Harvey Penick when the 1995 tournament started. But he held it together sufficiently and memorably, with Jackson's great help, to win his second green jacket.

Certainly, Augusta National was making life harder for Rory McIlroy as his week progressed, and by Saturday afternoon he was leaning more heavily on his caddie, J. P. Fitzgerald, for guidance, with his scores rising from 65 to 69 and then to 70 on successive days.

But still, McIlroy was in the final pairing on the Sunday afternoon, sitting four shots clear of the rest of the field. In the previous 20 tournaments, only once had the winner of the Masters not come from the final pairing. Accordingly, it looked like McIlroy's tournament to lose.

Or else, could it be the craftier Cabrera? The top-heavy Argentinian, known as 'El Pato', which unfortunately translates into 'The Duck' in English as befits Cabrera's waddling gait, was joining McIlroy on the tee in the final group on Sunday afternoon. Cabrera had had rounds of 71, 70 and 67. While McIlroy's scoring was going up, Cabrera's was moving ominously in the other direction.

CHAPTER SIX

The Final Round

As he teed his ball up on the first hole, Ken Venturi felt that he might have to throw up the little amount of food that lay in his stomach. He had never known such nerves. He had spent an hour on the practice tee, but nothing in his body or in his arms felt settled or calm or at all relaxed. It was the morning of Sunday, April 8, 1956, and another breezy, testing and unnerving day beckoned at Augusta National Golf Club for the concluding round of the 20th staging of the Masters tournament.

Venturi stood at six under par, and he had a solid four-shot lead over the defending champion, Cary 'Doc' Middlecoff, with just 18 holes between him and the comfort of that magnificent green jacket.

While walking to the clubhouse before making his way over to the first tee box, a man briefly stopped Venturi in his tracks. He asked a simple enough question.

'How does it feel to be the first amateur to win the Masters?'

That was it, politely put to him.

Venturi struggled to reply. He said it would feel good if he did win it. He said he hadn't won anything yet. He actually didn't know what he should have said, and as he continued about the business of reaching the first tee, Ken Venturi, for the first time in his life, felt overcome, overpowered in fact, by a swirling mixture of unrecognisable emotions.

There were tears in his eyes before he even hit his first shot of the afternoon. The thought of officially becoming the greatest amateur golfer in the world since Bobby Jones suddenly enlarged itself. He thought of all the money he would make after his victory, and he thought of his parents.

Long after the 1956 Masters had ended, Venturi was to discover that Eddie Lowery, his employer and mentor, had $5,000 on him to win the tournament, $5,000 to come first or second and $5,000 to finish in any one of the top three places, at extremely favourable odds of 12-1, 10-1 and 8-1 respectively. There was enough pressure on Venturi without having even a hint of that information in his dizzying head.

Venturi, all the same, should still have had his wits about him when he came to play the first hole, with its slight dog-leg to the right. After all, he had bogeyed it the previous day.

'A drive that is long and straight,' wrote Alister MacKenzie, the architect of Augusta, in the very first Masters programme, 'will be in a favourable position for the second. It is difficult to obtain par figures from any other position.'

Venturi hit a decent drive down the middle of the fairway. It should have been a straightforward par. His uphill second shot to the undulating green, however, gave the first clear indication that adrenalin was running amok through the upper half of his body.

He knocked the ball over the green. His chip back offered some hope of a par, but his putting was hopelessly out of sorts and, for the second day running, he walked off the first green with a bogey. Mostly, he felt embarrassed by his start. The chip back and his putting were poor efforts. It wasn't him, it wasn't Ken Venturi who played those shots.

On the second hole, the longest par-five on the course, a slight draw off the tee usually serves up the opportunity of getting on to the green in two shots, although the two large bunkers hugging the green at 45-degree angles can catch those who mis-read the wind or who don't get enough club behind the ball. That was something that Bobby Jones wanted, a hole early on that would challenge the best players, but that would also offer itself up to those with the stomach to take it on.

'It was one of our guiding principles in building Augusta National,' Jones once told *Sports Illustrated*, 'that even our par 5s should be reachable by two excellent shots.' Venturi had birdied the hole on day one, bogeyed it on day two, taken his par on day three. His final round was just minutes old, but it was already time to summon some courage, somehow, from somewhere. Venturi pulled himself together as best he could, and steadied himself with another par on the hole.

His legs strengthened a little after that, but danger seemed to lurk at every hole, and so it proved. The third hole, the shortest par-four on the course, had remained at 350 yards since 1934, although a clutch of four bunkers would be built just off the left of the fairway in 1982. It was a hole where MacKenzie clearly decided to have some fun with the mind of the visiting golfer. The majority of players opt for position off the tee, taking a one-iron or a fairway wood, though the small green that slopes from right to left is not entirely visible when that second shot is played. MacKenzie narrowed the left-hand side of the green, and did so alarmingly, whereas the right side is broad and long. On his fourth visit to the hole in the 1956 tournament, Venturi struggled with every shot, and was relieved to see his putt disappear for another par.

After three holes, Ken Venturi had dropped just one shot, and stood at five under par. He may not have felt it in his body, or in his mind, but on the leaderboard he was still, completely, in control of the Masters.

Rory McIlroy awoke early in his house in 'Chubbyville' on the morning of the final day of the 75th Masters tournament in 2011. His manager, Chubby Chandler, had block booked 20 or so private houses for the week, for his stable of players, their wives, his ISM staff, and friends. Ricky, Mitchell and Harry, McIlroy's three best friends, had been sharing one of the houses with him all week, and on the morning of Sunday, April 10, 2011, they had an early game to watch on the giant TV screen in the main living room.

They had all awoken at nine o'clock the previous morning to see their favourite football team, Manchester United, win at Old Trafford in the English Premier League, and they had also watched the Grand National from Aintree, which ended up as something of a horror show, with two horses dying on the course and being covered by green tarpaulins during the remainder of the race.

On Sunday morning they had a rugby match to see. They had to be up by 8 a.m.

'Good luck Ulster Rugby!!' tweeted McIlroy to his followers as the European Cup quarter-final between Ulster and Northampton kicked off in Milton Keynes, just north of London. McIlroy added to his tweet for good measure, 'Watching here in Augusta. Let's do the double!!!'

Ulster, the team McIlroy has supported all his life and who play their home games at Ravenhill, just a short spin from his home in East Belfast, lost 23-13 to their English opponents and, in truth, it was hard for McIlroy and his friends to watch because, after leading 13-10 at half-time, Ulster took a fair pounding in the second half. Rory, Ricky, Mitchell and Harry had to pick themselves up as the game wound down to a sorrowful conclusion in the final five minutes.

McIlroy, however, immediately put the rugby match to the back of his mind. He was full of energy, and confidence. Rugby or no rugby, he was about to live the greatest day of his life and nothing could dampen another minute of that day. During stoppages and breaks in the Ulster game, he and the boys had flicked to the golf channels, to see what everyone was saying, and to check who was doing what at Augusta National, the tournament that McIlroy led by four shots, and was set to win by early evening.

His was the biggest 54-hole lead at Augusta National since Tiger Woods led by nine shots in 1997 en route to his quite unbelievable 12-shot victory. McIlroy, on this pre-coronation Sunday morning in 2011, was standing at 12 under par for the tournament. The 2009 champion, Angel Cabrera from Argentina, was leading the chase at eight under alongside three others, South Korea's K.J. Choi, Australia's Jason Day and Charl Schwartzel, from South Africa. Tied for sixth, one shot further back, was the best-placed Englishman, Luke Donald, and another Aussie, Adam Scott. American Bo Van Pelt was standing alone on six under, and five men were tied for ninth on five under: Fred Couples, Ross Fisher, Geoff Ogilvy, Bubba Watson and Tiger Woods.

If Rory McIlroy had not been so far out in front, the morning of the final round of the 2011 Masters tournament would have been full of anticipation of an exciting day's golf. But McIlroy did look virtually out of sight. He had nine shots on the defending champion, Phil Mickelson, who surely was too far back to contend for victory. Winning would make McIlroy the second youngest Masters champion of all time. At 21 years, 11 months and 23 days, he was eight and a half months older than Woods had been in '97.

And McIlroy had simply looked too good. He led the field in driving distance at 303 yards. He was second in hitting greens in regulation, with 43 out of 54. He was averaging the paltry total of 27.6 putts per round, and he was one of only four players who had not three-putted one green in the previous three days.

McIlroy, with his three pals, made the short drive to Washington Road and up Magnolia Lane for lunch. He felt good. He felt cool. There was no great pressure that he was aware of, and when he joined his caddie, J. P. Fitzgerald, on the practice range he was swinging beautifully and true. He chatted and smiled, and his fellow players and some well-wishers he knew by name were welcomed into his company. McIlroy felt great, in fact.

And the day was perfect, with hardly a breath of wind to complain about. He soon whacked his drive down the first fairway, and began the walk that he believed would include 18 holes before taking him to the scorers' hut, and then quickly enough to the Butler Cabin, where a green jacket would await him. There, the defending champion, Mickelson, would be seated, with the new jacket for the 2011 winner draped across his lap, the most precious item of cloth in the whole wide world of golf clothing, ready for one champion to courteously help a new champion into. 'It was the easiest last day I remember at the Masters,' wrote Colin Byrne, the caddie and best-selling author, 'with little wind, reasonably accessible pins and putting surfaces that didn't look like polished marble.'

Angel Cabrera was paired with McIlroy for the final round and he, too, hit a clean shot down the middle of the first fairway. The first hole had been lengthened since Ken Venturi had also hit a clean tee shot in 1956. There were a number of adjustments, including moving the tee back 20 yards and extending the yardage from the 400 it had been when Alister MacKenzie had finished with it, to the 445 yards it became in 2009.

Like Venturi in the 20th playing of the Masters tournament, McIlroy was fuelled to the brim for the 75th tournament and, although he had smartly parred the first hole in each of his previous three rounds, this time, like Venturi had done, he over-hit the green with his nine-iron.

McIlroy's chip back was good all right, and it left him with a five-foot putt back up the hill. But, nervously, bullishly, he missed it to the left.

The last thing that McIlroy had imagined, all morning long, was bogeying the first hole. Cabrera holed out for his par and got one shot back on McIlroy immediately, sitting at eight under to McIlroy's 11 under – but, a little earlier, on the same green, Charl Schwartzel had birdied with a magnificent chip and run from the right of the green. The South African was on nine under. In the space of one hole at the very start of the final round, McIlroy's four-shot lead was reduced to two shots. Walking off the green, McIlroy felt ruffled, but he still looked confident.

His store of confidence had been large all week long, and one foolish hole was not going to dramatically reduce his levels of calmness and his utter self-belief. He parred the second hole but, somehow, it appeared more difficult than it had all week, and he had twice birdied it in his three earlier efforts.

The par-five second hole at Augusta National, even if it's the longest on the course, is a hole that McIlroy expected to birdie every time he played it. This time, however, he found himself in a bunker off the tee, and his third shot also found sand in one of the two large greenside traps.

He was happy to salvage a par and move along, quickly, to a new hole, and perhaps a fresh start to his final round. Beside him, Cabrera had moved to nine under after taking his birdie, but he would immediately give it back to the course when bogeying the short third.

However, on that par-four third hole, Schwartzel had already holed his iron from the middle of the fairway for an eagle, which had had more than a stroke of destiny attached to it. 'I heard the big roar for Charl,' McIlroy would remember. 'I knew then that my lead was gone.' The South African had moved to 11 under par. By the time that McIlroy had monstered his drive down the middle of the third fairway, given himself a birdie chance, but again been forced to settle for a par after another shaky putt, he was no longer sitting alone at the top of the leaderboard.

McIlroy's lead had indeed gone up in smoke.

For the first time since early on Thursday, he had someone for company at the top of the Masters field. And that someone was his ISM stablemate, Charl Schwartzel.

Ken Venturi was still only one over par for his final round heading to the ninth hole. He had parred the fourth, fifth, sixth, seventh and eighth holes, but he had to fight for every stroke on every one of them, and the final day's play of the 1956 Masters had Venturi climbing a mountain by an altogether different face, one that he had never known even existed.

The ninth hole at Augusta National measured 420 yards when it was unveiled in 1934 and, in its time, had never been one of the more forboding holes for players on the final day of the Masters tournament. A long drive straight down the middle would allow for a flat lie and an open shot to at least half the green. The putting surface slopes severely, however, and is the most testing feature of the hole in many ways, with any short approach shot usually rolling back off the green.

Ken Venturi looked sure of his par, one that would close out his front nine and complete a one-over-par 37. After a reasonable drive and a decent second shot, he putted the ball to about 18 inches from the hole. In his mind, he was already off the green and heading to the 10th tee. Inexplicably, he missed his putt. That put him out in 38.

He had not enjoyed the nine holes but, bizarrely, his lead had grown to five shots by the turn, because the defending champion, Middlecoff, was not having any luck at all with his game. Middlecoff, the most consistently brilliant golfer in the world for the previous 12 months, had remarkably blown his chances sky high it appeared on the fifth and seventh holes. He had four-putted the fifth for a double-bogey six, and two holes later he double-bogeyed again, after fluffing a relatively easy chip into the bunker he was attempting to pitch across. There was little time or room for Doc to charge for his title.

The only player making a reasonable move on Venturi was Jackie Burke Jr, but he had been all of eight shots off the lead when he hit his drive on the first tee.

'*I got this wrapped*,' Venturi told himself. '*If I can shoot 38, I win this tournament*.'

Even thinking of shooting another two-over-par score for the back nine was not Venturi's style. He was a swashbuckling golfer, not a cagey, conservative one. But he was definitely thinking, as he made his way from the ninth green to the 10th tee box, that another 38 shots would give him the Masters title.

Jackie Burke Jr had been four shots behind Doc Middlecoff and eight behind Ken Venturi at the start of play and had been playing the role of the invisible man during the first nine holes of his final round. After opening rounds of 72 and 71, he had fallen back into the pack when he closed his third round in the high winds with a 75.

On the morning of the final round Burke didn't fancy his chances of making any great headway in the appalling conditions, turning to Doug Ford on the putting green before commencing his round, and saying, 'I'll take a 77, and pull these shoes off right now.' Born in Fort Worth and a true son of Texas, Burke was liked by everyone in the game. His father was a professional golfer of the same name, and had tied for second place in the 1920 US Open.

Jackie Burke Jr had been admired for his tournament play for much of the previous decade, but like his father he seemed destined to have 'second place' most associated with his name, as he had never been able to muster a championship-winning performance in a major. 'Jack had played steadily and well, if not brilliantly,' wrote Herbert Warren Wind of the 20th Masters tournament in *Sports Illustrated*. 'Unregarded and unwatched, he had ghosted his way, when the leaders faltered, to within a shot of both Venturi and Middlecoff after the 15th hole.'

Burke was a quiet one all right. On one occasion some years earlier, he had been asked why he did not indulge himself more as a celebrity. He replied that he preferred the company of his wife and children at his home in Houston.

'Twenty years from now,' he memorably explained, 'I'd like to have a few other things in my life, other than just the joy of being recognised when I walk into a restaurant.'

Burke had made his way to his local golf course at a much earlier age than Ken Venturi had, and had played the game for five years before, at the age of 12, he put together a round of 69. He qualified for his first US Open at 16, and three years later he joined the professional ranks, just as his father had done, when he became the club pro at Galveston Country Club. He had not won a tournament in three years when he arrived at Augusta National in 1956 but, like Venturi, he had one of the game's older and most respected players in his corner. The three-times Masters champion Jimmy Demaret, who had been the assistant pro to Jack Burke Sr at River Oaks Country Club in Houston, had regularly baby-sat young Jackie for the Burkes.

But Demaret was only one of a large throng of outstanding golfers that young Jackie had known and watched as a boy. Upon being awarded the PGA's distinguished service award in 2007, it was noted: 'Burke reaped the benefits of his father's lessons on the practice range and at the dinner table, which was an "informal" classroom for such teaching and Tour legends as Jack Grout, Harvey Penick, John Bredemus, Byron Nelson and Ben Hogan, who gathered regularly to trade stories and advice.'

Young Jackie had joined the Marines when the United States entered the Second World War and he served until 1946. He would win 16 times on the PGA Tour during his career and, just like his father, his reputation as a teacher of the game grew during the second half of his life when he instructed or mentored some of the outstanding golfers of the modern game, including Phil Mickelson, Hal Sutton and Steve Elkington.

But Jackie Burke Jr would remain unashamedly old-school.

It was with a very straight face that he once informed his local newspaper that the 'worst day of my life' was the day they painted yardages on sprinkler heads.

Rory McIlroy's four-shot overnight lead had gone within half an hour, as long as it took to play the opening three holes, of his final round at the 2011 Masters tournament. He had dropped one shot, and had been joined at 11 under par by his ISM partner, Charl Schwartzel, who was five years older than McIlroy and came from long-standing farming stock in Johannesburg. Schwartzel was reared on his father's chicken farm.

McIlroy and Schwartzel had much more in common than the larger-than-life presence of their manager, Chubby Chandler. They both loved rugby; McIlroy cheering for Ulster, and Schwartzel being a big fan of the Blue Bulls and also his national team, the Springboks. The South African with the wide, toothy smile also liked to watch tennis, although, unlike McIlroy, he did not carry a tennis racket in his personal belongings at all times. Schwartzel's great love away from the game was flying, and time in the cockpit of his private plane, or hiring out a helicopter, helped him to ease the stress of his golfing career.

After turning professional at 18, Schwartzel had some excellent results on the Sunshine Tour in South Africa. By 2005 he was ranked 52nd on the European Tour's Order of Merit, but the early years of his pro career were workmanlike rather than spectacular. He had made it to Augusta National for the first time 12 months earlier, in 2010, when he broke par on the opening day with a fine 69, but then fell away with rounds of 76, 72 and 74.

But, after joining McIlroy at the top of the leaderboard on the final day in 2011, after shooting three under in his first three holes, Schwartzel immediately dropped a shot at the fourth hole when he three-putted the first par-three hole of the day to fall back to 10 under.

McIlroy parred the fourth hole, which was enough to regain a one-shot lead, but the biggest roar of the day soon came from the eighth green and grabbed the attention of the huge gallery following the leader.

Tiger Woods had smacked a three-wood to the green at the 570-yard par-five eighth, and his ball ran up the right-hand side of the green before rounding its way towards the flag.

Woods holed the putt for an eagle. He was five under par for the Sunday, and he would eventually take his par on the ninth after finding the sand and flopping out of the trap too heavily, before holing a monster 25-footer up the hill to completely disarm the front nine at Augusta National with a magnificent 31. 'I need a big front nine,' Woods had demanded of himself that morning.

Despite the shenanigans with countless women that had wrecked his marriage and badly muddied his career in the previous two years, the most feared golfer in the modern game had delivered. Woods stood at 10 under, one shot behind McIlroy, but worryingly for the young Northern Irishman and the rest of the field, Tiger Woods was only halfway through his day's work.

The pressure was on McIlroy from within, but with Woods moving his way up the leaderboard at breakneck speed and encouraging others to follow in his slipstream, big questions were also being asked of the leader from all corners of a course that was, for once, behaving benignly on a closing Sunday.

Not that McIlroy could feel any kindness coming his way. After parring the fourth hole, he went two over for the round when a tough breaking putt from six feet on the fifth green lipped out on him. That left a three-way tie at the top of the leaderboard. McIlroy, Schwartzel and Woods all stood at 10 under par. Behind them, there was also a three-way tie for fourth place, with Day, K.J. Choi and Cabrera all at eight under par.

McIlroy parred the par-three sixth hole, but almost lost the lead for the first time all week when Woods, playing the 10th, gave himself a birdie putt. The four-times Masters champion, however, could not carry his astonishing momentum from the front nine through to the first hole of the back nine and had to settle for his par also. On the 11th tee, Woods bombed his drive right down the middle of the fairway with threatening relish, and with the resounding approval of his growing gallery he appeared intent upon doing a great deal of damage through the three holes of Amen Corner.

McIlroy had managed a par at the 450-yard par-four seventh in each of his first three rounds, and on the surprisingly narrow fairway, which often takes players by surprise after they have just got used to the broad expanse of the opening holes, a safety-first approach was paramount.

The seventh hole was also 110 yards shorter when Alister MacKenzie originally designed it in 1934. It had been the subject of much further work down through the decades, with the green relocated and bunkers added in 1938, and then in 2006 the tee box was moved back 40 yards, and those tightening trees were introduced to both sides of the fairway, thereby ensuring that the seventh would offer up fewer birdies than ever before.

McIlroy safely found the fairway, but still faced a testing second shot to the elevated green that is protected by a ring of five large bunkers. His second shot was more like the McIlroy of days one, two and three, and his line was exactly right for a birdie.

He was back in the lead by one shot, at 11 under and, with his confidence stoked by his sureness on the seventh hole, he soon smacked his best drive of the day down the eighth fairway.

McIlroy had come away with a par five at the eighth hole in all three rounds so far that week, and after his excellent drive at the fourth time of asking he aimed his blind uphill second shot for the green with a three-wood. It looked good from where McIlroy was standing, but the huge shot bounced unluckily and went through the back of the green.

After fluffing his chip back, he had a lot of work to do for his par, but he managed it to retain his narrow lead. Four holes ahead of McIlroy, on the par-three 12th, Woods, meanwhile, was 18 feet from the pin. His first putt was fair, but short. His second, for his par, looked little more than a lengthy tap-in, but the ball dived left at the last second. Woods had three-putted for the sixth time in the week.

McIlroy parred the ninth hole. Woods parred the 13th hole.

At the turn, McIlroy remained a neck ahead of three players tied for second on 10 under par. Schwartzel was dead calm after his roller-coaster ride over the first four holes, and he parred the remaining five holes to the turn to remain one shot back from the leader. McIlroy's playing partner, Cabrera, birdied the seventh and the eighth, and breathtakingly just failed to deliver another birdie on the ninth after a splendid approach, to join Schwartzel on 10 under and remain right in the hunt for his second Masters title in three years. Birdies on the seventh and ninth holes for Choi, in a faultless front nine, also left him on the same number for the tournament.

McIlroy was at 11 under. Schwartzel, Cabrera and Choi were 10 under. Woods, Luke Donald and Adam Scott were right behind. It looked as if McIlroy had just about managed to hold his nerve. His giant lead was long gone but he had found his feet.

There was no sign of impending doom.

****

Ken Venturi held a five-shot lead as he stood on the 10th tee. Five shots clear, and nine holes from home, the prospects for a first victory by an amateur player at Augusta National still looked good, although Venturi was feeling unhappy and uncomfortable in his own body, and couldn't work out what to do about it.

Nevertheless, he drove the ball well enough down the 10th, which historically has ranked as the toughest hole of all at Augusta, and which became the monster it is when the green was moved, a couple of years after Alister MacKenzie's death in 1934, from the bottom of the fairway, back a further 65 yards. At 495 yards, the par-four demands a hard hook to gain extra distance off an elevated tee.

A drive that is too far to the right will not take advantage of the slope and can leave a long second shot downhill to the green. Left is better, and a good drive down this side can make it possible to play a second shot with a medium iron, or even shorter if there is any wind at the player's back. Go too far left, however, and there is trouble with trees.

On the 10th tee box, as he surveyed Augusta National from one of the highest points on the whole course, Rory McIlroy knew that he simply had to turn the ball around the corner of the fairway, which was lined with those towering cathedral pines.

He had parred the hole on Thursday and Friday, but bogeyed it the previous afternoon. With such a pent-up need to get his game back on the same tracks on which it had moved so smoothly for the three preceding days, he maximised every single element of his drive.

But the ball started a little to the left of where he was aiming. The snap hook went way left, in fact and, disastrously for McIlroy, his ball hit the trunk of a pine tree and finally nestled 100 yards off the 10th fairway, between two of the 10 cabins on the grounds of the golf club, which are used by club members and their families.

'He still had the lead at the turn and that is when he made a big error in judgement, going with the driver,' wrote McIlroy's first Ryder Cup captain, Colin Montgomerie, in The Daily Telegraph *the next morning. 'I know he was driving it well, but under pressure a straight-faced club is just more difficult to control than a club with loft. The previous 11 players through the 10th used a three-wood, including Angel Cabrera, who drives the ball with a big, high hook, perfect for that hole.'*

The Eisenhower, Butler and Roberts Cabins stand alone on the course, but to the east of the 10th fairway and west of the Par 3 Course are seven cabins that form a semi-circle. That's where McIlroy's ball lay, between the Peek Cabin, named after Burton F. Peek, one of the founding members of Augusta National and a former president of the agricultural equipment manufacturer John Deere and Company, and the Berckmans Cabin, so called after the Belgian horticulturalist Baron Louis Berckmans who purchased the 365-acre property in 1857, and who established the original nursery there.

'Is it out of bounds?' asked McIlroy.

Nobody answered immediately. Nobody knew. Nobody had ever seen a ball landing between the two cabins in the history of the Masters tournament.

As it transpired, he was not out of bounds and, finding a small opening back to the fairway, McIlroy pitched out, but remained about 250 yards from the green. He now needed to make sure of his bogey, and hold on to a share of the lead, but he pulled his second shot, with a metal wood, into the trees. His ball rolled down into the valley left of the 10th green. McIlroy's fourth shot was a delicate chip, but the ball conked against a tree and settled to the left of the green, slightly closer to the hole. He forced another chip, and the ball reached the green, coming to rest 30 feet from the hole.

Venturi had parred the feared 10th hole on the Friday and Saturday, after bogeying it and dropping his only shot during his opening round. This time, he had another par in his sights, with a shortish putt left in front of him. But he forced it, and I would expect a pushed putt to go to the right not left. He bogeyed the hole and slipped to three over par for his round, and three under par for the Masters tournament. Venturi slowed in his walk to the 11th tee, and the official commencement of Amen Corner.

A double bogey on the 10th was McIlroy's single fervent hope. But his putt from 30 feet slid past the cup. He knocked in the three-footer for a triple-bogey seven, his lead not just lost, but obliterated. The lead had instead transferred to Schwartzel, Cabrera, Choi and Scott, who all stood at 10 under par.

Woods was at nine under and McIlroy shared joint sixth position on the leaderboard, at eight under, with Jason Day.

'His brain is guacamole now,' Peter Alliss, the BBC's revered golf commentator, informed his viewers.

Both Venturi and McIlroy knew that the 11th hole, which had been lengthened by more than 100 yards between 1934 and 2011, and was the only par-four on the course measuring more than 500 yards, was not one to offer up much in the way of salvation to a golfer bothered by self-doubt.

Venturi had parred it on the Thursday, but bogeyed it on Friday and Saturday. McIlroy had actually birdied it on Thursday, but settled for his par in his second and third rounds.

A slight fade was needed in order to reach the fairway, with still a lot of difficult work lying in wait. The second shot usually required a three-iron, or more, with Bobby Jones, many decades earlier, advising that a 'great many players play this hole safely to the right, relying on getting a long putt or chip dead for the par'.

Venturi found the fairway all right, and gave himself another decent chance of taking a badly needed, and settling, par.

McIlroy, temporarily, found some composure on the 11th tee and smacked his drive to a spot on the fairway he would have hand-picked at the start of his round. His approach to the green was stunning. For the second time in four days, he had an excellent chance of a birdie on Augusta National's third most difficult hole.

For the second green in succession, Venturi missed with a short putt for his par. He put another five down on his card. He had now bogeyed the ninth, 10th and 11th holes. His lead in the tournament was down to three shots.

Somehow, McIlroy contrived to take three nervous and debilitating putts before walking off the 11th green. Four holes ahead of McIlroy, on the 15th, Tiger Woods had walloped his drive down the middle of the fairway and then struck a towering, perfectly balanced five-iron to three feet for an eagle opportunity, which, bizarrely, he lost to the left of the hole.

Instead of taking the outright leadership of the 75th Masters, Woods had to settle for a share of it with Schwartzel and Co. On the par-three 16th, which Woods had good reason to love from his past, Tiger's tee shot looked set for the hole, before rolling 12 feet past. Tiger had another birdie close at hand but would again disappoint the noisiest gallery on the whole course by just, agonisingly, missing it.

Venturi and McIlroy both bogeyed the short par-three 12th, the shortest hole at Augusta National, in their earlier rounds. On the tee, both men knew full well that the wind sweeping down along Rae's Creek, at the front of the green, was always a sinister hazard. But, with Amen Corner offering scant protection from the stormy weather that had been rocking the course all day long, the 12th was especially terrifying for Venturi, who had to make absolutely certain of hitting the ball clean and true.

Venturi did so rather too well and knocked his mid-iron up against the bank of azaleas at the back of the green. He recovered and gave himself an awkward chance of a par. He needed to stop his string of bogeys in their tracks.

McIlroy, for every split-second that he stood on the 12th tee, needed to remember the trickiness of that wind down the creek. He hit his tee shot straight at the flag, giving himself a rare birdie opportunity, and also a merest glimpse of redemption, but his putt never looked like dropping, as he left the ball six feet beyond the hole. When his putt back missed the hole by several inches, a maddening panic gripped at McIlroy's heart. He missed with his third putt also.

McIlroy four-putted the 12th green for a double bogey. He had dropped six shots on the opening three holes of the back nine.

Venturi wanted his par on the 12th so badly he willed his ball into the hole, even before he made contact with his putter. His hold on his putter tightened. The ball trickled to the hole. Venturi waited for it to fall.

The ball stayed out.

Four bogeys in four holes – the ninth, 10th, 11th and now the 12th. He had been one over for the same four holes in his first round. In his second and third rounds, he had been two over each time as he made the always difficult turn at Augusta National. He felt all at sea, and sickened by his distrust of almost every piece of his game.

He knew he needed help. He was now one under par for the tournament, and still leading, but barely, and without the authority or the natural instinct of a true leader.

With six holes left to play, the worst was over for McIlroy. His four-shot lead had been wiped away hours earlier. He had dropped from 12 under par for the tournament down to five under, losing seven shots in 12 holes, and while his drive off the 13th tee was wild and unsynchronised, it actually called a halt to his half-hour of rapid disintegration.

He would drop only one more shot, on the par-five 15th, which he had birdied twice in his three earlier rounds, but which was beyond his reach in his final round.

Moments after he delivered his wicked drive on 13, McIlroy rested his head in the crook of his left arm for several seconds, offering the posse of photographers still feasting on his collapse, on his pained face, on his polo shirt untucked and unkempt, a moment that perfectly captured Rory McIlroy's roughest, and most punishing day, ever on a golf course. As he briefly hid his face in his arm, McIlroy told himself it was over. He accepted that it was all at an end, and although momentarily he felt like crying, he quickly regained his composure.

He actually felt calmed. He was tired, but he was coming back to himself again, and he knew there was nothing more to fear over the remaining holes.

On 13, he recovered to make his par, and he safely and assuredly parred five of the last six holes of Augusta National late on the Sunday afternoon. He would finish his final round with an 80 and, unbelievably, on a day that was kind and perfectly accommodating for playing golf, he would finish 15 shots worse off than his opening round of 65.

The 75th Masters title had nothing much to do with Rory McIlroy as he walked those final few holes back to the clubhouse. Beside him, on that mournful final trek, Angel Cabrera said very little to his young companion. The Argentinian was naturally consumed by his own game. When he had the time, or the inclination, to look in McIlroy's direction, Cabrera was as nonplussed as the next person in the gallery, but he did not have anything in particular he wished to say to the young man.

'Did I feel sorry for him?' Cabrera asked himself in a busy press room after it was all over. He said he did not.

'Because, when I play bad... nobody feels sorry for me,' he said honestly, and coldly. 'It was a shame. But I didn't feel bad for him.'

As the pair shook hands on the 18th green, however, Cabrera did think it necessary to say something of a positive nature. 'This is a tournament you can win many times,' he reminded McIlroy.

The 20th Masters title, however, was still Ken Venturi's to win or lose as he exited Amen Corner. He had dropped five shots in the opening 12 holes, but he was still out in front of the rest of the field.

Like Rory McIlroy, Venturi found some peace at the par-five 13th, parring the hole to stay at one under for the tournament. But, just as quickly, the slide in his game recommenced, and he dropped further shots at the 14th and 15th when he three-putted both holes. Venturi gathered himself again on the par-three 16th by holing out with some courage. However, the 17th hole would take the tournament into its hands, and do so with real intent.

'The par-four 17th, which measures exactly 400 yards, requires that the drive be accurately placed between two hefty pines which patrol the landing area of the uphill fairway,' wrote Herbert Warren Wind in *Sports Illustrated*, shortly after the tournament, 'and then demands a skilful approach to the slightly plateaued green, especially when the pin is located, as it was on the final day, some 20 feet directly beyond the forward edge of the bland, white trap that guards the entrance to the green.'

Doc Middlecoff, after seemingly ruining his chances of a successful defence of his title midway through the opening nine holes, was, somehow, still in the picture. So, too, as Venturi discovered when he arrived on the 17th tee, was Jackie Burke Jr. 'Late Sunday afternoon, with the wind still prowling over the course as the fourth and final round wore on, the three leaders came to the 17th – Cary Middlecoff, Jack Burke Jr, and Ken Venturi, in that sequence and almost in succession,' wrote Warren Wind.

Middlecoff was only one shot off the pace. However, the Doc, after doing such a good job in getting back into the hunt, mis-hit his approach to the green, and his chip was equally poor. He three-putted once more, and this time it was a killer double bogey. Middlecoff parred the 18th and finished with a total of 291.

Then, 10 minutes later, Burke arrived at the 17th hole. Helped by the wind at his back, Burke struck a longish drive up the hill, and then used an eight-iron for his approach to the green over the trap, to land 15 feet from the pin. He sank his putt for a birdie three. 'I didn't think the ball would reach the cup,' Burke later told the press. 'That wind just absolutely took the ball in.' His playing partner, Mike Souchak, put his big arm around Burke.

'C'mon man!' Souchak ordered him.

'They're still making bogeys out here. Let's go!'

With two holes to play, Ken Venturi realised that he needed two pars to force an 18-hole play-off with Burke. Venturi hit a perfect drive on 17, and then took out his eight-iron to aim at the pin that was tucked behind the bunkers minding the front of the green. *Forget about par*, Venturi thought. *I could make birdie, par the 18th and win this thing outright.*

His ball looked close to the hole, but the 17th at Augusta National has the toughest, hardest-surfaced green on the course, and Venturi's ball seemed to stop at the top of the little hill on the green before the wind caught hold of it, and sent the ball scurrying seven or eight yards down the bank.

Venturi had to chip back to the hole. He then missed his six-footer for another bogey. As Venturi went to retrieve his ball, he heard a monstrous roar coming from the 18th green, and he would later learn that Jackie Burke Jr had managed to get down in two from the greenside bunker and finish for a brilliant, somewhat improbable, 71 and a four-round total of 289, in the most atrocious playing conditions anyone at Augusta National that day had ever experienced.

A par on the last would mean that Ken Venturi, like Rory McIlroy, had lost a four-shot lead and the Masters title by recording an 80 in his final round. Venturi needed a birdie on the last to force a play-off.

The double bunkers that would eventually become such a critical feature on the left of the 18th fairway did not exist as Venturi aimed his tee shot down the middle. Those two bunkers, which have lured so many pressurised golfers, were not constructed until 1967, and the extension of the hole by almost 50 yards did not happen until 2002, further adding to the drama that has enveloped the 18th at Augusta National in more recent decades.

Venturi had parred the old 18th in his second round, and with the tournament no longer pressing down hard on his shoulders, he felt that he could bring his round back to life, finally, with one magnificent closing hole. His approach shot to the green looked good, but ultimately disappointed in landing 30 feet from the pin.

Venturi saw the line of his putt.

He struck through the ball, and it looked good. But then the ball moved sharply to the left, and went by the hole. The crowd hugging the green moaned loudly as Venturi's ball slid by.

The amateur, who everybody had willed to win the Masters tournament, to become the first non-professional to wear the green jacket and thereby reawaken the glory days of Augusta National's own revered Bobby Jones, didn't deserve the title. At the end of the final day, even though he had hit 15 greens in regulation, his four-round total rested at 290, one ahead of Middlecoff, but crucially one behind Burke.

He may have taken the highest winning score in Masters history, but Jackie Burke Jr was a worthy, and popular, champion, and he had taken his first Masters title in the last tournament that was played without a cut after two rounds, and in conditions that Bobby Jones would later describe as 'the hardest playing conditions we've ever had in this tournament'. Burke, no doubt, earned every cent of his winning cheque for $6,000.

However, he had one big advantage over every other competitor in that, on his bag, Burke had the one man every golfer playing Augusta National on such a wild day would surely have wished to have with them for guidance. Willie 'Pappy' Stokes had worked the same land when it was still a nursery owned by the Berckmanses, and had first caddied at Augusta National as a young boy. Pappy was the father figure among the club's family of white-clad caddies, and by bringing Jackie Burke home safely, as one of only two players who broke par for the final round, Pappy Stokes got to celebrate in the caddie shack *his* fifth Masters title in 18 years with four different champions.

Venturi swallowed his disappointment as he walked off the green and signed his card, but he was fighting a losing battle against his tears. Before he met the waiting press, they finally came. He then cleaned up his face, remembering that his mother had always told him that a man should never cry in defeat. He smiled when he sat down in front of the nation's journalists.

Venturi knew that he had blown it. He had three-putted seven greens in his final round, whereas the new Masters champion had not three-putted once. Each time, nerves frayed to paper-thin, he had tried to leave the ball just close enough to the hole to ensure that two putts, and nothing more, would do the job. Each time he had needed three.

Jackie Burke Jr had decided early on during his final round that, with the wind hitting 50 miles per hour at times, he should only worry about one hole at a time. 'Well, I mean, I thought Venturi was going to win,' he remembered. 'But with that wind... you could only play your best and hope you didn't shoot a hundred.'

Burke didn't realise he was in contention for the title until he walked off the 16th green. 'Going to 17, I knew I had a chance,' he revealed, 'because Mike Souchak told me they were all falling dead behind me.

'The 17th, I hit this big old high slice over those people sitting on that mound, and my ball stayed on the front edge. Got my birdie.

'I had to par 18 to win, but the wind was blowing, and if you went left of the green, you'd make double bogey, because you were chipping with the wind.

'So I put it in the bunker... got out of the bunker and had a downhill putt. I took one look at that putt... and hit it. Didn't look at it twice.'

The 75th Masters tournament had long been over by the time Rory McIlroy hit his final putt on the 18th green, as Ken Venturi had done, for a final round of 80.

It was absolutely of no interest to McIlroy, whose head felt as though it had been rocked about in a tumble-dryer for the last hour out on the course, but the final holes of the final day turned into a real helter-skelter ride for almost everyone near the top of the leaderboard.

The 2006 US Open champion, Geoff Ogilvy, from Adelaide, got himself into contention and, after he had birdied the 16th hole, he shared the lead for a time with his fellow Aussies, Jason Day and Adam Scott. Ogilvy began his back nine on five under par, but then went par, par, birdie, birdie, birdie, birdie and birdie! As he sped up the leaderboard, he didn't even have time to bid McIlroy the time of day as the overnight leader came tumbling down past him.

Then Scott, playing two holes back from Ogilvy, birdied the 14th to take the lead outright. Scott was 11 under par for the tournament, and by then Woods, Ogilvy, Bo Van Pelt, from Indiana, Day and Schwartzel were all tied on 10 under par.

With a birdie at the short 16th, Luke Donald, from England, also joined the growing number tied for second place. However, Tiger Woods was already on the 18th tee and he knew he needed a three to get himself into a position where he might stick for a possible play-off.

'Bite. Bite!' Tiger yelled after his drive.

Woods struggled with his approach to the green and could only par the 18th, to finish his day with a 67. He was stuck on 10 under, and with such frenzied activity out on the final holes of the course he knew that it would not be enough.

Scott parred the 15th and then struck a stunning tee shot on the par-three 16th that offered him a gilt-edged birdie chance from less than two feet for a two-shot lead in the tournament. It looked like Scott's to lose, as his fellow countryman Ogilvy managed only par figures on the final two holes and was soon left sitting in the clubhouse, with Woods, on 10 under.

Donald, disastrously, dropped a shot on the 17th and fell back to nine under, and needed to birdie the last to get a share of the lead in the clubhouse.

As he walked on to the 15th tee, Charl Schwartzel had five pars at his back and needed to make something happen in his round if he was going to hold on to Adam Scott. After a birdie, an eagle and a bogey in his first four holes of the day, Schwartzel had settled into safety mode, parring the last five holes on the front nine, and then doing the same on the first five holes on the back nine. Ten pars on the trot was fine, but it was hardly going to be enough to win the Masters tournament.

Schwartzel, finally, got his birdie on the 15th, and took a share of the lead, but a few moments later on the 16th green, Scott dribbled in his birdie putt to move to 12 under par. Schwartzel rose to the challenge. On the 16th, he hit an aggressive tee shot and his precision putting earned him another birdie.

Scott and Schwartzel were both on 12 under par for the tournament. Woods and Ogilvy were in the clubhouse on 10 under, while

Donald joined them there on that number by birdieing the last. Also on 10 under, and still out on the course, were Day, Choi and Cabrera, but the title looked more and more like it was going to be earned by either Adam Scott or Charl Schwartzel.

Scott found the greenside trap on the 17th, and needed to get up and down in order to stick on 12 under. Jason Day, also on the 17th, birdied to take second place on his own on 11 under, one behind Scott and Schwartzel. Scott's broom-handle putter never looked bigger or more ridiculous to the large gallery, but he made his difficult putt to save his par.

Day drove spectacularly down the middle of the 18th fairway, while at the same time on the 17th, Schwartzel saved his bacon after a leaky drive down the left. Partially blocked by the trees, he floated his nine-iron second shot over a bunker and gave himself an excellent chance of a birdie from 12 feet, and of taking the lead on 13 under par.

Back down the 18th fairway, Scott's second shot looked beautiful, and when it hit the green it started to make its way towards the pin. But then it stopped in its tracks all of 20 feet away from its destination.

Schwartzel grabbed his birdie on the 17th. That was three birdies in a row. He was leading the Masters on 13 under par, all on his own, with one hole remaining.

Scott had to make his putt on the 18th. As he lined it up, Schwartzel hit another magnificent drive, this time off the 18th tee. Scott's putt was a little left, and it was far too long. His second putt was tricky, but he held his nerve and saved his par.

Day, also, showed a rare mixture of daring and defiance for someone making their Masters debut, to get down in three on the 18th, to join Scott in the clubhouse on 12 under par as the tournament's leaders.

Schwartzel now, suddenly, had the Masters to lose. The pressure that, over time on the 18th hole at Augusta National, had consumed Arnie Palmer exactly half a century earlier, and obliterated the hopes and prayers of so many of the finest golfers in the world before and after Arnie, bore down on the South African. With three birdies directly at his back on successive holes, he had the momentum, and he also had a rhythm to his walk, which helped.

He looked loose, relaxed, and his disposition was that of a man who was running an everyday errand. But, everybody present at Augusta, and the millions of TV viewers all over the world, were watching extra intently, because they thought that Schwartzel might crack.

They wanted Schwartzel to crack. They wanted to see one more golfer go up in smoke; one more round of golf at Augusta National sunk, without trace, in a single shot.

He found the middle of the green with his second shot, however, and he looked so close to home. Two putts and the Masters title, and the green jacket accompanying it, belonged to him.

Behind him still on the course was Rory McIlroy, ready and willing to end his humbling experience of leading a Masters tournament. But the players who had been out in front of him, and who were all now mustered inside and outside the clubhouse, were all filled with some regrets.

Seven golfers besides McIlroy had held a piece of the lead in the final round. Woods had bowed down to a couple of small putts on the back nine. Choi had bogeyed three of the last seven holes. Scott, miserably, had failed to birdie either of the par-fives on the back nine. Day was unable to make the most of relatively easy pin positions on the 15th and 16th holes and had to take his pars. Cabrera had bogeyed the 12th and 16th. And Ogilvy, after a great drive on the 18th, and needing a birdie, failed to find the green with his second shot from 145 yards.

On the 18th green, Schwartzel maintained his pace and timing, and managed somehow to put the roars of welcome and congratulation from the gallery moments earlier far behind him. He stroked his putter through the ball. He birdied the last.

Four birdies in four immaculate holes, a feat never before achieved by a winner of the Masters tournament. 'We've seen in Europe and Africa that when he has a chance to win, he usually does,' observed the three-times Masters winner, Phil Mickelson. 'He's a closer!'

Schwartzel had won the 75th Masters tournament with rounds of 69, 71, 68 and, finally, a slick, tidy 66. The lanky 26-year-old Charl Schwartzel, on the 50th anniversary of his countryman Gary Player's first victory at Augusta National, won himself a cheque for $1,440,000, and also earned a great big bear-hug from Chubby Chandler.

PART TWO

From Augusta To Bethesda

CHAPTER SEVEN

Eight Years, Two Months, Twelve Days

Ken Venturi stood over the man at his feet.

Ken still had a bottle in his hand. His rage was uncontrolled, and sodden with alcohol. 'Make one move... and I'll kill you,' Venturi shouted.

Only moments earlier, the bar-room acquaintance had slapped Venturi on the shoulder as he walked by. Venturi turned and snapped, warning the man not to touch him again.

'Anybody can touch you,' the drunk laughed back.

'You're a bum, a washed-up has-been.'

Venturi had jumped off his stool. He punched the man in the stomach and, as he doubled over, Ken had thumped him on the back of the neck, forcing him to crash to the floor.

Quickly, several people rushed in and pulled Venturi away, and got him out of the building.

In his autobiography, *Comeback*, Venturi would bravely recount the frightening incident in detail. He had become quick-tempered. He had been drinking too much, and drinking far too often, sometimes for a few days on end, over the previous 12 months. He was unhappy with his life. Stubborn and belligerent, he was often looking for fights, and regularly finding them. In restaurants where Conni and he would always have been offered a table immediately, he fumed at being left to wait. Worse still was being ignored for a few minutes. His golf game was close to ruin, and he was brutally dismissive when Conni, his beautiful wife and ardent supporter, sought to comfort him or lead him to a safer place in which to deal with his pain and unhappiness.

It was the early months of 1963. And Ken Venturi had no idea what his future held as a professional golfer.

After hitting the pro tour full-time 12 months after his dramatic loss in the 1956 Masters, he and Conni had enjoyed a good life, driving all over the country in a fancy car, and reeling in sufficient tournament wins and decent pay-days to ensure that most of his fellow professionals viewed his life with some envy. For five years, everything was just so good. Then it all unravelled.

His winnings petered out. His game had slumped, and his confidence was left in tatters. Physically he was suffering also, feeling the effects of a car crash in September 1961 and experiencing upper body spasms that meant he was often in pain. Mentally, he felt as though he was being slowly crushed, as though every portion of his life was contained within some stranger's fist. His pride did not allow him to turn up at tournaments for the qualifying rounds. He wanted to step straight into tournaments proper, on day one. But officials and sponsors didn't want Ken Venturi any more than they wanted to have the name of any other down-and-out professional taking up space on their playing list. He blamed himself, but he was not going to admit to that in front of his wife, or anyone else for that matter.

Venturi also blamed Augusta National. The magnificent old course and its grandiose sense of itself and its history had gently ensnared him, like so many other outstanding strikers of a golf ball who felt at home there. It had then torn the man apart.

There was the personal wreckage of the 1956 Masters, of course, but two years later he was once again only a handful of holes away from victory in the tournament when Arnold Palmer's bullishness, combined with Clifford Roberts' carefree attitude to the rules of the game, knocked him off his feet once again. Two more years down the road, Augusta National doled out yet more blatant cruelty when he was defeated on the final hole in the 1960 Masters tournament. This time Palmer did the damage without the help of Augusta's own rulers.

Three times in five years he had only to reach out, it seemed, for that green jacket. And three times he sat in the locker room on the Sunday swamped by a grevious sense of loss. It was no wonder he turned to drink.

****

When he awoke on Monday, April 9, 1956, Ken Venturi felt deeply scarred. He felt angry and bitter. He felt brutally humiliated by what had happened to him at Augusta National the previous day. His sleep that night, and for several weeks to come, was fitful. He longed for the US Open in June, so that he could close a door or, if not that, so that he could at least leave the space in which he felt imprisoned by what had occurred at the Masters.

He thought of what winning the US Open would be like, and how victory at Oak Hill Country Club in Rochester, New York, would end his terrible memories of every single stroke he played on the last day of the Masters tournament. In his mind, since leaving East Georgia, he had played the final round about one hundred times and each time with a huge variety of smarter, better shots, and each time ending with a score that was nothing like 80.

Venturi didn't win the 1956 US Open. He opened with a disappointing 77, but fought through the rest of the tournament with rounds of 71, 68 and 73 to finish in eighth position, eight shots behind the winner. That was Cary Middlecoff, the man who had helped Jackie Burke Jr into the green jacket at Augusta minutes after Venturi's collapse had been noted for the game's history books.

By the end of the year, Venturi had taken the decision to turn pro, after first turning down a hugely generous offer from Eddie Lowery, who wanted to give Ken his own company, Lake Merced Motors. Taking on his own car business on the coast would certainly have been the safest bet possible for Ken and Conni, a still young married couple with no savings and payments to be made every month. 'I knew how tough being a touring pro was, that it can be Heartbreak Hill,' admitted Venturi. 'But I was determined to test myself.'

Lowery was more than happy for Ken to pay him back for the business with his future profits, but Ken turned him down.

'I can't do that, Ed,' Venturi told Lowery.

However, after announcing his decision to join the ranks of professional golfers, Venturi stayed working with Lowery, because the PGA Tour's pompous rules prevented any new professional from picking up a winner's cheque for a period of six months.

During that waiting period, Venturi returned to Augusta National for the 1957 Masters, where he finished tied for 13th with Bud Taylor and Britain's Henry Cotton, 11 shots behind the winner, Doug Ford.

As Ken prepared to be a fully-fledged touring pro, he and Conni bought a new car for the road, and placed $3,350 in their bank account to meet future travelling expenses, until some winnings started coming in. Until then, the couple had $5.50 left in their savings account. However, within weeks, at the Carling Open in Flint, Michigan, Venturi finished fourth and his first official pay-cheque was for the sum of $1,450. After two and a half months out on tour, with Conni travelling with him and occasionally offering encouragement to him between shots, Venturi won his first tournament, the St Paul Open, which had $2,800 as first prize. He scored in the 60s in each of the four rounds.

'When we drove out the gates and rolled up the window, we were absolutely delirious,' Venturi remembered. 'I was singing at the top of my lungs. And Conni, her big eyes shining, was squealing and laughing... the miles seemed magically short. We never stopped giggling all the way home.'

In 1958, as Ken and Conni, and sometimes with their two-year-old son Matt for extra company, continued driving from tournament to tournament in one of Eddie Lowery's new Lincolns, the couple felt that life could not have been rosier. Venturi had arrived on tour. He looked the part when he played, donning his Ben Hogan-trademark white linen, short-billed cap to announce his intentions. He was, also, a winning professional, and someone the older tour members knew they had to beat before they could get their hands on some of the decent money. At the Thunderbird Invitational in Palm Springs, the first prize was another cool $1,500, but the Ford Motor Company had a new four-seater Thunderbird, which they wished to show off, so the keys to the T-Bird were also thrown into the pot for the winner. Venturi was full of confidence, touching upon arrogance. 'Isn't that beautiful,' Conni sighed, when she glimpsed the prize car.

'Hon, just be patient for a couple of days... and I will give that car to you on Sunday night,' Ken replied.

He did too.

And the next week he took the title at the Phoenix Open. In less than a fortnight he had won $3,500 in prize money, and the glimmering T-Bird. Venturi had seven top-10 finishes in seven starts.

Back at Augusta National, which now meant more to him than any other course on earth, he maintained his sparkling form and shot a 68 in the first round of the 1958 Masters tournament, to take a one-stroke lead over a quartet of players including Jimmy Demaret. Two back were Arnold Palmer and Cary Middlecoff.

In warm temperatures, Venturi had putted almost perfectly, stroking the ball 28 times in his opening round. On day two, though, Venturi once again found how Augusta National could suddenly bite back. He took 40 on the front nine and had to knuckle down hard to score 32 coming home, but he was still at the top of the leaderboard at the halfway mark, with one shot to spare over Billy Maxwell and Billy Joe Patton. Palmer and Middlecoff were three back. But that situation was turned on its head on the Saturday when Venturi could manage only two 37s and fell three shots behind Palmer, who, untouched by self-doubt, marched his way around the course in 68 shots.

On the Sunday, Palmer, who would go on to win seven majors, including four Masters titles in a 62-win pro career, and become the most celebrated golfing star of the dawning TV age, was, like Ken Venturi, eyeing the first major win of his career.

Venturi knew only Palmer really stood between him and the green jacket. Ken sparkled on the front nine, shooting a 35, to Palmer's 36. The lead was reduced to two shots. On the 10th, Palmer bogeyed and Venturi parred. There was one shot between them. Venturi, however, felt that he had the momentum and that he had a degree of control over what was happening out on the course.

Both players parred the 11th and then, on the 12th, Venturi found himself witness to a controversy that was none of his making, but which possibly cost him the Masters title.

On that par-three 12th hole, Venturi opted to send the ball to the back edge of the green, about 20 feet from the cup. It was a safe play, especially with the Sunday pin placement far to the right and only a few yards behind the water. Palmer followed, striking his shot over the green. Palmer's ball landed in the bank.

It looked embedded and, under the rules of the game, the player seemed entitled to a free drop. However, the rules official, Arthur Lacey, disagreed. He ruled the ball to be 'half embedded'.

Venturi, like Palmer, thought that the wrong judgement. As Palmer continued to argue his case, Venturi informed those present that he was going to hole out. He didn't wish to become distracted. He just missed his birdie putt, and then Venturi sat down on his bag while resolution was still being sought regarding Palmer's ball.

Venturi was on Palmer's side, even though he knew he would gain more from his playing partner's misfortune.

Angry, Palmer finally played his shot. He fluffed his chip. The ball did not even reach the putting surface. His next shot went five feet past the hole, and he duly missed the return as well. Palmer finished the 12th hole with a double bogey and Venturi was back in the lead, by one shot.

But Palmer wasn't finished. He declared that he did not like the ruling. 'I'm going to play a provisional ball,' he insisted, but Venturi knew that Palmer was not entitled to play a second ball.

'You can't do that,' he told Palmer forcibly. 'You have to declare a second ball before you hit your first one. Suppose you had chipped in with the other ball? Would you still be playing a second?'

Nevertheless, Palmer decided he was going to play a second ball. As he did, Venturi turned to his caddie and calmly informed him that Palmer was in violation of the rules. He told his caddie that they had probably just won the Masters tournament.

Palmer took his drop to one side of the 12th green. Twice he dropped the ball and twice it rolled towards the hole, so Palmer was allowed to place his ball instead.

Now, at the second time of asking and with a better sense of the speed of the green, he almost chipped in, before finally tapping in for his par. Venturi walked to the 13th tee, certain in his own head that Palmer's original five shots on the 12th hole stood, and that he was leading the tournament by one stroke.

Palmer eagled the 13th. Venturi parred the same hole and believed they were now sharing the tournament lead. Walking up the 14th fairway, however, a member of Augusta National and one of Cliff Roberts' assistants, Bill Kerr, came running towards Venturi.

'They gave Arnold a three at 12,' Kerr shouted, before repeating, 'they gave Arnold a three at 12.'

Venturi told the official to get off the fairway. And then, inside, Ken began to fume.

He told himself to settle the incident when they got into the clubhouse. But, somehow, Ken could not get what had just happened out of his head, and started replaying the 12th hole and convinced himself that Palmer was wrong. Troubled and badly distracted, Venturi three-putted the 14th, three-putted the par-five 15th after getting on the green in two, and he also miserably three-putted the 16th.

Palmer would win the tournament by one stroke over Doug Ford and Fred Hawkins. Venturi tied for fourth, two shots back. In the scoring tent, however, he confronted Palmer one last time.

'You're signing an incorrect card,' he said.

Arnold Palmer disagreed. The officials had made their local ruling, Arnie stated matter-of-factly.

After signing his card, Venturi immediately sought out Cliff Roberts. He sought fair play, in his eyes, if not for himself, then for Ford and Hawkins. He poured out the events on the 12th green to Roberts, who did not appear to be overly interested in Venturi's thoughts.

In desperation, Venturi asked for the official, Arthur Lacey, to be brought forward for confirmation of what had happened. He was quickly informed by Roberts that Lacey had already left the golf course.

An agitated Venturi then asked Roberts to bring in Palmer. Arnold knows the rules, Venturi continued. But Roberts decided to end the conversation.

'I don't need to know the rules,' said Roberts curtly. 'I make the rules.'

It was many years later before Bobby Jones apologised to Venturi, explaining that he had attempted to have Palmer's five on the 12th hole stand but was overruled by the chairman of Augusta National. Venturi always believed that Palmer had been in the wrong and, more importantly, he believed that Arnie knew that Ken believed he had been in the wrong. The two golfers never again discussed the 1958 Masters tournament.

Remaining confident and consistent in his game, despite the mockery that he felt he had witnessed at Augusta National, Venturi won four more tournaments before the year was out, finishing up with victory at the Gleneagles Open, where he beat Jackie Burke Jr by one shot, and took the first prize, a mind-blowing $9,000, which meant that Venturi finished his second season as a pro as the third-highest money-winner on the PGA Tour, with a total of $36,268 for his year's work.

Venturi was enjoying the exciting new twist in his career, but he always reminded himself of how he had arrived at such a place in his life by carrying two warnings from Ben Hogan with him in his wallet at all times.

Every day you miss practice will take you one day longer to be good, Hogan believed, adding a rider for good measure, *There isn't enough daylight in any one day to practise all the shots you need to.*

****

In 1959, it was a leaner year and Venturi was 10th on the money list, picking up $25,887 in official earnings, before other bits and pieces, and endorsements, were added in. At the Masters he was never in contention, shooting rounds of 75 and 76 and missing the cut.

But moving into 1960, Venturi began to think more and more about winning a major. It was foremost in his mind, and if it was to happen he thought there was no reason in the world why his first major win should not come back at Augusta National. With his game hot, and his intentions sharpened, Ken Venturi didn't know it but he was soon heading back to East Georgia for more anguish and heartbreak than he could really handle at that point in his life.

Venturi shot 73 in his first round at Augusta in April 1960 and was six shots behind the leader, Arnold Palmer, by the close of the day. Venturi blazed his way through the front nine in 31 shots, but found the back nine a whole different proposition, hitting the ball 42 times, including four shots from the edge of the 18th green.

That night, in the historic Richmond Hotel on Greene Street, Venturi felt the eyes of every single player, as well as the more venomous hangers-on, darting in his direction. He knew they all doubted his ability to walk, and play, Augusta National under the most glaringly intense pressure imaginable. He also knew that he had to attack the course the next day.

In his second round Venturi shot a 69, to Palmer's 73, and by the finish of the third round he had taken back another stroke, by scoring a 71. He was one shot behind Palmer and on the Sunday afternoon he was paired with Dow Finsterwald, from Athens, Ohio. Venturi birdied three of his first six holes, while Palmer went in the opposite direction, and when Arnie bogeyed the fourth hole, Venturi was at the top of the leaderboard.

Finsterwald, a close buddy of Palmer's, was a scintillating short-game player, possessing such skills within sight of the green that he finished in the top five on 50 occasions before his pro career ended. Venturi and Finsterwald went toe-to-toe over their final round. The pair were tied at the top of the leaderboard as they teed it up on the 18th hole. Venturi hit a great drive and his approach landed 15 feet from the pin.

He faced a smooth downhill putt.

He knew a par would leave him in the clubhouse at five under par for the tournament, and that would put all the pressure back on Finsterwald, who was eight feet away for his par. Venturi left the ball six inches from the hole. He had his par and finished with a two-under-par 70. Finsterwald missed his putt. Venturi led the tournament in the clubhouse by one shot, with only Palmer still out on the course to worry about. Palmer was even par for his round and needed two birdies to stop Venturi from finally taking the green jacket.

Venturi watched what happened next on the television set in Cliff Roberts' cabin, with the place packed out with about 40 or 50 officials and writers. The rules at the time allowed a player to leave the pin in the hole while putting on the green, and Palmer did just that on the 16th hole. His putt was too hard and long but, unbelievably, it bounced off the pin and up into the air. The ball finally stalled two feet from the hole. Billy Casper, playing with Palmer, later explained that if the ball had not hit the pin it would have gone over the green and, perhaps, into the sand trap on the other side.

Palmer saved par on the 16th hole, but he still needed birdies on the 17th and 18th to win. On the next hole, Palmer's approach was timid and short, the ball stopping 52 feet from the hole. But Palmer holed it anyhow. A par on the final hole would mean a play-off.

The room in the Roberts Cabin had hardly anyone left inside, only Venturi and a couple of friends. Everyone else had headed out to the 18th green to watch what would happen next with the amazing Arnie.

Conni was there with her husband when they were invited to join Bobby Jones in his private room to watch the final hole. As they sat down, Conni and Ken saw Palmer's approach shot to the green land eight feet from the hole.

But the putt was downhill. And it had a severe break to the right. It was not going to be easy.

Venturi could not watch. He left Conni with Jones and walked outside, but he had not gone 20 yards when he heard a monstrous roar in the distance. Palmer had won the 1960 Masters by one shot. Venturi felt tears flow and he walked blindly into a room where he stumbled upon his old friend and believer, Byron Nelson, who wrapped his arms around the younger man's shoulders.

Again, there was no sudden redemption to be found two months later at the US Open at Cherry Hills Country Club in Denver, where Palmer boldly grabbed his second major in a row with a blistering final round of 65. Palmer's round was sufficient even to blow away the challenge of a 20-year-old amateur from Columbus, Ohio, called Jack Nicklaus.

Augusta had left Ken Venturi a broken man a second time, and even though he recorded his 10th win as a pro by the close of 1960, had collected 18 top-10 finishes in 24 starts, and had finished second on the money list with handsome earnings of $41,230, it was still a deeply unfortunate year for a man who felt that destiny had cold-bloodedly ruled against him.

Four years into his life as a professional golfer, Ken Venturi suddenly felt that neither his energy nor his desire were up to scratch. He felt at a loss. The certainty that he always carried in his head was, somehow, sapped, or entirely removed.

He was not the same man he once was, it seemed. Or, perhaps, he had never been that man… that champion… at any time?

****

Something was not right. By April of 1961, Venturi felt deeply troubled by his professional life. He had started the year with three straight top-10 finishes, but at Augusta National he managed to break par only once in four rounds. With the tournament nearly at an end, it was Gary Player's turn to sit with Bobby Jones and watch Arnold Palmer attack the 18th in his inimitable manner.

The South African was the clubhouse leader. Palmer needed only a par to retain the Masters title, but this time Arnie's approach found the sand on the right side of the final green. Palmer, still, could win by getting up and down in two shots. Two putts for a bogey would still leave him in a play-off. Inexplicably, Arnie's bunker shot cleared the green.

He chipped it back, missed his putt and recorded a double bogey. Watching this unfold, Ken Venturi felt tortured, and ridiculed, and his bitterness sank even deeper. 'I was a distinctly troubled man plagued by my own misgivings, angers and anxieties,' Venturi would admit. He finished 1961 with $25,572 in earnings, 14th on the list but a long way down from Gary Player, who pocketed $64,540.

At the beginning of the next year piercing pains and spasms in his upper body left Ken Venturi moving like a complete wreck. His injury was freakish in nature. He was on the 10th green, during the fourth round of the Palm Springs Classic, when he went to pick his ball out of the hole, as he had done a hundred thousand times before. This time, however, he experienced a sudden piercing pain, as though someone had stabbed him in the chest.

Mentally half-broken, he now felt a physical deterioration as well, and for several months he struggled to lift his right hand over his head. He refused to miss the 1962 Masters tournament in the spring, however, and stubbornly finished in the top 10.

But the following month, in Cleveland, when he was being driven from a golf course to a department store for an appearance for a manufacturer he represented, his career was left in further turmoil when his driver ran a red light. Another car struck Venturi's door and sent him spinning inside the car. He was left banged up, damaging his back and ribs, but there was nothing broken and he still tried to play every week. He took whirlpool baths, he gained some comfort from heating pads and tried cortisone injections. He needed to keep playing. He needed to make money.

In June, he tried to qualify for the US Open, but without any success for a second year in succession.

In that summer of 1962, Venturi started drinking regularly, shots of Jack Daniel's being his choice of cure in the bar-rooms he visited throughout the country. Before then, he had limited himself to a couple of glasses of white wine on a Sunday night, and a Bloody Mary with his lunch on Monday, but for the remainder of the week he was a completely focused, sober young man. Now, however, he began to drink during the week as well.

Doctors had talked him into wearing a brace. Day and night he did so, to pull his shoulders back and ease the spasms while he tried to sleep. His awful year held the added misery of Venturi being fired by the Palo Alto Hills Country Club as their touring professional. He sued the club, and got them to pay compensation, but, too often, to find his way through every week, Venturi needed a few drinks.

His golf game was slipping. His swing had become too flat, too short, too fast.

Ken felt desperately unhappy. His life was spinning negatively, and straying out of his control. And soon, he needed those few drinks every day.

****

By the end of 1962, Venturi's year's winnings totalled $6,951. In 1963, his mental and physical well-being plunged even further, to depths unknown to him previously. The perfect swing, which Byron Nelson had helped Venturi develop into a smooth act of wonder to most other professionals on the tour, had pretty much fallen apart and become a laboured, fractured action. Venturi felt ashamed of his game.

Palmer was now the king of the fairway. Nicklaus had emerged, and wasted absolutely no time in capturing the US Open in

Above: Ken Venturi and his first round playing partner, Billy Joe Patton from North Carolina take time out during the 1956 Masters at Augusta National. *Getty Images*

Below: Patton and Venturi both spectacularly eagled the 13th hole in their first round, at the end of which the amateur player and West Coast car salesman, Venturi, led the tournament. *Getty Images*

Above: Ken Venturi, Clifford Roberts and Bobby Jones watch as Jackie Burke, Jr. receives a Green Jacket from Cary Middlecoff during the 1956 Masters Tournament Presentation Ceremony. *Getty Images*

Left: Venturi, who led Burke Jnr from Texas by eight shots at the start of the final round in Augusta in '56 before shooting a gut-wrenching 80, congratulates the champion at the end of the day's play. *Press Association*

Right: Venturi holds his medal for best amateur after finishing eighth in the US Open at Oak Hill, New York, in '56. *Press Association*

Left: Venturi reacts after sinking a 30-foot birdie putt in winning the St. Paul Open golf tournament in St. Paul, Minn., in August 1957. In his first year as a professional Venturi won the St. Paul Open title with a record-equalling 266, or 22 under par. *Press Association*

Above: After his 12-foot putt nestled into the cup on the 18th green, Ken Venturi throws up his arms in celebration of his winning the 1964 U.S. Open golf title at Congressional CC in Bethesda. *Getty Images*

Left: Ken Venturi gets a kiss from his wife Conni as he accepts the title holder's silver cup of the U.S. Open. *Press Association*

Below: Ken Venturi on the practice green with his two 'corner men', his loyal coach Byron Nelson (centre) and his great mentor Eddie Lowery. *Getty Images*

Above: Fred Venturi, pro shop manager at San Francisco's Harding Park Golf Course, shows off the headline that his son had won the U.S. Open. *Press Association*

Below: Venturi came to Britain in October '64 as reigning US Open champion, but during the opening round of the Piccadilly World Matchplay Championship at Wentworth he noticed a serious problem with his hands. *Getty Images*

Above: Venturi, here teeing off on the second hole during the 1966 Masters, never did overcome the heartbreak of coming so close on three occasions to winning the precious title at Augusta National *Getty Images*

Left: Rory McIlroy, with his childhood sweetheart Holly Sweeney, attend the 2010 Ryder Cup Dinner at Cardiff Castle. *Getty Images*

Right: McIlroy described his opening round 65 at the 2011 Masters as 'more solid than spectacular,' despite coming within two shots of the course record and ending the day as the tournament's joint leader. He waits (right) on the second tee during that first round.
Getty Images

Left: The pride before the fall: Rory McIlroy waves to the gallery after a birdie putt on the 15th green during the third round of the 2011 Masters. He would lead the tournament by four shots at the end of the day's play.
Getty Images

Above: Rory shows his frustration as his round collapses at Augusta, on Sunday, April 10, 2011. *Getty Images*

Below: McIlroy stormed into the lead on day one at the US Open in Congressional Country Club in Bethesda, hitting 17 greens in regulation and his six under par left him three shots ahead of the field. He tees off (below) on the 16th hole in that opening round. *Getty Images*

Above: Rory McIlroy is bear-hugged by his father, Gerry, after sinking the last putt on the 18th hole to win the US Open. *Getty Images*

Below Passing the baton: Ken Venturi presents Rory McIlroy with the US Open trophy. *Getty Images*

Above: Rory McIlroy proudly presents the US Open trophy next to a beaming Chubby Chandler, his agent who was shocked at McIlroy's decision to walk away from ISM by the end of the summer of 2011, and Stuart Cage (left) his handler in International Sports Management. *Getty Images*

Below: Rory McIlroy, victorious with trophy, stands before the leaderboard. *Getty Images*

2011 WOMEN'S WORLD CUP: TEAM USA's TEST
BY GRANT WAHL
SLUGGER JOSE BAUTISTA: DO YOU BELIEVE?
BY JOE POSNANSKI
Sports Illustrated
RORY McILROY'S HISTORIC WIN AT THE U.S. OPEN
GOLF'S NEW ERA
By MICHAEL BAMBERGER

Left: *Sports Illustrated* covers from 1964 and 2011 celebrate the victories of Ken Venturi and Rory McIlroy at Congressional Country Club in Bethesda, Maryland. *Getty Images*

Palmer's backyard, at Oakmont Country Club, in 1962. Billy Casper was also on top of his game. The top of the leaderboard at most tournaments was a crazy, congested place in the early months of 1963.

Ken Venturi's golf career, in comparison, was moving into the small print in the daily newspapers. Venturi felt no better about his life in general. He had tried hypnosis, without any satisfaction or gain. Conni urged him to seek the help of a psychiatrist, but Ken reacted angrily to the suggestion and stormed out of their home. He did not return for four days.

Tensions in their marriage boiled over with alarming regularity, usually every time Ken returned home from a few weeks out on the road. His drinking and his moods gripped large portions of every day of his life, and there was nothing Conni, or any of his friends, could do to help. He was alone.

Having finished in the top 10 in the Masters tournament in 1962, Venturi had his invite to East Georgia in the bag for '63, unlike with so many other tournaments on the tour schedule which now requested him to qualify, something Venturi found galling and so damaging to his pride.

Augusta was different.

It was where he had so nearly been a champion, on three occasions, where there was still a sense of destiny, and where he had experienced every emotion possible in the book of a professional golfer, from exhilaration to despair, and back again. For the 1963 tournament he took a house in the city with Tony Lema and Bo Wininger for the first week of April. Venturi struggled through the four rounds, and ended up back in 33rd place. Lema came within a whisker of taking the green jacket, finishing one shot behind Jack Nicklaus, who celebrated the first of his six triumphs on the course. Two months later, for the third year in a row, Venturi failed to make the starting line for the US Open.

Off the course, the disharmony grew month by month in the Venturi home, where Ken continually poured out all of his anger and despair. Conni sometimes tried to avoid the constant arguments, but Venturi sometimes lived for them.

Conni could not always resist the temptation to join in. Once, she told her husband that his golf game was 'over the hill', three words he would never forget and for which he would never be able to fully forgive her. Certainly, he no longer lived to be out on the course. He was as unhappy there as he was in his own home. He was practising less than he had ever practised in his life. And he was spending longer and longer drinking. He would often happily call Conni to tell her not to expect him home and, in that home, there was very little trace left of a normal family life. He didn't fully understand what was happening, how everything appeared to have been lost. He felt guilty and that overpowering sense of guilt forced him to withdraw from his wife, and from the game he loved.

Conni sought help from Eddie Lowery. But not even Eddie, with all of his multi-layered abilities and way with people, could get through to Ken.

'Kenny had tremendous success but he was not able to handle it,' said Lowery, at the end of 1964 in a *Sports Illustrated* article. 'I had people come up to me and say, *Ed, you're a friend of mine and I know how you feel about Venturi, but I hope the s.o.b. shoots 100.*

'Kenny thought he knew all of the answers. He thought that he knew more about golf than anyone else around. He might even have resented the fact that everyone said he was the creation of Byron Nelson. I don't know.

'Anyway, Kenny decided that he had to lengthen his tee shot, so he took a more closed position. He thought he had to hook the ball in order to hit it as far as Palmer. He wouldn't listen to anybody. He wouldn't listen to Byron any more, and Byron was hurt.

'I remember one time I said to him, *Kenny, have you got a dictionary at your house?*' said Lowery, who told Venturi to go and look up the spelling of the word humble. 'H-U-M-B-L-E. I told him, *You have no idea of the meaning of the word.*

'Oh, he was sore at me… he didn't even speak to me for a while after that.'

Venturi was as quick with a rebuttal or an insult for his former boss and mentor as he was with his wife, occasionally advising him to mind his own business. He knew he was being cruel to the two people he loved most, and had needed most, in his life, Conni and Eddie. But, the more guilt festered inside him at this knowledge, the more Ken struck out randomly in the direction of those he deeply respected.

For several months, the drinking continued apace. The few cocktails and beers with the boys were fine, but he now needed a few stiff whiskeys to help him get through most days.

One afternoon, Ken arrived at a bar on Geary Street in San Francisco, which had long since become another safe place of refuge. He had left his car there the previous night. The bartender, a former University of San Francisco football player by the name of Dave Marcelli, whom Venturi had once admired, watched him come in and take his seat at the counter.

'Ken, what the hell are you doing?' shouted Marcelli, angrily. 'What's the matter with you? Do you have any idea what you did to yourself last night? You're making a total wreck of yourself.'

Marcelli told Venturi the last thing he needed was another shot of Jack Daniel's. He told him he needed to go home. He told him to go home to his beautiful wife and two great kids.

Venturi heard every word that was spoken. He thanked Marcelli but stayed sitting, and hoped that he would have another drink in front of him at any minute. He asked for a double Jack. Marcelli stared back at his customer, dumbfounded at Venturi's failure to understand what he had just been told.

Eventually, Venturi looked up at Marcelli.

'Trust me,' he said. 'Give me a double Jack Daniel's on the rocks.'

For the next hour, Venturi sat at the bar with that one glass in front of him, thinking hard. Finally, he called over to Marcelli and thanked him. Rising from his stool, he told the bartender that he was not going to have another drink until he had won a golf tournament again.

This time, Venturi had not responded by getting angry. He didn't feel like swinging in the direction of the man who was telling him he should be ashamed of himself. He had heard the bartender tell him that he had Conni, and his two boys Matt and Tim, and that he had the world by the tail. He heard all of that, and the words sank into Venturi's heart. And there they stayed.

But Ken still walked out of the bar feeling that he had nothing in his life, and telling himself that he was a nobody. However he wasn't angry and, for once, he didn't feel like blaming anybody else for what had befallen him. He also wondered what he should do next. Before going home, he drove to his home club, the respectable old California Golf Club, on the southern outskirts of the city, and with darkness enveloping the clubhouse and a few members pottering around, he mapped out a practice regime for the following day.

Shortly after a stay with the Nelsons, Venturi received a verbal invitation from the tournament director of the Sahara Invitational. It was a rare piece of good fortune in his golfing life. He and Conni flew out to Las Vegas with some hope of having a good week together. At the airport, the couple were picked up by their good friend, Ed Moore, and they headed straight for the course, to register.

Ken walked into the clubhouse, and with a happy, expectant voice, asked where he might register. But at the registrar's desk he found a man, deeply embarrassed, with a list in his hands.

'Ken, your name isn't on the list!'

Venturi thought someone was kidding with him. But there was no laughter, no smiles. Only embarrassment all round. Venturi tried to remain upbeat, and enquired about an 'invitation' to play the tournament? He was told there were no free places for another starter. Venturi stood there, in the silence, before walking quickly out of the clubhouse.

He didn't know that four of his fellow pros, including Mike Souchak, had heard about the incident, and had decided to meet the tournament director on Venturi's behalf and seek a late placement. The director was embarrassed into doing a U-turn, but when he phoned Venturi with the good news, Venturi haughtily told him that he had no intention of playing in his tournament.

Conni, back in their hotel room, talked reason into her husband. She knew they needed the money, and badly at that.

Roused by the events of the previous days, Ken held nothing back in the tournament and, even though he suffered a triple bogey in his final round for a 76, he still mustered sufficient quality in his game to win $675, which was more money than he and Conni had seen in some time.

In 1963, Venturi finished in the money on only eight occasions. He never placed higher than 18th position in any tournament, and by the end of his year's work he was 94th on the PGA Tour's money list. His total winnings stood at $3,848.

****

Ken Venturi knew that 1964 had the look of the longest, most punishing year of his life. He was performing like a loser every week. He was close to broke. He had Conni and his boys on one side, and his tattered golf game on the other, and he had been sitting in the middle, sometimes uncaring about his self-destruction, drinking like a fool to end the misery, which had descended upon his life as completely as the heaviest of blankets.

Most of his endorsement contracts were coming to an end. Too many tournament directors didn't give a damn about him any more. He knew, in his heart, however, that he might have one last chance left within him to try to win back the love, and respect, of his wife and friends.

Ken was 32 years old. Significantly, he reminded himself that Ben Hogan did not win his first major title until he was 34.

Three things, he knew for certain, would have to change. He'd have to keep to his promise not to drink. He'd have to bring some calmness, some self-belief, some confidence, back into his life in general. And, for sure, he'd have to get out on the practice range, and work harder on his golf game than he had ever worked in some years. All of that, he knew.

But bringing such change to his everyday life would not be easy. For starters, it would take real courage. And where was Ken Venturi, from where he was sitting, going to even start looking for that?

He started with one big question, asking himself if 1964 was going to be his last year as a professional golfer? There was only one straight answer to that question. It certainly looked like it might be. The honesty with which he faced up to that distinct prospect started a trickle of courage. But, Venturi also needed the humility to roll back the years, as far as they needed to be rolled back, and think and act like the young, ambitious man he had been in his early 20s. That was when he first met Byron Nelson.

He still had the notes that he had written down after the countless lessons he had received from Nelson, the man he respected more than any other sportsman he had ever known or watched from a great distance. Venturi read those notes, and brought them in his pockets to the practice range at the California club, every day, for several weeks, along with Nelson's book *Winning Golf*.

He practised, morning and afternoon, taking a break in between when he'd borrow a couple of towels for pillows and take a nap in the clubhouse. He went through every club in his bag, occasionally breaking up the sequence with a quick nine holes, or perhaps the full 18 on his own. Everyone in the club knew not to bother him. The only person allowed to observe, because he always did so without speaking, was the club president, Bert Schroeder.

Venturi began to shoot consistently in the 60s. The first step in rebuilding his life was to rebuild the long, slow, rhythmic one-piece swing that Nelson, magnificently, had helped create. With that, anything on the golf course, and within his life, would be possible.

In January of 1964, Ken, Conni and the boys travelled to Palm Springs for the Los Angeles Open. Money was short, but Venturi decided that his family would stay in the Beverly Hilton. He wanted to look the part. He wanted people to think he was back and, besides, he had decided that if the year was to implode, he may as well face the complete destruction of his golf career in stylish surroundings.

There was still tension in the family's rooms, of course. Venturi felt his wife watching him, closely, too closely, and always nervously, and at the same time trying too hard to give her husband the firm impression that she believed they had returned to the good, old travelling days of his early pro career. Eddie Lowery also came to Los Angeles to offer his unstinted support, telling everybody who wished to hear him or not that his 'boy' was ready to start winning again. Other friends were also on hand nearby in LA, and Venturi felt the pressure mounting up all around him, like giant glassed walls that might shatter at any second, and he found it difficult to breathe or even think straight until he had got a dreadful first-round score out of his system.

After that, Lowery became even louder in the clubhouse, and in the hotel foyer and bar. Ken told Conni that if Eddie didn't stop, he was going to blow up, for sure. Conni spoke to Eddie, and asked him to step back and tone it down. The next day, Venturi played a little bit better, but not good enough to know for sure that he had survived the midway cut in the tournament. He waited in the clubhouse with Conni until the very last golfer was off the course, and the tournament officials started totting up all of the numbers from the day.

Finally, they told Ken and Conni that he had missed the cut by one shot. That same evening, a man from Jantzen Inc, a clothing company that had been selling Ken Venturi swimsuits and sweaters for several years, asked for a meeting the next day. The contract was up. The next morning, Venturi was told he was being cut from the company as well.

As he returned to the hotel, to hook up with Conni and the boys, the strength had drained out of Venturi. His shoulders were visibly slumped. On the long drive back north, to their new home in San Francisco, Ken did not speak to his wife for more than five minutes.

The Venturis had moved from Westlake to the city's most expensive and exclusive suburb, Hillsborough, with the birth of their second son, Timothy. Their home was a fabulous ranch-style house on a wooded hillside. Parked in the driveway was a Lincoln Continental convertible, and a Mercury station wagon. The Venturis' neighbours were wealthy businesspeople, and showbusiness folk. Bing Crosby lived just a block down the road.

Ken and Conni pulled the car into the driveway shortly after midnight, in the early minutes of Sunday morning. Ken unloaded the car, while Conni got the boys into the house and into their beds. There was, still, hardly a word spoken between the two of them. Venturi, finally, carried his clubs down to his basement workshop where, in the past, he had spent hours playing around with different designs. He stayed down there.

Conni, worried at his absence, nervously came down the steps, slowly, to find her husband sitting there, looking at his clubs. Conni's normally sparkling eyes were wide, and frightened.

She suggested that he should come to bed. It had been a long week, and a difficult day. He should sleep and be ready for a new day, she advised. As she did so, Conni also looked distractedly at the gun collection, which her husband also kept in his basement.

'Only much later did she tell me that when I sent her back

upstairs,' Venturi would recall in *Comeback*, 'she waited hours in sheer terror, expecting at any moment to hear a shot and to find me lying dead in a pool of blood.'

When Conni went to her bed, Venturi took out each of his clubs and, slowly, intently, began to clean and polish each one. He then laid them, numbered in order and looking like new, on a bench.

When Conni reappeared, to check on him and ask if he'd like a coffee or a hot chocolate, she was quickly told to go to bed... to go to sleep.

'Leave me alone,' he told her softly.

As soon as she was gone, Ken was on his knees. Without thinking about it, he found himself praying. He asked God not to let him die as he was. He begged for another chance at getting his life back in one piece. He begged and promised. And he prayed, and he stayed praying, until he could no longer remember how long he had been on his knees. He had been on his knees for hours.

It was 4 a.m. when he finally stood up, turned off the lights, and joined Conni in their bed. He kissed her gently on the forehead. He felt at peace as he lay there. More significantly, he felt that he had forgiven himself for the previous years of wastefulness, and utter selfishness. He closed his eyes, and instantly fell into a sound sleep.

On Monday, Venturi lunched with his old friend, Bill Varni, in the Owl and Turtle restaurant. Venturi, in the cold early light of another hopeless-looking week, was feeling down on his luck again, and poured out his fresh doubts about his golf career over the table.

Bill wasn't having any of it. He shut Venturi up. He told his pal that he fully believed he was going to have the greatest year of his career, and he went further than that. He offered him $50,000, that same day, if Venturi agreed to hand over all of his winnings, and bonuses and new endorsements, to him for the entire year.

He offered the $50,000 by the end of their lunch.

Venturi shook his head. He liked the idea of fifty grand, and if Bill had not been such a close friend, he might even have thought seriously of taking him up on the offer. Nevertheless, the other man's faith had an impact on Venturi, and he walked out of the restaurant feeling infinitely better about what might lie in store over the next few weeks. Nothing much changed, however, and a mixture of self-pity and poor shot-making had him debating, once again, if 1964 was to be his last year as a competitive golfer. At the Lucky International in San Francisco, he won a cheque for $295, and was grateful to pocket it.

****

During the Lucky International tournament, Father Francis Kevin Murray, a local priest whom Venturi knew from sight, walked the final round with Conni.

Father Murray was the assistant pastor at the St Vincent de Paul Church in the Marina district of San Francisco, and after the tournament Father Murray also spoke with Ken. They agreed to meet up again soon. Venturi looked forward to it. He even asked the priest to call by his house at any time for their next chat.

It had been a more positive week, and in the following days Venturi expected to get some word from Augusta National that he would be receiving an official invitation from the club to play in the Masters tournament. He had not qualified for the trip to East Georgia. He needed Clifford Roberts and his officials to take a decent view of his past performances on the course.

'You will always be invited back to Augusta,' Roberts had informed him after the 1960 Masters tournament.

He finished well enough at the Pensacola Open, where he came ninth, and also at the St Petersburg Invitational in Florida. Small winnings were gained in each tournament, but he waited, every day, and called Conni every single day to hear if anything had come in the mail from Augusta National.

A month before the Masters, however, Ken and Conni had one more argument, and one more than either could handle. Ken had asked Conni to fly down to Crystal River in Florida, where he was intent on practising for five days before taking in the Greater Greensboro Open, and moving on to Augusta. Conni brought with her a sequence of photographs of Ken's swing, and as he studied and practised his grip and his stance, and every element of his swing, she sat there with him, for hour after hour. They then flew into Raleigh-Durham Airport in North Carolina, as they had intended to spend a few days with Mike and Nancy Souchak at their home, before heading to Greensboro. The Souchaks, however, had already left for the tournament.

In the airport, Ken picked up a copy of *Sports Illustrated*, in which he had heard that Tony Lema had written something about him. Lema wrote that Venturi was not open to advice from Byron Nelson or, for that matter, anybody else.

Ken fumed. He handed the article to Conni, to seek a supportive view, but Conni thought the piece was well written. He snapped at her judgement. That night, before dinner, he also picked up a newspaper. Ken, finally, got to read through the list of entrants for the 1964 Masters tournament.

His name was not there.

The club's final two invitations had gone to Dave Marr and Phil Rodgers. Ken lost it completely. Conni, however, had already reached the end of the road in listening to her husband vilify indiscriminately and complain about everybody and everything.

She asked him why he didn't just quit. Venturi said he was going to quit, there and then. As they flew home, Venturi also came to the conclusion that his wife and their boys would be better off without him. When they arrived home, he told Conni what he was thinking.

'We just can't live together any more,' he blurted. 'I have to do it alone. I can't live with anyone... not even myself! I've just got to get away by myself.'

Conni was also close to breaking point, and she informed Ken that if he was going, then he needed to make it permanent. None of this coming and going! She told him he needed to pack his clothes and go.

Venturi watched the final round of the 1964 Masters tournament, as Arnold Palmer won with a handsome six-shot advantage, on the television set at the California Country Club, where he spent the week hitting more balls than any other week in his entire golf career. He and Conni had been apart for a number of weeks, and when they met up next Conni informed him that he appeared to view her and his children as a handicap and, with that being the case, she had decided to consult a lawyer.

Conni was strong-minded about the situation. Ken asked for another three weeks.

She felt that they had had enough time, over the previous two years, to get their lives back in harmony and bring some happiness into their home, and that they had failed. Ken then asked for two more weeks.

When Ken left, there was no kiss, only a goodbye. He walked out of his home and away from Conni, Matt and Tim, thinking that his marriage might be over already.

While Ken was away, Father Murray stopped by and, finding Conni quite distraught, the priest decided to repeat his visits most evenings. By the end of the week, Father Murray had convinced Conni that Ken needed her more than ever before.

When Ken came home from his next tournament, Father Murray also sought him out and chatted to him. Daily, on occasions, they talked about everything, with Father Murray telling Ken how much Conni loved him, and how much a part of his life she and his boys could be. When they finished talking, Ken always felt that Father Murray had worked some wonderful therapeutic magic on him. He felt calmer, unloaded of his tension, and the mounting fear and doubt that grappled in his head every hour of every day.

He talked to the priest about everything. 'I could tell the troubles Ken was going through,' Father Murray would explain at the end of that same year. 'Sort of like reading between the lines. He didn't say anything, but I knew pretty much how he felt. Sometimes when Ken was away, I would send him a telegram just to let him know I was thinking of him and appreciated our friendship, that I believed he could succeed.'

The professional golfer and the priest walked together, and played a little golf as well. Understanding his life, and its recent events, allowed Ken to think about bringing an end to his selfish, self-pitying crusade, which had all but crushed his wife and was ready to wipe out their marriage.

Alone with Conni, Ken was becoming more able to quietly discuss their life. He said he would try to win some more money on tour for a few weeks, and if he failed then he would happily come home for good. He'd find a job in San Francisco, back selling cars perhaps. Conni told him she didn't care about money, or losing their lovely home. She just wanted them to be stronger and happier than they had ever been.

The day Ken left for the Oklahoma Open, he embraced Conni and trotted to the car, which had Father Murray waiting behind the wheel. He was not afraid of what lay ahead. For the first time in such a long time, there was no worry.

In Oklahoma, Venturi performed only okay, finishing 27th, and in Memphis a week later he could only manage 28th, but he didn't beat himself up about either performance. On the Monday after the Memphis Open, he had to stay put in order to take in the first stage of two qualifying trials for the 1964 US Open at Congressional Country Club in Bethesda.

In his bag, Venturi had a new putter. Actually, it was an old putter but a new addition to his bag, and it had been given to him a fortnight earlier by a friend, Bud Ward. It was a rare Ben Hogan pacemaker MacGregor centre shaft, featuring a leather grip. It had once belonged to the late Phil Garnett, a kindly man who bore a slight hunchback and who had been a member of the California Golf Club. The initials J. P. G. were still stamped on the bottom of the putter. Garnett, shortly before he died, had given the putter to Ward.

'Someday you will find someone who really needs this putter. You give it to him, and you tell him it will work,' promised Garnett.

It was the only putter in Venturi's bag for those few weeks, and it felt a natural fit in his hands. He felt he never needed to back off any putt, and in the two rounds in Memphis, Venturi shot 67 and 70, to become the third lowest qualifier for the US Open.

He called Conni immediately. He told her they were back on the right road, and that Bethesda was their next big destination. However, the next week, in the next tournament, Venturi missed the cut in Indianapolis, which was the gateway to the extravagant Thunderbird tournament. The Thunderbird had a prize fund of $100,000 and was being played the following week at the Westchester Country Club in New York.

This time there was no anger, no sulking reaction, no wish to scour his life to see if he could spot someone to blame. He took his failure in his stride. Ken also decided to do something about his situation, by picking up a phone and calling the Thunderbird tournament director, Bill Jennings.

'Bill, I really need this,' he said.

Venturi was on his knees, he was begging for his place in the tournament. And, as he did so he also knew that Jennings, who owned the New York Rangers hockey team, owed him nothing. Twelve months earlier, in the Thunderbird, Ken had shot an 80 in the first round, and in a state of utter disgust he decided not to turn up the next day.

'If I go home now,' he told Jennings, 'I'll never be back on tour. You've got to help me, Bill!' Ken felt he was simply doing what he had to do for Conni and his boys, and Father Murray, and Byron Nelson, and all of his friends who had never let him down.

Jennings said he didn't know if he could help. But, importantly, Jennings did ask for 24 hours, telling Venturi to call him back the next evening. He hadn't said no. As Father Murray had repeatedly told him, Ken did not need to believe that the whole world was teamed up against him.

He got his invite, and got on to a plane for New York the next day. The first man Ken went to see, and thank, was Bill Jennings. In the tournament, Venturi fought every single hole to prove to everybody that he was still a good golfer. Tony Lema and Mike Souchak had the tournament wrapped up between them on the back nine of the final round, but Venturi was in the hunt for third place. The cheque was worth $6,250.

He needed every dollar of that cheque. He had arrived in New York virtually broke.

He kept his nerve after the turn. On the difficult par-three 16th hole, he wondered for several seconds whether he should play conservatively. He could hit a four-iron, and make a certain bogey. That might be good enough for a share of third place? But the thought did not sit well in his head. He knew that he had been backing off for far too long. Too often, when the time arrived to make the big shot, he'd failed to take on the challenge.

'I thought about Conni, and I thought about the money… and how badly we needed it. I told myself, *You back off now, you'll back off for the rest of your life*.' He took his three-iron into his hands.

His ball landed safely on the green. A birdie was a possibility, but Venturi two-putted for his par. It was a par, however, which had the strength, if not the salvation, of an eagle. He had made the right decision. He had shown that when he needed to, he had the guts to go for it. Venturi birdied the 17th and parred the 18th, and won third place outright.

In the locker room, he phoned Conni to give her the good news. The tears streamed down his cheeks. Every hour, all evening long, he kept calling his wife.

After the Thunderbird, Ken Venturi needed to be in Franklin Hills, Detroit, for the second qualifying competition for the US Open at Congressional Country Club in Bethesda, Maryland. He had never played Franklin Hills before.

The wind blew hard. Venturi shot a 77 in the first of his two rounds on the day. He looked well out of the qualifying spots for Bethesda. After lunch, Venturi was back on the first tee again, and the wind was still hitting his face hard as he stared down the narrow fairway of the first hole.

He needed to be strong, and to fight for what he wanted in the rest of his life, and he aggressively drilled his tee shot right down the middle, before knocking a one-iron into the heart of the green. He holed his putt for a birdie.

There was no stopping him. He shot a 70 and made it through to Congressional and the US Open by three shots. In making the journey to Bethesda, Ken Venturi was on his way to a first US Open in four long, puzzling years.

CHAPTER EIGHT

Seventy days

When Rory McIlroy turned 20, he bought one of the many cars of his dreams. He made a quick one-day trip with his father, Gerry, to Birmingham, in the heart of England, and purchased a Ferrari F430. McIlroy was quick on the draw and immediately let readers of his blog, and his followers on Twitter, which numbered 490,000 at that time, making him one of the most popular sportsmen in Ireland and Britain, know of his purchase.

'It's gun metal grey and it's absolute class,' he wrote. 'We drove it up to Stranraer and then on the ferry to Belfast... seriously exciting day.'

McIlroy also mentioned that he'd 'picked up' an Audi RS6, more of an estate-type car, so that he and his girlfriend, Holly, could travel around with their dogs (the couple had just got a black Labradoodle puppy, which they called Theo). He already had an Audi S5, 'in black with every extra imaginable' which was a little treat for himself upon making the top 50 in the world in 2008.

One year before that, after one early big pay day on the professional tour, he had sauntered into a local car dealership in Belfast and bought Gerry a C-Class Mercedes. McIlroy's first car had been a BMW 1 Series, which trumped the teasing of his father and mother, who had promised him a respectable, compact Ford Ka if he ever passed his driving test. Three years, almost, into his professional career, McIlroy liked to tell people, with a touch of humbleness, that he owned '11 or 12' expensive cars.

In the final month of 2011, however, Rory McIlroy sat at a press conference and stated matter-of-factly that he had sold the 'few cars' that he had owned. Unlike so many other golfers he knew personally, he didn't feel the need to have a large trophy garage of fast, expensive toys. Other golfers down through the years, as competition for television rights, as well as the bragging rights of global corporations, poured outrageously large amounts of money into the game, had often spent extravagantly on playthings. In 1996, for instance, as his mighty ambition of one day winning the Masters was about to go belly-up once again, Greg Norman had declared that he had no idea how many Ferraris he actually owned.

Put on the spot, the 41-year-old Aussie thought the number was six. But he definitely possessed a custom-built $18 million Gulfstream IV jet, a $4 million Bell 230 twin-engined helicopter, an 87-foot fishing yacht called *Aussie Rules*, a few smaller boats, three Harleys, two jet-skis, a Rolls-Royce, a Bentley, a Mercedes and six Chevrolet Suburbans.

****

Ten days before he teed up for the first round of the US Open at Congressional Country Club in Bethesda, Maryland, in June 2011, Rory McIlroy changed his Twitter profile picture. For a couple of years, the page had shown McIlroy as a tiny boy swinging a miniature golf club, which was a cute, if not very cool, way for one of the world's greatest young golfers to present himself. But on Monday, June 6, it was gone.

Instead, there appeared a picture of McIlroy holding up to the camera a beautiful little Haitian child with the biggest eyes and most hopeful smile. McIlroy had flown into Port-au-Prince, the still reeling capital of the Caribbean country, earlier that morning from the East Coast of the United States. McIlroy was making a visit as UNICEF Ireland's newest goodwill ambassador. He planned to spend 48 hours in Haiti, to see for himself the effects of an unimaginable tragedy, and to catch a glimpse of the still impoverished lives of millions of people who had survived a catastrophic 7.0-magnitude earthquake in the second week of January 2010.

The quake had occurred in the late afternoon. More than one million people were left homeless. The Haitian government reported that more than 300,000 people had died, though whether this total erred by 100,000 or so, nobody seemed quite sure.

McIlroy had taken up his UNICEF appointment one month before arriving at Augusta National to compete in the 75th Masters tournament. He had no idea, none whatsoever at that time, that his decision would not only be of remarkable benefit in highlighting the still pressing needs of the people of Haiti, but that by helping the charity he was also helping himself. He had been afforded a unique opportunity of rapidly coming to terms with the vastly exaggerated drama of throwing away a Masters title and, privately, having the ability to label it as really nothing more than one bad day's golf in a rich young man's life.

In Haiti, McIlroy saw enough. When he touched down in Washington, the week before the US Open at Congressional, he had hopped into an expensive 'pick-up' car and found himself on a freeway of impossible comfort, compared to where he had just been.

'I'd been in a four-wheel-drive whatever-it-was for two days,' McIlroy informed the world's media. 'There's no roads, no streetlights, no infrastructure at all. There's nothing.'

In Haiti, he had seen rubble, and looked upon thousands and thousands of people living in tents in every direction from where he stood. He walked by the Presidential Palace in Port-au-Prince, standing there with its domed roof still caved in.

He took photos of everything he saw, and they remained on his phone as he switched his thoughts to the golf tournament, which, soon enough, would have to grab his complete attention. 'There's stuff there that I never thought I'd see in my life,' he tweeted. McIlroy had played some soccer with children during photo opportunities for UNICEF, and he had looked through a maternity ward, chock-a-block and resembling a ward from a different century. Eighteen months after the quake, the people had still to come to terms with what awaited them in the remainder of their lives, but their spirit, McIlroy noted repeatedly, was intact and as strong as it had ever been, possibly stronger.

'A little bit of perspective now and again is a good thing,' McIlroy noted for an inquisitive media.

McIlroy had never played Congressional before, or ever taken in, from up close, the size of the clubhouse, in all its grandeur and opulence. However, after travelling from Haiti to leafy Bethesda, just beyond the Capital Beltway that surrounds Washington, DC, he played the course twice in 48 hours and described it as 'fantastic'. He planned to return on the Monday of tournament week, play nine holes on the Tuesday, another nine on the Wednesday, and then tee off in the US Open the following day.

'I feel comfortable on it,' he said. 'It's long... you've got to fly the ball. The greens are getting firm already... you've got to shape it, primarily right to left, which is fine with me.

'I think it's great.'

Forty-eight hours earlier, on the Tuesday morning before flying out, McIlroy was supposed to travel to the Petionville Club, a nine-hole track outside Port-au-Prince that once was Haiti's only golf course, but which dutifully served as a tent city for thousands of refugees, their homes destroyed in the quake. The previous night, a tropical depression produced heavy rains across Haiti. Flooding and mudslides ensued, and two dozen people died. Many tents at the Petionville Club were washed away. McIlroy abandoned his plans to visit the former golf course.

'You didn't want to intrude, because after a night like that happens, spirits in the camp are not going to be very good,' McIlroy said.

'It's hard. It would've been great… well, it wouldn't have been great to go and see it, but… If you ever hear me moan about a hotel room again,' McIlroy had told his ISM aide, Stuart Cage, 'shoot me!'

****

On the Sunday evening, in the hour immediately after his loss at Augusta National, Rory McIlroy had remained in a state of shock. The minutes flashed by. He could not remember walking off the green. Before he knew it, he was facing Peter Kostis. The CBS analyst was apologetic, but nevertheless enquired if Rory was prepared to say something?

'Right now, all I need is a hug!' McIlroy replied.

'Give me a hug, and we will do the interview.'

Kostis embraced the fallen, shattered hero. Then they spoke for one minute and 40 seconds about McIlroy's final 18 holes.

It was not until the following morning, when he was closeted back in the house that Chubby Chandler had booked for him, and when he got the chance to have a long chat with his mother, back at home in Northern Ireland, that he felt a torrent of emotion. He had spoken to his father the previous night, within half an hour of ending his round. Rosie and Gerry were so far away from him.

Rosie and Gerry had also endured a 24 hours that they had never imagined or anticipated. Early on Sunday evening, Rosie's nerves were all-consuming, and finally she determined that she had to escape her own home. She drove across Belfast city to a pizza restaurant. But one slice of her favourite pizza was all that Rosie could manage. Her stomach had closed.

Gerry, knowing that his wife would be agitated and frayed by her worries, had already driven to their son's beautiful home. He decided to watch the final round from Augusta National on his own, and at the same time look after Holly and Rory's two dogs. Rosie and Gerry repeatedly phoned one another through the evening. Each tried to build up the other's spirits. But Gerry knew by the way Rory walked, by the way he held himself when he prepared for his next shot, that something was wrong. Between the 10th and 13th holes, Rosie's tears and sobs were uncontrolled. Gerry could say very little to his wife.

When he spoke to them both on the Monday morning, Rory, quickly, felt like a little boy, their only son... their baby son. The boy they had worked so hard for: all those long nights Rosie had worked in the 3M factory; her few hours' sleep before Rory came home from school; Gerry coming home from his two day-jobs, taking his tea, then tending the bar at the sports club until midnight, by which time Rosie would be back at her night shift. He felt he had let them down.

At the end of 2011, he would honestly recount those most private of conversations with his parents.

At the time he had felt a surge of self-pity, and sorrow for himself as he heard his mum's voice and her softly encouraging words, 'It'll be okay... Rors... you'll get plenty more chances.'

Before he knew it, McIlroy was sobbing his heart out.

No... it won't be okay! McIlroy thought to himself as he listened, and cried. 'I felt like shouting down the phone, *But I won't get plenty more chances! That was it. I blew it. I choked.*'

The agony of losing the Masters title, which he had been absolutely certain was his just 24 hours earlier, when he sat and chatted on the same telephone, was now overwhelming him. He felt so sorry for himself. But, at the same time, he didn't want to be one of those players whom everybody else feels sorry for. Everybody had watched him choke.

'I hate using the word *choke*, but that's exactly what happened,' he would concede. But, that Monday morning, he knew that everybody was trying so hard to be so nice to him, and while he was thankful, and appreciative, he also felt their words were next door to pity.

Jack Nicklaus, the most successful golfer in the history of the Masters tournament, had been in touch. So, too, Greg Norman, the biggest loser in the tournament's history. It came from all sides.

It was good to cry. He'd felt like crying since the previous afternoon, when he lost control of his game and also lost his grip on the title. After the disastrous 10th hole, when he recorded his awful triple-bogey seven, he had still told himself that there was some hope of gathering everything back together for the remaining holes, but his drive on the 13th, when he hooked his tee shot into Rae's Creek, had pinched any of that slim prospect to death. That's why he rested his face in the crook of his arm. That's when he first felt like crying.

Amen Corner had been mortifying, and the one hour and 15 minutes that followed contained the mocking roars of the galleries just ahead of him, as Charl Schwartzel began his long victory march. McIlroy, luckily, had been spared the sight of Chubby Chandler beaming with satisfaction as he grabbed Schwartzel in a bear-like embrace as he came off the 18th green. That would have been hard to watch.

But, despite everything that happened on the back nine, the one shot McIlroy wished he could retrieve more than any other from that Sunday afternoon, every time he revisited his final round at Augusta National in his head, was his second shot at the first hole. 'That was the first time in the tournament that I made a very tentative swing,' he admitted, recalling how the pin had been on the left of the first green, and how his approach had foolishly missed the green on the same side.

'That's when I knew I didn't feel the same as the previous days.' That's when he knew that something had happened, in his head, between leaving the course on the Saturday evening when he held his four-shot lead, and bringing that four-shot lead back to Augusta National the next day.

'I'd a lot of time between getting up on the Sunday and going out to play. Even after watching Ulster in the Heineken Cup quarter-final, I still had time to kill,' McIlroy realised.

'If I turned on ESPN or the Golf Channel, all I could hear were people talking about me. Greg Norman told me after the Masters that any little outside influence you let into your bubble can be detrimental.'

McIlroy vowed no more TV. No more Twitter, either, not on the morning of the final round of the greatest golf tournament on earth, and not on the morning of any final round, anywhere, ever again.

McIlroy had appreciated, but felt embarrassed by, the applause of the people who had lined the final few holes, and who did their best to ease him through the desolation as he sought to bring his final round to some sort of close. Augusta staff were lining up five rows of chairs for the awards ceremony when he finally emerged from the side door of the scorers' hut near the 18th green, his expression still weary and bedraggled, his polo shirt still untucked at the back, but the gang of spectators packing the clubhouse balcony insisted on soundly clapping him for the entire 20 seconds it took him to trudge from the hut to the locker room. That was nice of people, too. But all that did for McIlroy was further seduce him into a state of deepening sorrow.

Chubby Chandler, when he got to speak to McIlroy, was sympathetic and uplifting, but when he appeared before the world's media, the boss of ISM was rather more businesslike. He spoke about golf being a funny game.

'One moment you're on top of it, and the next moment it bites you,' explained Chandler. 'He knows there's a problem, but it's not an insolvable problem. It's just learning and... he's a smart lad.'

However, Chubby appeared less sympathetic, as he rattled on over the next few hours, about what had happened to the hottest young golfer on his books. 'The problem with Rory is that he doesn't play a lot, so you don't get that much practice at winning. And that's the balance, how many times you play.

'You have to stay fresh and focused... it was great he came in fresh as a daisy, but you've got to learn to do certain things around a golf course,' continued Chandler, saying a little too much and using words and issuing judgements that McIlroy, at the most vulnerable point in his adult life, would remember.

One of the problems, possibly the biggest problem, in McIlroy's game was his putting, which had not been glaringly apparent during most of his time at Augusta National in 2011 considering he had not three-putted any green until he arrived at the 11th hole on the Sunday. On closer examination, however, McIlroy could have closed out the tournament and also, perhaps, stepped well back from his moment of self-destruction, if his putting had been that tiny bit sharper, and as absolutely perfect as a champion's putting needs to be if he is to benefit from the excellence of the remainder of his game, and close out tournaments consistently.

On the Saturday, McIlroy had one-putted greens on 12 occasions, and over the whole tournament he had the fourth best putting statistics of the entire field. However, in his final round, he had missed with eight putts from inside seven feet.

During his 2008 rookie season, when he was bothered by his putting stroke under pressure, McIlroy had sought the help of short-game specialist Dr Paul Hurrion. One year later Hurrion summarised his young pupil's stroke.

'Rory is a naturally gifted player, no question,' said Hurrion. 'But really, with the putting, he was relying on an awful lot of hand-eye co-ordination. Science basically says that you can't rely on hand-eye co-ordination to get you through time after time. It won't be repeatable when the pressure comes on. You just can't depend on it.'

McIlroy, after Augusta National, had more work to do on his putting technique but, luckily for him, at his sprawling, new, luxurious six-bedroom home outside Belfast, he had built three practice greens within a personal golf facility that contained a 330-yard driving range. He had two greenkeepers working on his three greens, paying particular attention to the speed and the demands of upcoming tournaments.

In the first half of 2011, Hurrion, who had been so instrumental in Padraig Harrington developing a winning edge, had visited the new McIlroy home three times for intensive sessions. More help was needed, however, and a few weeks after the Masters tournament McIlroy met the former US Ryder Cup captain and two-times major champion Dave Stockton at Quail Hollow, where he sought to defend his title. McIlroy decided to take his advice on board officially as well.

'It was nice to get the call, and he's certainly neat to work with,' Stockton said. In between their first and second meetings, Stockton was amazed at how much McIlroy had changed for the better. The young man had told the veteran that he didn't really practise much, but Stockton found that hard to believe. 'I'm just trying to make it natural,' explained Stockton who, himself, had walked away from Augusta National a beaten man when he lost a two-shot lead to Gary Player in the final round in 1974. Stockton liked what he was seeing in McIlroy, in every sense.

He especially liked the fact that McIlroy had missed all of his crucial putts to the left of the hole, which Stockton believed is a problem that is much easier to fix than if someone is missing putts to the right.

More than anything else, however, the coach believed that his new pupil needed to become more patient. 'On longer putts, 12 feet and out, Rory's relaxed and rolls it.

'I see a different kind of approach, almost on attack mode, on a five, six or seven-foot putt… he's just trying too hard to make it.'

It was also agreed that McIlroy was taking too long, taking three looks at the hole while making his practice strokes. It was decided that there should be no more practice strokes of any kind. He should instinctively take one look at the hole and let the ball roll.

But McIlroy's tee shots on the 10th and 13th holes of his final round at Augusta National could not be forgotten either. There were, in truth, plenty of putts and shots from all over the course that McIlroy privately wished he could retrieve. It was not just his second shot to the first hole that, repeatedly, he replayed in his brain for more than two weeks after he had left East Georgia.

'The only shot I'd take back was the tee shot on 10,' he told the press a few days after first lamenting his second shot on the first hole. 'That tee shot on 10 was the first bad drive I hit all week.'

McIlroy's swing, for as long as most observers could remember, was a work of art, and a quite magnificent one at that. It was beautiful and true, and unsullied by any of the demonic forces that eventually come to visit, and occasionally reside, at different times in the heads of almost every man who has ever been a professional golfer.

McIlroy's swing was all innocence, but still it would be wrong to think it was solely the property of Rory McIlroy. Just as Ken Venturi's natural-looking movement with a club in his hand had actually been partially bullied into him by Byron Nelson, one of the greatest golfers ever to play the game, McIlroy's swing was largely constructed in a tiny back room in the pro shop at Bangor Golf Club, the workplace of Michael Bannon.

It was at the back of Bannon's small, untidy shop that Rory McIlroy spent hours, and days and weeks, if not half his young life, building his golf swing; standing on the hitting mat, with Bannon watching him, and with five video cameras trained on every angle of his moving body.

There, too, on the two old leather-bound chairs, Bannon and McIlroy sat together, as coach and young boy, as coach and young man and, later, as coach and world No.1 in the making. Sitting there, the two of them watched the results of their hours and hours of diligent work on the large plasma screen on the wall facing them.

Bannon had been friends with Gerry and Rosie McIlroy for years. He'd been a guest at their wedding and he'd watched their boy grow up. 'When he joined Holywood aged eight, Gerry handed him over to me and we started working him properly,' Bannon explained to the Irish golf writer, Paul Gallagher. 'It wasn't long after that that I moved to Bangor and he followed me here.'

Bannon, who had had the slightest brush with the big time himself when losing out in 1980 to the former European No.1 Ronan Rafferty in the final of the Irish Close at Royal County Down, and again 17 years later when being beaten in the Irish Professional Championship by three-times major winner Padraig Harrington in a play-off at Powerscourt, would spend quality time over the next 15 years working with Rory McIlroy, as his swing coach and as his friend.

As a boy, Bannon played Ireland's oldest native sport, hurling, as often as he could, and that certainly helped him develop an eye for a small white ball, so when his father Sean, a recreational player at the local Kirkistown Castle Golf Club, introduced his young son to the game, there was only one direction life would take him. Bannon became his own teacher, turning for guidance only to a well-thumbed edition of *Jack Nicklaus: The Best Way to Better Golf* and by watching better players.

When he lost to Rafferty, Bannon was holding down a job in a local bank and, such was his heightened excitement in making his way to the first tee at Royal County Down that day, he forgot to pull on his golf shoes and duly arrived to take on the young, bullish Rafferty wearing his everyday footwear.

McIlroy, in the very early years, was always hanging around Bannon's shop. He always wanted to learn, and play. He also wanted lots of attention, nearly all of the time.

'LOOK AT THIS!' he'd yell, before hitting a ball.

Bannon could see that from a young age McIlroy could shape his shots in a way that was far beyond any boy that age or size. 'He could hit the ball low, high, left, right… it didn't matter,' recalled the coach. 'And the thing was, he always liked people to see him doing it.' That was back at a time when he also loved signing his autograph as 'Rory Nick Faldo McIlroy'. He loved the questions that his incredible golf talent, as well as his cute, puppy-dog face, drew from visitors to the shop.

'So that's the wee fella then?' they'd ask Bannon, before having a few words with little Rory himself.

Over the years the mechanics of Rory McIlroy's swing would become the most valuable bundle of information on Michael Bannon's PC, stored as they were with the swings of members and visitors to Bangor Golf Club who paid Bannon the sum of £75 for 45 minutes' tuition.

Bannon had given up his day job and become one of the game's hard-working club pros in his mid-20s. All of the hardest work with McIlroy was done in the earliest years they spent in one another's company. In 2011, Bannon's main preoccupation was in not doing anything too drastic; just refining, adjusting, making certain everything looked and felt as easy and true as a great golf swing can sometimes be.

'I suppose people like the look of it,' Bannon had concluded 12 months before. 'Aesthetically, it looks nice. But his "good-looking" swing is a result of what he is able to do, a decent bit of coaching, and lots of practice.

'That's what it is, pure and simple.'

****

On the Monday morning after his loss in Augusta, McIlroy had to face up to the prospect of spending 25 hours in the company of the new Masters champion, Charl Schwartzel. A private plane was waiting at the airport to send the two protagonists on their way to Kuala Lumpur for the Maybank Malaysian Open. It was a commitment that McIlroy could not break. It was also a golf tournament that many people reckoned was worth €350,000 in a personal appearance fee, before McIlroy had to even think of how he might hit a ball.

On the plane, McIlroy and Schwartzel, the latter wearing his Masters green jacket over a white T-shirt and trying to contain his full-throttle of a smile and McIlroy posing casually and smiling much more naturally than his ISM buddy, posed for a photograph. Moments later, McIlroy proudly tweeted the image, pouring out even more graciousness in a one-line caption, which read, 'Flying to Malaysia with Charl! Glad one of us has a green jacket on!!!' Upon landing, however, McIlroy quickly discovered that his luggage and clubs had gone missing between airports on their 10,000-mile trek across 12 time-zones. He did not fuss unduly. Lost luggage was not a big problem; he had already lost something a billion times more precious than clothing and clubs.

But, in the immediate aftermath of Augusta, he had also gained something too, in the surprise appearance of his long-time girlfriend, Holly Sweeney. Four months earlier, Rory and Holly had announced that, after six years together, they had decided to take a break from their relationship.

That had been just before Christmas 2010. McIlroy admitted then that he had made the toughest decision of his life to date. 'I think we both understand what we want,' he sought to explain at that time, 'and that's basically what it is. I didn't have a great couple of weeks before Christmas, but you got to do what's right for yourself.' He said that he wished to put all the time he could into his golf game, rather than his private life. He was a 21-year-old man who had completed more than a decade of growing up on the golf course, but, in his personal life, McIlroy had known and loved only Holly, who was busily completing her studies for a degree in sports technology at the University of Ulster.

He was clearly confused in his own head. In November, one month before the split, he had happily announced to the world's media that one of the reasons he had decided not to compete on the full USPGA Tour schedule in 2011 was because of his desire to spend more time at home in Belfast with Holly and his parents and friends. Then in December, he sought to step out of his relationship.

Four months later, he looked the most relieved man at Augusta National when he found Holly waiting for him inside the clubhouse.

On the Saturday morning at her home in Belfast, as McIlroy had still to be roused from his bed in Augusta to face his third round, Holly had hurriedly grabbed a bag and chased a plane. Kerrie Sweeney knew not to ask too many questions of her daughter.

The previous night, she and Holly, and Kerrie's parents, had been enjoying a quiet night in at their home, keeping an eye on what was happening in Augusta, keeping close to the edges of their seats. But everything changed in the early hours of Saturday morning. Holly and Rory's people at ISM got chatting, and both sides thought it would be entirely proper, as well as a fantastic surprise, if Holly was present on the 18th green to embrace her man, as so many wives and partners, and girlfriends, of newly crowned champions have done at Augusta National.

It seemed wrong for Holly to be so far apart from Rory if, and when, he won his first major title. She had been at his side, on and off the course, for those six years. How could she be left tweeting in a whole different time-zone?

'Well played @McIlroyRory... beautifully done!' she had declared on her Twitter account at 1.07 that Saturday morning, but by then she already knew that she would be flying out to the US that same day. A few hours later, with only a tiny bag packed, her grandad drove her to Belfast Airport.

Holly and Rory had talked on the phone every day since their amicable break-up. They both had admitted publicly that they wanted to remain the closest of friends and that was clear to see. Among other things, they had shared a home together, and they'd also shared custody of their two lovable dogs.

Holly felt as lost and pained as Rory did, when the Masters tournament was ripped from his grasp late on that Sunday afternoon. They had lived each other's lives since their early teens. Each had never known anyone else intimately.

They'd both grown up in Holywood and both attended Sullivan Upper School. By the time Rory was 16 and Holly 14, they were pretty much inseparable. In his earliest days on the pro tour, Rory made sure that Holly was usually included in his entourage, properly cared for and chaperoned, and looking nothing like any of the other glitzy, glamorous partners, as she wore her natural blonde hair long and girly.

When Holly passed her driving test at the first time of asking, Rory bought her a new car. 'She quite likes little dinky cars like the Fiat 500 but I've refused to get into one of those,' said McIlroy. 'We've seen a really nice Mini and a nice two-door Mercedes.'

When McIlroy announced himself among the world's greatest players, during Europe's victory over the United States in the 2010 Ryder Cup at Celtic Manor in Wales, Holly took the full glare of the world's press in her stride, a 19-year-old woman looking as though she had been living a relaxed life of privilege all of her life, her hair further highlighted and cropped tight, her extra-smart and sophisticated appearance finished off by her Louboutin shoes. Out on the course, and at the gala dinners at Celtic Manor all that week, her freshness and beauty outshone all of the European and American women in all of their expensive finery.

****

For the week following the Masters, McIlroy wanted Holly to stay with him, and fly to Kuala Lumpur, even though she had not packed sufficient clothes. They could buy clothes, he assured her. In Malaysia, for the crucial days after the Augusta ordeal, Holly offered him the comfort and support he needed in his time of personal turmoil. She was the dutiful girlfriend and life partner again. She also appeared happy and excited to be back with him in the public glare. Always one to look firmly on the brighter side of life, and known to her closest friends as 'Positivity Sweeney', she sounded so content with life.

On Monday, Holly tweeted, 'Off 2 Malaysia 2day, got to get a bit of shopping in cause I only packed an overnight bag… Mainly consisting of sweats!'

The next day, she updated, 'In transit to Kuala Lumpur… didn't bring much to augusta so gotta 1) get a suitcase and 2) fill it!' Later the same day, she announced, '30 hours travelling completed!'

Rory, likewise, was tweeting daily with messages to close friends and fans that were consistently upbeat. When they came home to Ireland a week later, Rory returned the compliment, turning up to watch Ulster play at Ravenhill, and in particular to cheer on Holly as she danced in the middle of the field as one of the club's cheerleading troupe, the Rockettes.

****

McIlroy's golf clubs did not arrive at his hotel in Malaysia until Wednesday evening, a little over 12 hours before he was due to tee off in the first round. However, lulled into a safe place by the thought that he had nothing more to lose after throwing so much away in Augusta, he went out in that round and shot an absurdly low 69, which was followed by a 64 the next day to give himself the tournament lead on 11 under par.

However, deep down, he was still a nervous wreck from the events of Augusta National, and on the Sunday he once again blew a four-shot lead sky-high, allowing the 17-year-old Italian, Matteo Manassero, to step in in front of him and claim the title. Manassero's winning cheque was €288,466, while McIlroy had pocketed his €350,000 for turning up in the first place, and the additional sum of €108,349 for third spot. His finish also moved McIlroy up two places in the world rankings, to seventh, just behind Tiger Woods, who was journeying in the opposite direction.

There followed a two-week break for McIlroy and his entourage, during which time it was decided that he should have a proper sit-down and discussion with Chubby Chandler about the remainder of the season. But little did Chandler know that such days with the most valuable player in his pack at International Sports Management were numbered.

In the first week of May, McIlroy arrived back in the United States for the first time since getting out of Augusta fast, when he jetted into Charlotte, North Carolina, to defend the Wells Fargo Championship at Quail Hollow. He looked relaxed within himself. Mostly he looked strong, and not someone who had been beaten down and left physically drained after his severe defeat on the final day at Augusta National. Since starting to work out with a new trainer, Steve McGregor, in the preceding year, McIlroy had increased his muscle mass, and his level of body fat had fallen impressively. McGregor and McIlroy, together, were quite a double act.

All of the analysis of McIlroy's diet, sweat composition, fluid loss, and the results of the GPS tracking device that added up the distance he covered during rounds, were making a marked difference. Equally, all of McGregor's intense and quite brilliant work on McIlroy's golf swing – the print-outs from the biomechanics laboratory that showed the force he produced during that swing, and the muscles he packed into his action – were bringing results. Like Tiger Woods a decade earlier, Rory McIlroy, who had gained three kilograms of muscle and lost one kilogram of fat, and was busily upping his weight from 76 kilograms to 80, was already becoming a whole different physical specimen of a professional golfer.

On the eve of defending his title at Quail Hollow, McIlroy had taken his football boots out of his travelling bag. Traditionally, in the build-up to the tournament that he had won the previous year with a sumptuous closing 62 to leapfrog Phil Mickelson, there was a football game between the pros and the caddies. McIlroy's enthusiasm during the game, as was always evident on any tennis court he strayed across on his travels, was boundless for over an hour.

He also turned 22 years of age the day before the first round in North Carolina. To everyone tackling him, and looking to take the ball from him, McIlroy looked a fairly happy young man. 'No one died… I'm very happy with my life… very happy with my game,' he quipped, when asked about coming back to the United States for the first time since the Masters tournament.

He had decided to miss out on the $9.5 million prize pot at the Players Championship at Sawgrass in Florida the following week. His schedule was taking in Quail Hollow and the Memorial tournament and, after a week of rest, which nobody knew at that time would actually include a couple of days in Haiti, he was going to arrive in Washington for the US Open. But, in Quail Hollow, McIlroy's golf game, unlike his football game, didn't sparkle. He was three over par after his first two rounds, and 15 shots adrift of the halfway leader Pat Perez. He duly missed the cut and found himself with even more time on his hands.

****

At Sawgrass, the Spanish flag flew for the full week, replacing the South African one that had been due to flutter over the Circle of Champions, commemorating Tim Clark's win in 2010. The world of golf was in mourning after the death of 54-year-old Seve Ballesteros, who had endured, over three years, a long and bravely stubborn battle with a brain tumour. In Europe, at the Iberdrola Open at Pula Golf Club in Majorca, black ribbons were attached to flagsticks for the tournament's pro-am.

At the end of May, a month in which Tiger Woods dropped out of the world's top 10 for the first time in 14 years, McIlroy met his countryman and closest friend on tour, the reigning US Open champion Graeme McDowell, in the last 16 of the Volvo World Match Play Championship in Spain. McIlroy was unable to hide his annoyance in going down 3 and 2, flinging his putter after a missed putt cost him the long 11th hole, and then kicking his ball away on the next when he also failed to hole out. For more than two years, McDowell, who had looked so certain of winning before making a horse's dinner of his final round in the Players Championship the same month, had been telling everyone who cared to listen to him how he had grown accustomed to getting 'beaten up' by McIlroy whenever they practised together.

After their first tournament head-to-head, however, all of those comments from the fancifully branded 'G-Mac' seemed, in retrospect, little more than soft, idle praise for his young friend.

A week later, at Wentworth, at the BMW PGA Championship, a huge iconic image of Seve Ballesteros was put up behind the 18th green, showing the Spanish hero at his most disarming, in his favourite navy jumper, looking down upon all the game's professionals with that charismatic grin, and with that great fist pumping the air. But McIlroy, playing alongside his mentor and own personal hero from his childhood, Darren Clarke, remained hopelessly sluggish in his actions, and he watched the portly Clarke, 20 years his senior, shoot a 69 to his own slovenly 76. The next day, McIlroy got up and down from a greenside bunker on the 18th hole to secure a birdie for a 70, which allowed him to sneak into the weekend's action.

By the end of the same week, McIlroy showed that he had more than golf on his mind. On the Saturday evening, he darted from the course and made it to London in double-quick time in order to cheer on his beloved Manchester United in the highlight of the European football season, the Champions League final, an occasion and a title as historically endearing to football supporters as the Masters tournament is to golf fans. But, at Wembley Stadium, McIlroy could only grimace as his football heroes, and some of them his new-found buddies on Twitter, were treated like errant children by Lionel Messi and his amazing Barcelona team-mates, who produced some mesmerising ball-work that would not have looked out of place on the same stage as the Cirque du Soleil. The Spanish wonder team won 3-1, and McIlroy had to return the compliment to Manchester United's manager, Sir Alex Ferguson, who had texted him on the evening of his own personal implosion in East Georgia. McIlroy offered Sir Alex his sympathies and his thanks.

The week ended on a slightly happier note for English sports fans, however, as the status of world No.1 was handed over from one Englishman to another, when Lee Westwood lost to Luke Donald in a sudden-death play-off. The highlight of Rory McIlroy's Sunday, however, was heading back to London a second time to see another of his favourite group of entertainers, Swedish House Mafia, perform.

There was two weeks to go to the US Open Championship at Congressional Country Club, which was kicking off on June 16. McIlroy had Jack Nicklaus's Memorial tournament at Muirfield

Village in Dublin, Ohio, first of all. He reminded journalists how he liked to take time off before a major in order to get the course fully into his head. 'I like to take the week off before a major, to go there and really suss the place out,' he emphasised, further reminding those around him how such manoeuvrings had worked for him in four out of his six previous major tournaments.

There was absolutely no mention of a quick trip to Haiti. He said he was happy with his game. He was adamant that he could not ask for more from himself in his driving, or any of his ball-striking around the course for that matter.

In Nicklaus's own neck of the golfing woods, McIlroy shot 66 on the undulating course, made up of seven birdies and one bogey, to hold the overnight advantage after the first round with the American, Chris Riley. At the end of the next day, he was three shots off the lead after he struggled to a level-par 72, with an eclectic mix of six birdies, four bogeys and a double bogey.

He fell five shots further behind Steve Stricker with his third-round 71, and there was more roller-coasting on the Sunday in Ohio when he helped himself to five birdies on the outward nine, and birdied the 11th and 15th coming home, but also dropped shots at the 10th, 13th and 14th holes.

Thirteen months had passed since McIlroy's last win on any tour, but he remained upbeat. He knew that, at Congressional, the fairways would be even less generous than those at Muirfield Village. But he knew the rough, and the oppressive heat, would be the same.

He decided to be in Bethesda, to make sure of all that, on the Wednesday and Thursday of the following week. And then, with Congressional Country Club locked safely away in his head, he would fly to Haiti.

PART THREE

The US Open

CHAPTER NINE

Congressional Country Club

Since Man first learnt to open his mouth and babble in search of power over other men and women, politics has always partly glorified itself in being a dirty game. In the time of the 29th President of the United States of America, Warren Gamaliel Harding, the son of a farmer who doubled as a physician in Blooming Grove, Ohio, that game had an explosive mixture of ingredients and characters at work.

President Harding's place in American history, as deplorably evidenced in his re-entry into the consciousness of his people through the cut-throat HBO series on power and politics, *Boardwalk Empire*, was never destined to age well. Harding was either a puppet, or a puppet-master. In either role, the self-made newspaper publisher, the first person from such a profession to be elected President of the United States, was in Washington, DC, to put on a show aimed at entertaining and distracting the people who had voted him into office in the first place.

Harding, at the age of 57, died of a heart attack on August 2, 1923, while visiting San Francisco, two years into his first term as president. That was the year after the tumultuous mid-term elections for the Republican Party. Dissatisfied at the recession of 1920-21, voters had let loose their anger at the Repubican-led House and Senate in Washington, and the GOP saw its majority dramatically shrink overnight from 166 seats to just 20. The Republican edge in the Senate dropped from 24 to 10.

Two of the losers in that massacre were congressmen from Indiana, Oscar R. Luhring and Oscar E. Bland. Both were lawyers and good men, to all intents and purposes, and both, during President Harding's two years, had sat in the 67th Congress from March 4, 1921, to its dissolution in the spring of 1923.

Harding's time was also the time of prohibition. In 1919, the manufacture, sale and transportation of alcohol was banned right across the United States, and would remain so for 14 prosperous years for some, mainly those up to their eyeballs in criminal activity, until the Eighteenth Amendment was repealed on December 5, 1933. Prohibition was big business for some, and a hot issue for others, such as President Harding, who was never going to make it to the White House without sufficient money behind him, in addition to some strong-armed support. The prohibitionists, or 'Dries', saw the new way of life as a victory for public morals and good health, but the 'Wets', or anti-prohibitionists, who were more city-based, more Catholic and swelled by newly arrived immigrants, believed the alcohol ban to be an outrageous intrusion upon their lives by a white, rural, mainly Protestant people, who actually included Methodists, Northern Baptists, Southern Baptists, New School Presbyterians, Disciples of Christ, Congregationalists, Quakers, and Scandinavian Lutherans. Temperance associations had been forming in large numbers through rural communities throughout the 19th century, and where men did stick to their drinking, women grouped together to accentuate the belief that true motherhood included a definite intolerance of alcohol. The American Temperance Society had 1.5 million members in its ranks by 1835 – with women often constituting up to 60 per cent of individual chapters – which was more than 10 per cent of the country's population when excluding those living in slavery. The United States census of 1840 would count 17,069,453 people resident in the country, including 3,204,313 slaves.

The Prohibition Party was formed in 1869, and four years later the Women's Christian Temperance Union was founded, arguing that a ban on alcohol would reduce the number of abusive spouses. Although denied universal voting privileges, the WCTU saw temperance as a method to enter politics, and tackle sensitive issues, such as the labour laws. Kansas, in 1881, was the first state to ban alcohol in its constitution, and soon others followed, states and individual counties, though not always with the same streak of madness of Carrie Nation, who was famed for marching into saloons in Kansas, where she would scold customers and, occasionally, smash bottles of liquor with her hatchet. Most women's groups chose to enter saloons in song and in prayer.

In addition to the moral climate, the difficult economic conditions at the beginning of the 20th century meant that, quite clearly, prohibition had reached its time and place in American life, though enforcement of the ban was hopeless.

Organised crime in America flourished in a divided nation. Corruption in political circles, and through the police forces in all of the major cities, prospered year by year, and in 1925, in New York, it was thought that there existed 100,000 'speakeasy' clubs, selling liquor illegally. Four years later, at the height of the prohibition-era conflict between crime gangs, America would formally record the St Valentine's Day Massacre, when five members of the North Side Gang, led by Bugs Moran, and two of their associates were lined up along the inside wall of a garage at 2122 North Clark Street, in the Lincoln Park neighbourhood of Chicago, and were gunned down on the instructions of Al Capone.

The shooting, and its spectacular coverage in the nation's press, turned the stomachs of the American people as a whole, though by the close of the Roaring Twenties Capone had collared 10,000 speakeasies in Chicago for himself, and was the king of the bootlegging business from Canada right down through New York and Atlantic City, and into Florida.

In the 1916 presidential election, the Democratic incumbent, Woodrow Wilson, and his Republican opponent, Charles Evans Hughes, each chose to ignore the prohibition issue. Both parties had strong support from Dries and Wets, and neither candidate cared to step out of line with his support base. By the time President Wilson suffered a stroke in 1919, which left him an invalid, America was leaving a ghastly world war at its back, and there was a desire among its people for a simpler, more peaceful era. Warren Harding, an inconsequential backbench senator from Marion, Ohio, hit the mood on the head by declaring, 'America's present need is not heroics, but healing; not nostrums, but normalcy; not revolution, but restoration; not agitation, but adjustment; not surgery, but serenity.' In 1920, he enjoyed a comprehensive victory over the Democratic Party's progressive nominee, James M. Cox, in the biggest presidential election landslide, a whopping 60 per cent to 34 per cent, since such voting was first recorded in 1824.

Americans had become disillusioned by President Wilson's global idealism. Harding's election, the first presidential vote in which women were allowed to participate, was happily received, and he maintained that standing by ending wartime controls, cutting taxes and tightening regulations concerning immigration.

He also kept his campaign promise of 'economy in government', but what the people didn't know at the time was that Harding's administration was sullied by widespread corruption, and among the dishonest members of his cabinet was the Interior Secretary, Albert Fall, who accepted bribes from private oil interests for naval reserves, in what became popularly known as the 'Teapot Dome scandal', named after an oil reserve in Wyoming. Fall received more than $400,000 in gifts and loans from such business interests, and the President knew all about it. Harding had rewarded too many friends and political contributors, whom commentators called the Ohio Gang, with powerful roles.

Included among some of the rascals he had appointed to his cabinet was the Attorney General, Harry Dougherty. Fall and several of the President's other appointees were at different stages tried and imprisoned for bribery or defrauding the federal government. The Teapot Dome scandal itself did not become public knowledge until after President Harding's death, when there were also sordid claims that he had had affairs with four women, two of them close friends of his wife's. Two of the women, Susie Hodder and Nan Britton, were furthermore believed to have given birth to daughters of the Baptist President.

After the death of her husband, Harding's wife Florence made her way back to Washington, DC, and stayed in the White House as a guest of President Coolidge and his wife, during which time it is understood that she gathered and burned as much of her husband's correspondence and documents, both personal and official, as she could get her hands on.

****

In December, 1921, Congressional Country Club in Bethesda, Maryland, just 10 miles from downtown Washington, DC, was incorporated with the expressed intention of mixing politics with big business – on tee boxes and over short putts. Such a vision would not survive the absolute correctness of modern-day politics, but the visionaries and founders of this place for talk and action were Oscar E. Bland and Oscar R. Luhring, the two congressmen from Indiana who thought it a spanking idea.

The 'two Oscars' were driving through Bethesda, accompanied by their wives, all enjoying the peacefulness and quiet beauty of the surrounding farmland, when they decided they had found the right place for all politicians to get away from the pressures and all-seeing eyes of Washington. They imagined, according to their 1921 prospectus, a spot 'where talk has no fetters and where exchanged opinion leads to clarity'.

Bland and Luhring were indeed serious that Washington needed an informal place where politicians and businessmen could meet on an equal footing, as peers, with no red tape interfering with their friendship, and their doings, and where everyone 'could discuss freely the state of feeling in their respective communities regarding problems awaiting government action', confirmed *The Washington Post*. That meant lots of lobbying. The two Oscars carried their idea for a very special golf club to Herbert Hoover, then Secretary of Commerce, and solicited his support as an honorary founding president of the planned club from 1922-23.

The construction of Congressional Country Club was quite painful. Luhring and Bland sold $1,000 life memberships to the fattest of industrial cats and 'robber barons', gentlemen who were not shy in letting it be known how they fast-tracked their way to hideous amounts of wealth. So, Congressional's first membership list included the names of Astor, Carnegie, Chrysler, Du Pont, Firestone, Guggenheim, Hearst and Rockefeller. That helped, of course, but the place still took two and a half years, from concept to completion.

By the time Congressional formally decided to show off to the world of golf what exactly had been created off River Road, in Bethesda, Oscar E. Bland and Oscar R. Luhring were long gone from their personal seats in the most powerful house in the land, though both gentlemen stuck around Washington and got to play at the golf club of their dreams on occasions. Both were counted among the bodies of those who had been kicked out in the massacre of Republicans in the 1922 mid-terms, though President Harding looked kindly at some of his defeated colleagues, including the two lawyers from Indiana.

The President appointed Bland to a federal judgeship and he served in the United States Court of Customs Appeals until his resignation at the tail end of 1947, when he resumed practising law privately for four more years in Washington before his death in 1951. Luhring, also at the pleasure of President Harding, was eased into a position at the Labor Department, where he served as a special assistant to the Secretary of Labor for three years, but his career subsequently moved through the hands of two further presidents. Harding's successor, John Calvin Coolidge, appointed Luhring to be Assistant Attorney General of the United States, and President Herbert Hoover later moved Luhring to the job of Associate Justice of the Supreme Court for the District of Columbia, which he did until his death in 1944.

****

Congressional Country Club was officially fit for play by 1924, just over 12 months after the death of Warren Harding, who remains listed alongside Taft, Wilson and Coolidge as one of four presidents of the United States to be founding members. Three others – Hoover, Eisenhower and Ford – would also enjoy membership in the exclusive hideaway for politicians, their business friends and, of course, their business friends-to-be, in the stunningly beautiful, calm leafiness of Bethesda.

More than 7,000 people attended the official opening on May 23, 1924, in the stately building with its enticing Mediterranean-style architecture. President Coolidge and his wife, Grace, were there, naturally. They were joined by cabinet members, Supreme Court justices, army generals, foreign diplomats and gangs of US congressmen and senators. The next morning, Congressional presented a celebration fourball. The main attraction was Gene Sarazen, a New Yorker by birth, and one of only five men, alongside Hogan, Player, Nicklaus and Woods, to win all four major championships in his career. Freddy McLeod, the Scot and pro at nearby Columbia Country Club who had won the 1908 US Open and who would also be made to feel at home at Augusta National when it opened a decade later, teamed up with Sarazen. They beat Congressional's first pro, James Crabbe, and the reigning US national champion, Max Marston.

Bethesda, as one early resident pleasantly explained, was no more than a 'wide spot on the road' to begin with. In the distant past, that road was a ridgeline trail through ancient woods, carrying the first settlers, the Native Americans, as they hunted for food on the lands near the Potomac River. At the end of the 17th century the road brought the English to newly granted plantations. For centuries, farmers hauled their produce along the road, sacks of wheat and barrels of tobacco that would bring them reward in the port of Georgetown. Livestock travelled it; British regiments marched it; wooden-wheeled wagons laboured along it.

The road is now widely known as Wisconsin Avenue.

Downtown Bethesda was built upon the shoulders of a small stone tavern, which was found on a bend in the road in the middle of the 18th century. It welcomed travellers, and offered a stiffening drink to them. A century later, however, the old road was in some disrepair and the Maryland legislature had to charter a new company in 1805 to do something about it. It would be another 20 years before the road received its first hard surface, and its upkeep was maintained by a small, wooden toll-booth, which collected 'twelve and a half cents for a score of sheep or hogs', as recounted by Mark Walston in *Bethesda Magazine*, 'six and a quarter cents for every horse and rider, and 25 cents for a coach or stage with two horses and four wheels'.

With enough people living in the area, a post office was called for, and after that a name for the place was necessary. The postmaster, Robert Franck, was the holder of that idea, and he petitioned the government, with the consent of the whole community, to name the village Bethesda, originating from 'beth hesda', or 'house of mercy', in Aramaic, and so named after the Presbyterian meeting house standing on a nearby hill.

Two things quickly changed everything in lovely little Bethesda, which had endured slow, grinding movement down through the previous two centuries. By 1890, the newly formed Chevy Chase Land Company had begun to add to its huge property portfolio to the east of Bethesda, with the desire of creating an attractive enclave for Washington's social and professional elite. The following year, in 1891, the trolley, or electric railroad, arrived.

The quality of rural life in Bethesda, however, remained in place. That was until Henry Ford introduced his affordably priced Model T in 1908. In the first year of production, more than 10,000 of the vehicles were sold, and within the next 20 years nearly 15 million Fords were breezing their way up and down the growing cities and towns, of the East Coast of the United States especially. Cattle and sheep had been roaming contentedly in fields on either side of Wisconsin Avenue, but the industrial age and Ford's babies put an end to Bethesda being a rural retreat of any kind.

New residents needed places to entertain themselves, and country clubs soon littered the place, and prospered. The older Chevy Chase Club, formed in 1892 as a hunt club, and the Columbia Country Club, which hosted the US Open in 1921, were soon joined by others forming a wide ring around the town of Bethesda. The Montgomery Country Club was formed in 1913. It was soon joined by Town and Country Club, founded by members of Washington's German-Jewish community. On River Road, Congressional Country Club came into being in 1924, as did Burning Tree. Kenwood Golf and Country Club was up and running in 1928, and one year later the Montgomery was converted into the National Women's Country Club, enticing *The Washington Post* to note, 'women have a club of their own now – one of the finest nine-hole courses in the country.'

Bethesda was doing the business, finally, with the nouveau riche needing a growing town, and even the Great Depression of 1929 failed to batter the spirit or appetite for advancement of the urban areas surrounding Washington. President Franklin D. Roosevelt's New Deal programmes brought further additions, including a 20-storey National Naval Medical Center, which would become known the world over as a place of medical excellence.

Several years before the Great Depression descended upon people's lives, and within 12 months of opening, Congressional Country Club met with financial woes. And things only got worse after that. Membership dues were hard to pocket, and even harder to deposit in a bank without a great number of them bouncing all over the place like errant golf balls. In 1940, the club's lien holder foreclosed. A public auction was held of the club's assets, and some members clubbed together and put up the sole bid of $270,000.

The Second World War also helped to get the club back on its feet. The Office of Strategic Services leased the club for the war's duration, at a cost of $307,000, and the magnificent clubhouse and course became a training ground for spies and commandos for an organisation that would later evolve into the Central Intelligence Agency. The course was designated 'Area F'. There was hand-to-hand combat training, firing ranges and paratrooper exercises. The money was most welcome but there was a cost to pay too, as the training ripped the course to shreds.

Congressional Country Club never looked back. Financially it was secure, but the club's creation, as a place for politicians and businessmen to cosy up to one another, took a change of direction.

By the end of the 20th century, Congressional existed for business and family only. No sitting member of the Congress or Senate, despite its near perfect location just outside Washington, would have his name in Congressional's membership book, which had a cost per individual, after many years of waiting for the nod of approval, of $110,000. It was no longer sound financial management for the club to offer discounted membership to politicians. Equally, it was no longer prudent for politicians to accept discounted membership.

Besides, Washington's most powerful people always knew that they'd get a club invite, or a call from friends, if they really wished to stand on that first tee box.

****

The area around Bethesda was indeed graced with a fine choice of golf clubs and courses. None, however, would hold a candle to the Blue Course at Congressional Country Club, which was first designed by a New Yorker, fancifully named Devereux Emmet. In addition to building one of the most amazing courses in the country just off River Road, Emmet was feted throughout the US, from the late 1800s to the 1920s, in what became known as the golden age of golf course architecture.

Emmet's name, however, as time passed, slipped between the floorboards as contemporaries such as Donald Ross and Alister MacKenzie were instead chosen to enrich the writings of golf historians through the remainder of the century.

Emmet did present to the golfing world a remarkable total of 130 golf courses. His problems, in truth, were twofold. He worked on too many courses in and around New York, and too many of those courses 'have long since been plowed under in the name of progress', wrote Barry Svrluga in *The Washington Post*. There was another problem, however.

It had to do with Emmet's style, his eye. He liked offering future golfers lots of surprises, lots of blind shots, par-sixes, for instance, and other offbeat bits and pieces, which were destined to lose their appeal after initial periods of curiosity and wonderment.

Emmet had the first nine at Congressional ready in 1922, and the second nine in June of 1923, and both front and back featured a par-six opening hole. When he was finished building the Blue Course, he also created an adjacent and shorter Gold Course for the club. Big-shot members of golf clubs and their fawning committees, however, usually preferred to grade themselves against more conservative, more serious architects such as Robert Trent Jones and his ilk, and that wish precipitated the downfall of Emmet.

Donald Ross took a look over Congressional's Blue Course in the 1930s and moved things around. In the '50s, Robert Trent Jones changed even more, and his son Rees Jones also got his hands on Congressional in the late 1980s. By the time the latter Jones was finished, shaving down several fairways, eliminating almost all of the blind shots, nobody would know that Devereux Emmet had ever laid out the course in the first instance. 'I don't think there's much left to be honest,' Rees Jones reflected. 'Back in those days, you didn't really move a lot of earth. We're able to do a lot more shaping.'

Congressional Country Club's Blue Course had seen so many changes. It has also enjoyed hosting three US Open Championships: in 1964, 1997 and 2011. But the greatest change of all had still to come. That change came after the club hosted the second of those championships, in 1997.

When he had finished with the course in the 1950s, Robert Trent Jones had left Congressional with a most wonderful par-three finishing hole, which called for a gutsy tee shot over a lake with the full glory of the clubhouse as an awe-inspiring, and sometimes stomach-wrenching, backdrop. The members liked their finishing hole. However, the rulers and bosses of golf in the United States took a different view. They didn't like the idea of a major championship ending with a par-three. They preferred the sight of a golfer having to take out his driver on an 18th hole, and having to hit a more complete range of shots in order to get home safely and win a championship.

In 1997, the club briefly arched its back at that pressure from the game's bosses, and demanded that golfers competing for the US Open title should finish up on their chosen par-three 18th. That's what South Africa's two-time US Open champion Ernie Els duly managed that June in his one-shot victory over Scotland's hapless big-time competitor, Colin Montgomerie.

However, back in 1964, when Ken Venturi sought the US Open title at Congressional, it had been decided that the Blue Course should temporarily borrow two holes from the adjoining Gold Course, in order for the tournament to end on a par-four, the club's normal 17th hole.

Instead of looking at a glorious 218-yard par-three finishing hole over water, Ken Venturi had to face what is universally regarded to be the best hole on the course, that sumptuous old 17th, a downhill 480-yard par-four, which has a green surrounded on three sides by water.

That was Ken Venturi's 18th hole at Congressional in the 1964 US Open. Forty-seven years later, long after the club had decided to make the 17th its 18th for good, and with the hole lengthened to a mammoth final test of 523 yards, it was also Rory McIlroy's closing hole in the 2011 US Open.

CHAPTER TEN

June 1964

Washington was melting under a weighty heat, even by mid-morning, when Ken Venturi walked off the plane that Monday. It was already close to 100 degrees. The air had a breathlessness to it, but Venturi still didn't hang around. He had been absent from US Open week for four brutally long years, so he legged it immediately to Congressional Country Club, and didn't bother checking into the Governor's Motel in downtown Washington until after he had completed his first day of business in Bethesda.

The United States Open Championship was to be played over three days, from June 18 to 20, with the final 36 holes waiting to snap the ambition and focus of the leaders on the Saturday morning and afternoon. It was to be the last time the most stubborn and powerful officials in American golf would decide to play two closing rounds back-to-back to end a major championship.

Stretching the championship out over four days rather than three would provide an additional day of growing revenues from clambering television executives. That helped the officials to make their firm decision, though, of course, the welfare of their own golfers might also have come into those same set of heads. The 64th staging of their championship could have killed somebody.

Even if temperatures had not scooted past the 100-degrees mark, the Saturday of the championship was destined to be a punishing day for golfers possessing even the most supreme levels of physical and mental fitness.

Conni Venturi was due to fly into the city from San Francisco on the Tuesday evening, so Ken knew that he had two days, totally alone, to settle himself and to really get a feel for the full 7,053 yards, the longest course in US Open history.

Ken's clothes were clinging to his body when he reached Bethesda. Once in the Congressional clubhouse, he found the locker rooms, but discovered that there were few players hanging around the place. Nobody had any desire to get out on to the monster that was the Blue Course and start testing themselves in what promised to be an open-mouthed furnace by the time they had completed the first and second holes.

Ken had already registered upon arrival. His personal items were in his locker, and he was ready to go. All he needed was a playing partner.

Ten minutes passed before he ran into a part-timer, Paul Harney, who had tried out the pro tour for seven years and won six events. He had had his best finish in a major tournament when he tied for fourth place in the US Open the previous summer. But, in 1962, Harney had decided to take a step back from putting all of his time and energies into the professional game, and was happy to be holding down the job of club pro at Pleasant Valley Country Club in Massachusetts.

'Aren't you going to the White House?' asked Harney, surprised to find Venturi hanging around the place.

Ken hadn't been told that the White House was hosting a lawn party for the championship favourites, as well as past champions. He had not received any such invite from President Johnson, but he didn't mind in the slightest. All that mattered to him at that moment was that Harney was also good to get out on to the course with him. Having taken a week off club duties, Harney wasn't liking the idea of spending even one day of US Open week sitting in a swanky air-conditioned clubhouse, even if the manicured grass did appear to be sizzling in the heat when he stood and stared out through the large windows at Congressional.

Yeah, Harney was good, and so too was Ken, and they struggled through the front nine on the Blue Course, and managed another four, slow, sapping holes before readily agreeing with one another to get back to the clubhouse fast.

****

In the caddie shack at Congressional Country Club, at the start of that same week, the men on the bags talked about everyone's prospects. They too knew that it was going to be a scorcher of a long week.

They all had their likes, and their dislikes, but they knew their hopes of making a few extra dollars by Saturday evening depended entirely on the luck of the draw. The pros didn't get to bring their own bag-man with them to the US Open in 1964. It would be several more summers before that would change. The right pro teaming up with the right caddie was down to pure unadorned luck, and the No.1 caddie in the shack at Congressional, William Ward, like everyone else around him, would have been happiest of all with Mr Palmer.

Out of as many as one hundred caddies on occasions, William Ward had a better pair of eyes than anybody. He was the man at Congressional Country Club. Like *Sports Illustrated*'s Rick Reilly once wrote of Pinehurst's finest bag-man, Fletcher Gaines, Ward could pretty much 'look at any green for the first time and tell you grain, speed, break and the approximate weight of the guy who mowed it last.' That's how good William Ward also was in 1964.

Yes, Mr Palmer would do just fine for William Ward.

Arnold Palmer, or Jack Nicklaus, or the defending champion Julius Boros, or Gary Player, who'd had three top-10 finishes in the championship over the previous three years; it didn't matter which one really. Palmer had, after all, just won the Masters tournament two months earlier by a whopping six shots, but Ward then went and... damn it... he drew out the name of Ken Venturi, which seemed an entirely worthless effort.

It was sure to be, he thought, a poor week for him, his wife, and his seven children, who would now watch him making the few miles' ride to Congressional every morning with a heavy heart, and that look of annoyance on his face. When Ken met William Ward, he, too, could see what was written on that face.

'I didn't have to be a detective to observe that he wasn't too elated over getting me,' admitted Venturi. A losing golfer never paid a bonus, only the caddie's dues for his working week. All of the work that William Ward had been getting through for the previous number of weeks seemed lost. Why, the best caddie to be found at Congressional Country Club had even decided to take a tape measure to the course he already knew almost by heart, to make absolutely certain that every distance he offered during the US Open would be inch-perfect for Mr Palmer, or the next champion he might have in the making walking beside him for three days.

Ken felt he had to say something to the man. They chatted some and, finally, Ken admitted to his caddie that he could not promise a US Open victory, but that if he did go out and amaze everyone by winning the thing he'd hand over $1,000 as a bonus to Ward.

William Ward smiled at that. It was a beaming, wide smile, behind which were still to be found the same number of large, probably insurmountable doubts. Nevertheless, he would be able to tell the boys back in the shack that his man had more confidence than he thought. *The bag might, after all, hold some worth*, he thought. Ken Venturi was never going to win the championship, Ward knew that for certain in his heart, but if he did well, and finished among the leaders, there might be a nice little bonus in that bag.

'Don't worry your head about William,' Ward replied. 'I know we'll give it a good, hard try, Mr Ken.'

****

Venturi was in a completely different place to William Ward. Actually, he could not remember when he last felt so strong in his own head about what he was doing, and why he was in Bethesda.

On Tuesday morning, he got out on to the course early, again with Harney as his partner. They needed to beat the heat, and it was an open race to get through the holes they needed to encounter in their practice session. Venturi was back in the Governor's Motel by 3 p.m. He was picking up Conni at 6 p.m., so he rested a while on his bed. When he headed off to the airport to collect his wife, Ken was never more certain that Congressional's Blue Course was indeed monstrous in every tiny detail. His practice round had not been all that good that morning. He had made mistakes, and repeatedly he had failed to get to grips with the shot required, but at the same time the round left him with a firmer understanding of what must be done.

Congressional would reward anybody who produced excellence in their long-iron play. Venturi was happy with that, even though he realised fully that the cost of even the slightest error would be doubled in size. No doubt about it, Congressional was demanding pinpoint precision. It was asking for absolute certainty in shot-making. Demanding and threatening, continually, as it twisted and turned.

Anyone not on top of their game was destined to end in a heap, somewhere on the course, between teeing off on Thursday morning and rounding everything up on Saturday evening. Peculiarly, for one who had experienced struggles and frustrations aplenty, Ken

Venturi was readily accepting of that deal with the course. He felt he had already gained some understanding of where to hit his shots and, just as importantly in the week ahead at Congressional, he felt he knew more about where it was safest to miss with shots. He feared less for himself and more for others, and it had been many years since such a selfless thought had resided with him before the start of a tournament.

Meeting Conni, the first words out of his wife's mouth were of concern about the course. She smiled the fullest smile Venturi had witnessed from her in weeks when he told her, with the happiest, most certain face, that Congressional was right up his alley. Conni, also, had no memory of the last time Ken had talked to her about a course without ending with some quibble or long note of caution.

****

On Wednesday, it was still blistering out on the beautiful golf course in the heart of Bethesda. The temperature hit 100 degrees, and moved even higher shortly after midday. Venturi, like so many others, decided to take in nine holes only. He stuck to the back nine.

That left him having played both nines twice in his three days, but he had only 36 holes on the Blue Course under his belt. He would have liked more. Nevertheless, that clear understanding of the course remained with him all the same. He felt that he had started a relationship with the place. He was getting there.

That night, he and Conni went looking for a church in Bethesda, and needed a cab to take them the eight blocks from their motel to the nearest place of prayer.

It was just after 8 p.m. The doors of the church, however, were locked when they arrived. Venturi looked around and found the parish priest working in his office in the nearby rectory. The priest was surprised but opened the side door of his church and put on all the lights. Conni sat at the rear on one of the long pews. Ken moved towards the altar.

He knelt. Over the course of the next 15 minutes he didn't ask God for victory in the US Open. All he prayed for was confidence, lasting confidence in himself, for three long, hot days.

Leaving, he stopped and dropped a few dollars into the box at the rear of the church before thanking the priest, and walking back to the motel.

Conni slept peacefully. Beside her, Ken shut his eyes and without a single lingering thought about the next morning's play, he also drifted into a deep, nourishing slumber.

****

Ken Venturi teed off in the first round of the 1964 US Open at noon, with the sun at its highest point in the Washington sky, and still with no air offering even a few seconds of kindliness upon his face. His heart was beating faster than at any point over the past three days. There was a slight terror rumbling in the background, in his head. But it only rumbled there, nothing more.

He understood, still, what had to be done. Drawn with little Billy Joe Maxwell, from Texas, and local golfer, the six-feet-five-inches tall George Bayer, who had been drafted by the Washington Redskins from college and had not turned to life as a golf pro until he was 29 years old, Venturi liked being on that first tee. That understanding of where he was in his life was strong. He had clarity, and that clarity propelled him towards a state of calmness. For several years he had played golf with no such understanding.

Then, that Thursday morning, the front nine holes at Congressional sucker-punched him. He went out fairly dismally in 38 strokes, which left him at three over par. Twice he had found himself in bunkers, and bunkers never worried Ken Venturi, not ever, not even at his lowest point in the years just passed. But twice in his opening round he left his ball in a bunker at the first time of asking.

On the 10th tee, he checked himself, looked to pull himself back together. But the strangest thing of all was that Venturi felt pretty much the exact same mixture of emotions he had felt when he was standing on the first tee, a couple of hours earlier, his card then clean and blemish-free. Nothing much had changed within him despite playing fairly wretchedly for those nine holes.

On the back nine, the tougher of the two nines at Congressional, he made eight pars and shot one birdie for a 34 and an 18-hole total of 72. He was two over for the championship, and four shots behind his former nemesis Arnold Palmer, which was not great and which did not exactly fill Conni with the same confidence she had experienced upon greeting her husband two days earlier at the airport. However, Arnie's opening 68 was the only score of the entire day that had dipped below the Blue Course's par of 70.

After eating back at their motel, Ken told Conni that he needed to go back to the church. The priest was happy to see them, and more prepared on this occasion. Again, Conni sat at the rear and Ken knelt at the altar alone. He wanted to know that he was not talking to himself. He *believed* that he was not there alone, but he just wanted to be certain. A sign would be nice, he thought. Something. He prayed for another 15, 20 minutes, and then he and Conni made their way back to their motel in the unceasingly heavy, pressing heat of the evening.

****

Friday was the hottest day of the week. It seemed an impossible heat in which to play a round of golf, but Venturi shot an even-par 70 for a two-round total of 142. He had had a solid view of what he needed to do. Apart from the first hole, he drove the ball without using a tee. These 'sliders' off the ground, importantly, helped to eliminate the left side of the course. With his approach shots he repeatedly found the right side of the greens.

He made his share of important putts, too. The championship lead after 36 holes, however, was in the hands of the Denver-born Tommy Jacobs, one of the two Jacobs brothers who would play on the PGA Tour and someone Ken always called a friend. Ken and Jacobs had first bumped into one another while competing on the junior circuit in California, and a few years further down the line they sat across from one another in Austria, while serving in the army, eating an unsatisfactory Christmas dinner together.

Tommy and Ken talked about life after their military service, though that chat did not include going head-to-head over the final two rounds of the US Open ten years later. In his second round Jacobs had shot a 64, tying the record of the lowest round in the history of the US Open. Tommy had been one of those sensational young cubs, and in 1952 he became the youngest golfer ever to hit a golf ball off the first tee at the Masters tournament. He was 17 years old and that record would hold for an astonishing 58 years, until the Italian teenage sensation, Matteo Manassero, was invited to Augusta National in April of 2010.

Tommy Jacobs had turned pro in 1956 and eight years later he was still waiting for his first major title. He had only four tournament wins in those eight years, the latest coming the previous February in Palm Springs. After 1964, Jacobs would not win another tournament on the PGA Tour, although he would come agonisingly close at Augusta National in 1966, when he lost in a Masters play-off to Jack Nicklaus. Like so many other talented golfers, Jacobs' primary wage came from his duties as a club pro during his thirties and forties, when he was working at two clubs in California, during which time his golf game was at its absolute peak.

But, by the Friday evening of June 19, 1964, Tommy Jacobs was sitting pretty in the Congressional clubhouse on 136 after two rounds. Arnold Palmer was also sticking to his guns, and had shot another sub-par round with a scintillating 69, just one back from

Jacobs. In third place was tall Bill Collins, from Pennsylvania, on 141 after his two rounds. Ken Venturi was six shots back, joining Charlie Sifford on 142, but, sitting in the locker room, Ken heard two of his fellow professionals around the corner talking about him.

They both thought it good to see Venturi put up a good showing, and they both agreed he was playing better than they had ever expected. Their conversation then tailed off, without offering any ending or even the slightest clue about what either man expected from Ken Venturi the next day over the final 36 holes.

****

As he left the clubhouse on Friday evening, Venturi stopped to pick up some mail awaiting his attention. Among the handful of letters was one from Father Francis Murray.

It was a six-pager, written in longhand and on yellow, lined paper. Father Murray had sat down to write to his new-found friend some days earlier, at the start of the week, while on a retreat at Redwood City in California. The letter, which was supposed to have been read by Ken before he began his opening round at the US Open, had taken its time reaching Congressional Country Club.

It began...

Dear Ken,

For you to become the 1964 US Open champion would be one of the greatest things that can possibly happen in our country this year.

Should you win, the effect would be both a blessing and a tonic for so many people who desperately need encouragement and a reason for hope.

Most people are in the midst of unremitting struggle, involving their jobs, their family problems, their health, frustrations of various sorts, even the insecurity of life itself. For many there is a pressing temptation to give up, to quit trying. Life at times simply seems to be too much, its demands overpowering...

Venturi read, and re-read the letter, through the remainder of that Friday evening. He had its core message fully digested and understood by the time he laid his head on his pillow next to Conni.

'When I got the message clearly fixed in my mind,' Venturi would admit in *Sports Illustrated* magazine the following December, 'I began to understand what had been making me back off… I felt at peace with myself, and I felt I could cope with anything.'

Father Murray, among many other things in his lengthy letter, had assured Ken that he was indeed a 'new Ken Venturi', and he had some particularly hand-chosen suggestions for Ken in order to secure the US Open title. He asked Ken to keep his mood centred, and to avoid either elation or disappointment during the three days. He told him to have a determined plan of action and to follow through with his decisions. Think of one shot at a time and nothing else, he advised. Trust in yourself, Father Murray said. And, lastly and most pertinently, Father Murray strongly suggested that Ken should look to get his birdies in the early holes of each round, thereby building up his spirit and conviction for the long fight ahead on each successive day at Congressional Country Club.

Father Murray concluded:

… If you should win Ken, you would prove I believe, to millions everywhere, that they, too, can be victorious over doubt, misfortune and despair…

… I'll be here, with your mother and father and the children, watching you on TV…

Your Friend,
Father Murray

Everything Father Murray had written was soundly based on good spiritual teaching, in addition to having a clearly brilliant psychological insight to a sportsman at work under the most intense pressure. Instead of practising on the putting green at Congressional with two or three golf balls, as Ken normally would, Father Murray had asked him to take out one ball only.

He wanted Ken to simulate on the practice green the same requirements and demands of a green during the round itself, always focusing on one ball, needing only one ball to go into each hole on the practice green, only one, and with each putting stroke and each hole being afforded the fullest of Ken Venturi's concentration.

****

Taking the short journey back to their motel that Friday evening, Venturi had pored over Father Murray's advice and wishes, and by the time he hopped out of the vehicle there had been a feeling of jubilation stirring within him. He had also gone back to the church in Bethesda for the third evening running, with the letter in his pocket, which he looked over, before and after his prayer. He thanked God for the letter, and stayed in the church for almost a full hour.

The United States Golf Association had always satisfied itself that two big, bold rounds on the final day of a championship was only right and fitting, if they were to find a champion of true worth.

On the first tee, for the start of his third round, 33-year-old Ken Venturi felt more alive than he had ever felt before as a professional golfer, though there were energies and a raw mixture of emotions tunnelling through so many parts of his body. At the breakfast table he had difficulty working his way through one poached egg. Downing his pot of tea was way beyond his capabilities.

Next to him on the tee box was a quiet, 21-year-old fellow by the name of Ray Floyd. He was a talented kid, who had shown some promise in his first three years on the tour, and Floyd would go on to win four majors in his time, including the 1976 Masters and the 1986 US Open. But, with Tommy Jacobs the championship leader, and with Arnold Palmer tracking him by just a single shot, nobody paid too much attention to Venturi and Floyd when they hit off. All eyes were on the two front-runners, with half a dozen others looking handily placed.

Venturi and Floyd were two groups ahead of Jacobs and Palmer, and on that first hole of the third round there was certainly some hope of a birdie. Venturi felt extremely confident at that moment as he stood over his ball. He drove the par-four beautifully, found the heart of the green and duly left himself with a nine-foot putt for his birdie, which he aimed straight at the hole. The ball found its target, but stood stubbornly short, on the hole's lip, and the ball didn't budge for what seemed like four or five seconds to Venturi. He refused to move after his putt, using up every half-second and quarter-second allowed under the game's rules, waiting for the ball to drop.

Finally, Venturi knew he had to give up on the putt. He needed to tap the ball in, and, disappointingly, he followed the line his putt had taken. But, before he reached the hole, miraculously, his ball decided to slip into the cup.

Heavy rain in the earliest hours of Saturday morning had clearly softened the greens and improved their holding qualities. It was possibly a day for attack. Venturi felt he had had a lucky shot handed to him on the first hole, maybe from on high, and, thereafter, he decided to gamble with that gained shot by firing boldly at every flag.

There is one you should not have had, Ken told himself. *Now you've got one shot to play with. Let's gamble until we lose it.*

At some stage, he fully believed the Blue Course, bad-temperedly, would grab that earlier shot back off him.

As Alfred Wright, of *Sports Illustrated*, explained, 'Instead of backing off shots he was ramming even the longest irons over the edges of Congressional's big traps and right to the pin. Some of the shots were so risky that ever-bold Arnold Palmer played them a little safe. It seemed lunacy not to. But Venturi hit for the pins like a golfer gone berserk.'

Venturi, already alive and buzzing with a crazy formula made up of all sorts of ingredients in his body, had gone slightly crazy with his shot-selection and shot-making, and by the time he had concluded his front nine his scorecard read 3-3-4, 3-3-4, 3-3-4. That added up to just 30 shots and he had matched the all-time record for nine holes at a United States Open Championship.

Five birdies and four pars! After 45 holes, Venturi was sharing the championship lead with Jacobs. They were both on three under par. Palmer was one under.

The walk from the ninth green to the 10th tee was a long one. As he marched, Venturi came upon Conni. She looked overcome with emotion, and she was also suffering in the deepening heat. When her husband came towards her, she was actually spilling a cup of iced tea on to her dress in an effort to cool down a bit. Ken told her to get back into the clubhouse. He didn't want her fainting. There could be no distractions of any kind for the next couple of hours, he told her, and he didn't want to be worrying about her while he sought to complete the greatest round, perhaps, in the history of the championship. Conni took his advice and disappeared inside.

From the 10th tee box, the shimmering heat distorted everything in view. It was being noted by those standing around the tee that the temperature was hitting 115 degrees in some of the low, valley-like sections of Congressional Country Club. The humidity was nearing 100 per cent.

Watching with his father that Saturday morning was Ben Brundred III, who would grow up to be co-chairman of the 2011 US Open when it returned to Congressional Country Club. He had turned up in 1964 to see Arnie and Nicklaus, more than anybody else, in the flesh. But the then 12-year-old boy would always be left with one abiding memory of the burning course. 'It was so hot that day, steam was rising from the ground,' he would recall in Bethesda Magazine.

'It was an amazing sight. The memory that stands out most was how hot it was. There had been thunderstorms at various times. It wasn't like it is now where they clear the course if weather threatens. Then you just ran for shelter anywhere you could find it. After the bad weather cleared, you came back out and play resumed.'

Venturi got his par on the 10th, and continued to hold his score tightly together. On the 13th, he got back into birdie action by aggressively targeting the hole. He stood at six under par for his round, and five more pars would have him tie Tommy Jacobs' course record of 64 from the day before.

On the 14th, Venturi again snatched a par. However, as he walked to the 15th hole he felt something was not quite right. His body began to shake and tremble ever so slightly. When he tried to steady and control himself, the shaking fought back even more aggressively.

He tried to suck in some air, to hold in his strength, and on the 15th and 16th holes he fought to control every shot. Two more pars were his. He still needed to do better, he told himself. He still needed that birdie.

Sweat was dripping down his chest and his legs.

He could find no air, none whatsoever, and as he reached the 17th, Venturi found that his legs had stiffened. Also, visibly, his hands had begun to shake.

He drove the ball down the right of the 17th fairway, and then managed to hit a nice iron to 15 feet from the pin. A birdie would take him to seven under par. He left his putt 18 inches from the hole. Venturi, ever so slowly, walked to his ball.

When he stood over it, something new happened.

He felt the green tilt from side to side.

He was now shaking, uncontrollably, and for a few seconds

he felt that he was going to collapse. He closed his eyes to try to balance himself.

The green was still shifting under his feet.

He opened his eyes again and examined the ball at his feet, and then looked at the hole one and a half feet away. Now, however, there were three cups to choose from! He could see all three of them, but he could not wait any longer to decide which one to aim at. He still feared collapsing at any second, and he quickly aimed his ball at the middle of the three cups. His ball went wide of the hole, and the first bogey of the day went down on his scorecard.

On the 18th hole Venturi drove his ball poorly, straight into the magnificent cluster of giant trees down the right side of the fairway. But a saving chip shot from 45 yards landed within three and a half feet of the hole.

By now, Ken Venturi was in the grip of a severe case of vertigo. Again, he missed his par putt. He lifted his putter over his head. His hands clenched his face, to stop himself from screaming out. He bit his lip. When he lowered his hands, William Ward could see that his man was as white as a sheet, but Venturi knew he had to move. Somehow, he had to get off the green without collapsing from the dizziness.

He started moving but soon found that he needed some help. Two first-aid workers raced in his direction. Someone grabbed him and shoved him into a nearby station wagon. Jay Hebert, who had won the PGA title in 1960, three years after his brother Lionel had won the same major, was sitting next to him. He was shocked at the sight of Venturi.

'Think you can make it back to the clubhouse?' asked Hebert. 'Your eyes are rolling in your head!' The car quickly brought both golfers back up the steep hill from the 18th green to the clubhouse. There, Venturi sat down, slowly. He was still trembling all over, and trying vainly to gain control of what was happening to his body. People hovered all around him.

The first-aid guys had grabbed buckets of ice, and they had begun icing him down. Ray Floyd stood and watched his playing partner, unable to do anything to help, before deciding to go outside and tell people what was happening inside. There he met Conni Venturi.

Ken Venturi was an ill man but, despite recording two bogey-fives on his last two holes, he had just shot a 66 in his third round. Scores of 72, 70 and 66 left him two shots back from the championship leader, who was still Tommy Jacobs. He had rallied in the tough conditions to hit a 70, and stand on 206 shots after 54 holes. Paired with Jacobs, Palmer had finally fallen back off the pace with a round of 75, finishing the morning's play six back from Jacobs, and four behind Venturi with 18 holes remaining.

Most of those in the locker room, however, were in agreement that Venturi looked finished for the day. The championship, too, was up in smoke. He probably needed to go to the nearest hospital, it was further agreed. Venturi's entire body was in a state of deepening distress. As he slouched on the wooden seat, his head pushed back against the locker behind him, Venturi felt just about gone. He was sickeningly dehydrated. Someone asked him if he had drunk any water. Had he taken any water at all? he was asked more aggressively. He shook his head. He didn't say anything. He couldn't.

It had never occurred to him to carry any water. Well used to the heat of San Francisco, and the cooling Pacific breeze on even the hottest of days out west, Venturi had never fussed in his life about being too hot. Neither had his caddie told him to drink any water.

All Venturi had thought about, all morning long, was maintaining the tempo and smoothness of his swing, and concentrating on every single putting action. Then, as he sat there, Venturi suddenly flinched, hearing someone shouting loudly to get a doctor quickly.

CHAPTER ELEVEN

June 2011

Fourteen years earlier, at Congressional Country Club, Tiger Woods had claimed the position of world No.1 for the first time. However, the subdued but always dangerous Tiger had to scratch his name from the entries for the 111th US Open championship, held in Bethesda in 2011. This time there was no more girl trouble. Tiger's problems were all down in his knees and his Achilles.

Rory McIlroy might have liked to talk about Haiti, and his two-day tour of the devastated country as Ireland's newest UNICEF ambassador the week before arriving in Washington, but every time he sat down in front of any gathering of writers and broadcasters he found himself being asked about Tiger Woods first of all and, after that, what else but Augusta National. With Tiger not around the place, of course, that meant that McIlroy's final round of 80 at Augusta National two months earlier and his perishingly fast meltdown when he appeared to have the Masters tournament locked down, his shockingly wide drive on Augusta's 10th hole, that crushingly errant drive on Augusta's 13th… Augusta, Augusta, Augusta was all he was asked about in practically every single conversation. Soon enough, the subject was even drowning out Tiger Woods' absence.

Rory chatted about Haiti as often as he could on the Monday and Tuesday. 'It makes you feel so lucky that I'm able just to sit here and drink a bottle of water,' he explained, 'just the normal things that everyone does... that you take for granted.'

But, heartlessly, the attending media could not have cared less for the young man's genuinely bleeding heart. They didn't want to talk about Haiti. They didn't much want to hear about it either. Their topic of choice was Augusta National, and repeatedly the richness of that great beauty in East Georgia intruded, forcing Rory to relive that week in early April again and again.

He strived not to appear at all irked, or defensive. 'It's hard... it was my first time in that situation... you're going to be feeling the pressure a little bit... and I certainly did... but, you just move on. That's all you can do.

'It's not the end of the world.'

****

McIlroy felt that his high ball-flight appeared tailor-made for the Blue Course, which stretched out over a massively unforgiving 7,574 yards. The monster of Bethesda had been lengthened since 1964, when it measured 7,053 yards when it hosted the US Open for the first time, to 7,213 yards in 1997 on the Open's return, when South Africa's laid-back Ernie Els beat Scotland's needy Colin Montgomerie. At the third time of asking, Congressional had also shifted up from a par of 70, to a par of 71.

McIlroy was not alone. The five-times runner-up Phil Mickelson was in confident mood. The new world No.1 Luke Donald felt sure about himself. The defending champion, McIlroy's closest buddy of all on tour, Graeme McDowell, was ready and waiting, but certain that the rock-hard greens were going to break hearts, and that they were not going to be choosy whether those hearts belonged to the championship favourites or some journeyman pro well down the rankings.

'It wouldn't surprise me if anyone did it,' insisted McDowell. 'I'm not ruling out any type of player, the long hitter, the short hitter, but you've got to control it off the tee to give yourself a chance coming into those greens.'

Rory's closest companion for the week ahead was going to be his father, Gerry. He and Gerry would stick together for the whole week. It was agreed that Gerry was to be the one person he talked to most of all.

There was no repeat invitation into a cosy lair in Washington for Rory's three pals, Ricky, Mitchell and Harry, who had been his constant companions through his week in Augusta two months earlier. By the Sunday morning, Rory would know that he had chosen well. 'It was more reassuring to hear things from my dad, rather than a sports psychologist or anybody else,' he said. 'They came from someone who knows me better than anyone else in the world.'

On the Thursday, McIlroy had begun his opening round on the watery par-three 10th tee. Soon, he hit a sand wedge approach to six feet to birdie the 12th, he hit an eight-iron to 10 feet to birdie the 17th and again hit an eight-iron, this time to 20 feet, to birdie the 18th for a superb back nine, or rather front nine, of 32. Another birdie at the first after a lob wedge to six feet moved him into the outright lead in the championship. He stretched that lead with another birdie at the fourth after a wedge left him four feet from the hole, and increased it further still at the par-five sixth, which was playing 573 yards but which McIlroy cut down to size with a blistering 320-yard drive, a three-iron approach to 15 feet, and then two putts.

At the end of the day in Bethesda, McIlroy had a 65 on his scorecard, chillingly the same number that he had effortlessly reached after his first round of the 2011 Masters tournament at Augusta.

McDowell began his title defence with a one-under-par 70. Even though the weather was more English than East Coast, with grey cloud cover and some soft rain at intervals, the British challenge had immediately spluttered, with Luke Donald shooting 74 and Lee Westwood, the pre-tournament favourite, managing only a 75. Mickelson, the United States' best hope and one of McIlroy's playing partners, kicked off his first round on the fairly scary 10th hole by hitting his first shot of the championship into the gaping water, before running up a double bogey. It was Mickelson's 41st birthday, which he celebrated with a resoundingly dull round of 74.

McIlroy had hit 17 of the greens on the ferocious Blue Course in regulation, and his six-under-par round left him three ahead of his nearest challengers, the reigning Masters champion Charl Schwartzel and the 2009 US PGA champion, Y. E. Yang, who was now a sprightly 39 years old having spent more time body-building than hitting golf balls until his 20th birthday.

'This golf course is only going to get firmer, and it's going to get harder,' McIlroy reminded everyone, including himself, before the end of a long first day.

'I think something around two, three, four under par, something like that, is going to have a good chance. Even something around level is going to come close on Sunday.

'It's a US Open… they know how to make the golf course a lot more difficult than it was today.'

****

On Friday, in his second round, McIlroy was even faster out of the blocks. But, first, he had to find himself a coin marker. He'd forgotten one and his handler at ISM, Stuart Cage, needed to go and borrow one from a television reporter. After that, McIlroy was out like a shot.

He parred his first three holes but then birdied the fourth and sixth. He then sent out a warning shot right across the Washington sky of what was to come when he eagled the 354-yard par-four eighth hole, the shortest par-four on the course, to complete the front nine in 32 shots, one better than his start to his first round.

Like everyone else watching, Mickelson stood and applauded on the eighth after McIlroy's 113-yard approach spun into the cup, making him the first player in the long and utterly respectful history of the US Open to reach 10 under par in the second round of the championship. It left him with a seven-stroke lead. It had taken just 26 holes.

That chasm expanded to an eight-shot lead after he hit his approach to four feet at the 467-yard 14th hole, moved to nine shots after he just missed a 10-foot eagle opportunity at the 579-yard 16th, and finally his lead reached the figure 10 when he sank a 12-footer on the 17th hole. The fearful reputation and the preciousness that Congressional Country Club had assiduously built up over the 87 years since its grand opening had been torn asunder by Rory McIlroy.

The full damage was done in just 35 holes. By then, the 22-year-old leader had passed Tiger Woods' landmark achievement and become the first man in the Open's history to reach 13 under par.

On the 18th hole, the longest of Congressional's par-fours and its signature hole, its pride and joy since the restructuring of the Blue Course had been completed by all the many pairs of hands that had fully wiped the work of Devereux Emmet off the face of the earth, Rory McIlroy was finally stopped in his tracks. He double-bogeyed his 36th hole, then quickly got rid of that particular Titleist ball by back-handing it into the lake, before scooting over the nearby pontoon bridge. But it mattered little to observers, or writers and broadcasters, how that double bogey happened. It had occurred by way of a hook into the rough, and a second shot that curled into the giant lake that, if viewed from the clouds, sits atop the 18th green at Congressional like a broad and splendid hat, which a lady might wear at the races.

But who cared for the details? At the halfway mark of the 111th US Open, McIlroy left Congressional Country Club to retire for the evening in the calm and private luxury of the accommodation that his manager, Chubby Chandler, had laid on for him and his father, and he did so standing at 11 under par, holding an eight-shot lead for the championship. Y. E. Yang, on three under par, was his closest challenger. Sergio Garcia, the sometimes happy and often very sad Spaniard who seemed destined never to win a major, was two under, with the American pair of Zach Johnson, from Iowa, and Idaho's Robert Garrigus for company.

With McIlroy safely tucked away in his new living quarters in Washington later that night, writers and broadcasters were still thinking and behaving more like white-haired historians. The names of Yang, Garcia, Johnson and Garrigus were not on anybody's lips. There were much bigger names being trotted out.

Like, for starters, the names of Jack Nicklaus and Bobby Jones. Nicklaus, some time before anyone thought of him as the Golden Bear, had been a young man full of hope, but with nothing truly outstanding to show for his fine ambition. In June 2011, McIlroy was still several months younger than Nicklaus had been when, also aged 22, he won the first of his 18 major titles when beating the heavily favoured local, Arnold Palmer, by three shots in an 18-hole play-off to win the 1962 US Open at Oakmont.

Nicklaus became the reigning US Open and US Amateur champion with that victory in his 17th start as a professional, and he had also been the youngest championship winner since Augusta National's own Bobby Jones, Nicklaus's great idol, had taken the title in 1923 at 21 years of age.

There was another old name in people's heads. The name of Sir Henry Thomas Cotton, born in 1907 in Holmes Chapel in Cheshire, north-west England. As a young chap Henry was a superb cricketer, who showed his early promise while attending Alleyn's School in Dulwich, south London. However, one day, Cotton and some others were ordered by six of the school's prefects to transport their cricket clothing back to the school using public transport. Young Henry was not amused. He wrote to the school headmaster, who, equally lacking in daily cheerfulness, decided that the promising cricket star, but aspiring upstart, should be caned as punishment for his letter.

Henry Cotton refused. Thereafter, banned from the school cricket team, Henry and his brother made their way to the nearby Aquarius Golf Club in 1920, and decided formally to get to grips with the game of golf. In 1934, at Sandwich, Cotton led by nine shots at the halfway mark in the Open Championship, thereby setting a record that would stand for ever more at the halfway mark of any major tournament. Tiger Woods has come as close as anybody to that amazing figure, in the 2000 US Open at Pebble Beach, when he led by six after 36 holes. In June 2011, Rory McIlroy had landed ahead of Woods, but just one shot back from Cotton.

Jones, Cotton, Nicklaus and Woods! They were the people being talked about... Jones, Cotton, Nicklaus, Woods and McIlroy! That's the sort of company Rory McIlroy was keeping in all newspaper reports and broadcasts, the evening before the third round of the 111th US Open Championship.

****

When anything reaches absolute purity on a great golf course, the massive danger of its foul disintegration, and ultimate destruction, is crazily heightened. McIlroy was playing golf on a high wire, as high and as perilous a place as there could be, and where only a handful of outstanding golfers down through the two previous centuries had found themselves. Tiger Woods had been there, and Jack Nicklaus; both of them in the half century that had just passed. And Nicklaus, more than Arnold Palmer or Seve Ballesteros, who both instinctively could play the old game magnificently and in an awe-inspiring way.

But… *purity*? Neither Arnie nor Seve naturally possessed it.

'It's been near the best I can play,' McIlroy had dutifully informed the attending media. 'The second on the eighth was a bonus, but I hit a couple of iron shots on the back nine which were so pure.

'I'm halfway there, but there's still a long way to go. It's a big challenge, but every time I put myself in position I am becoming more and more comfortable… and that's important.

'I felt much more at ease today. You are when you hit so many good shots.'

****

On Saturday morning, McIlroy awoke in sprightly form. He had Gerry to talk to. There was no fuss, no great laughter, no drama whatsoever. His Twitter account had been silent for several days, and would remain speechless until Sunday evening. There were no American sports on TV to get too excited about, or distracting images from home. Everything, just about, was normal, level, balanced perfectly, leaving a young man and his father to talk about everyday life as best they could.

It was decided by Gerry and Chubby and others who analysed what had gone so wrong, so suddenly, during the final 24 hours at Augusta, to keep talking with McIlroy. No highs, no lows, but good, lively, interesting conversation. Gerry McIlroy was tuned into that. So, too, was McIlroy's caddie, J. P. Fitzgerald, who had admitted after the great loss in Georgia that he and Rory had actually stopped chatting sufficiently to one another for lengthy intervals, as the pressure magnified hour by hour on that fateful Sunday afternoon.

Arriving at Congressional Country Club for the third round, only an absolute fool would fail to recognise that the very same pressure, which had caught up with him in Augusta and overpowered him by forcing him to break down every little element of his game, and seek to put it all back together with one swing of a golf club, was tailing Rory McIlroy.

But, on this occasion, because of what had happened at Augusta National two months earlier, there was even greater force to that pressure. The closing day at Augusta, and the first two days in Bethesda, combined to double or perhaps treble the danger of the US Open leader pausing, thinking about where he was, and wondering what he was doing so right.

****

It could happen to anybody. In 1992, midway through the US Open at Pebble Beach, one of the safest pairs of hands on the PGA Tour, Gilmer Bryan Morgan II, known as Gil Morgan to golf fans, and called 'Doc' by his closest buddies in the locker room as a result of earning himself a Doctor of Optometry degree before turning pro, became the first player to reach 10 under par in the history of the championship when he recorded a birdie on the third hole of his third round. Gil Morgan had had his game down pat for 13 years on tour, and was consistently one of the tour's top five finishers during this period.

Gil, routinely, got the job done on a golf course.

At Pebble Beach that summer, Morgan built on his good early work in the third round and reached 12 under par after seven holes. He led the championship by seven shots. Then, over the next 11 holes he dropped eight shots. He finished his third round, still leading the tournament, at four under for the championship.

The next day, Morgan shot an 81, which pushed him out to five over by the end of his final round, tied for 13th place, and eight shots off the winner, Tom Kite.

Such roller-coaster experiences were still fresh in the mind of Rory McIlroy as well. At Augusta, two months before, he had shot into reverse and gone from four ahead of everyone to 10 shots behind the eventual Masters champion. In July 2010, McIlroy had set a new record for the best opening round in the Open Championship, shooting a 63 on fine, old St Andrews. The next day, he tumbled off the biggest stage in European golf with a plump round of 80.

McIlroy followed his opening rounds of 65 and 66 in Bethesda with a 68 on the Saturday. He birdied the fifth.

The ninth.

The 11th.

The 14th, and he had one blemish on his third-round scorecard – a bogey at the 10th hole.

There were no great heroics during his 18 holes. Neither was there much unnerving drama, as he held tightly to his eight-shot lead in the championship. The records, though, continued to tumble at his feet. His three-under-par 68 took him to 199 for his three rounds, 14 under par for the championship, thereby going one shot better than the previous lowest three-round total for a US Open.

He did the job.

CHAPTER TWELVE

The Final Round

Ken Venturi was helped off his seat in the locker room at Bethesda's Congressional Country Club. He was left lying on his back, on the floor.

Over him stood Dr John Everett, a club member, a six-handicapper, but also a hard-working GP in Washington whose daily chores included clinic hours and lots of house calls. The doc was giving Ken iced tea, which he had loaded with lemon and sugar. He was telling Venturi to sip it slowly, but often.

Ken, despite his grogginess, could hear the doc's voice clearly enough. He was being told to forget about playing any more golf in the afternoon. 'If you go out there again in that heat, in your condition, it could actually be fatal.' That was Dr Everett's warning.

When Ken had finally entered the locker room some 15 minutes earlier, escaping the sauna-like effects of the course, his temperature was at 106 degrees. Anything over 105 degrees Fahrenheit and a human brain can meet with plenty of damage. Backing up the doctor's words, a second voice over Ken's head echoed, severely, the warning that he might die if he went back out on to the golf course. There was a second doctor in the room.

Also among the small group crowded too tightly around the golfer lying on the ground was Frank Murphy III, just 23 years old, just out of the military, and the son of a Congressional member who was chairman of the 1964 US Open. He had been allowed to help out in the locker room for the week by his dad. 'All of these people were working over him,' recalled Murphy to the New Jersey *Star-Ledger*. 'He didn't look good at... *at all*. It was a total blank stare. That's the best I could categorise it.

'It was like nothing registered.'

Murphy, nevertheless, heard Ken answer Dr Everett. His voice was faint, but quite clear.

'Whatever happens, it's better than the way I've been living,' said Venturi, who was now fervently promising that if anything should happen to him out on the course, his family would not sue Dr Everett.

Ken was now imploring him.

'Can you keep me going?' he asked.

Dr Everett was uncertain at first, but then committed to doing everything he could for Ken. 'My father told him he'd try,' Dr Everett's son, Richard, explained. 'My father gave him the benefit of many years of practice and dealing with heatstroke and dehydration.'

The evidence of the heat exhaustion and severe dehydration was in everyone's heads. Ray Floyd knew better than anyone how quickly Ken had faded in the blistering and oppressive conditions. Looking demented, and quite unsteady on his legs, Ken had turned to Floyd on the 17th tee of their third round earlier in the day.

'I don't think I'll make it, Ray!' he warned.

Floyd had told him he'd be okay. But not for one second did he fully believe what he was telling his playing partner. On the last two holes of that morning's round, Ken had been unable to grip his putter hard enough to hold it as still as he wished, and he had blown an 18-inch putt on 17, and then failed with a putt only twice that distance on 18. It was as he was coming off that final green that he had stumbled to his knees, before being taken to the clubhouse.

Dr Everett demanded that Ken continue to rest. He didn't need any food, he just needed to keep sipping liquid. But he needed a longer period of rest than the timetable for the day's play was going to allow.

Making one of the quickest decisions in its lengthy history, the USGA granted Venturi a 30-minute extension before he would have to tee off for the start of his final round. When he did finally make it to the tee to start that round, the doc demanded that his patient take in an additional quick period of rest, and laid him back down on the ground for a couple of minutes more.

The situation remained serious. The United States Golf Association knew that there was no room for foolishness, and therefore it had given its special permission that Ken Venturi would be allowed to play the final 18 holes under a doctor's care. There was actually quite an entourage. For starters, there was William Ward, Venturi's caddie. After that, there was Dr Everett, who was given a helmet with a red cross logo on the front, whose job was to administer salt tablets and ice packs, and keep Venturi alive and walking. There was a marshal with an umbrella to shield Venturi from the worst effects of the sun. There was a second marshal, who was equipped with a walkie-talkie, in case word needed to be dispatched double-quick back to the clubhouse that an ambulance was required on the course. The executive director of the USGA, Joe Dey, would stay with the Venturi group, and it was also felt necessary to have a police officer at hand.

A spectator at the US Open at Oakmont in 1935, Edward Stimpson, watched a putt from Gene Sarazen roll off a green. Stimpson was sure in his head that the greens had been made unreasonably fast by the championship officials. A week later, he set about proving that he was right and started work on developing a device called a Stimpmeter, which releases a golf ball at a known velocity so that the distance it rolls on a green's surface can be expertly measured. It worked splendidly. Everyone approved.

The USGA had targeted a Stimpmeter reading of between 14 and 14½ for the greens at Congressional Country Club for the playing of the 111th US Open Championship.

On the eve of the first round, Congressional officials had met members of the USGA to present their thoughts on how things looked in Bethesda. Everybody wanted firm and fast putting conditions. Pebble Beach, the summer before, had been 11 to 11½ on the Stimpmeter when Graeme McDowell claimed his first major title. At Oakmont, in 2007, when the Argentinian, Angel Cabrera, was victorious, the Stimpmeter reading was between 14½ and 15.

But the week before the players arrived in Bethesda in 2011, local officials looked out on their course being prepared in the already oppressive heat. The heat index was at or over 100 degress for five days solid, and that left them cutting back on the number of mowings, the number of rollings, and also to cutting back on the mowing heights on each green.

When the players arrived at Congressional Country Club on the Monday of championship week, the course had not yet become as fast and sharp as everybody wished it to be, but 48 hours later, Tom O'Toole, chairman of the USGA Championship Committee, was delighted with what was laid out in front of the magnificent field of golfers. 'In my 20 years officiating at the US Open,' he stated, 'the putting greens, their firmness, their smoothness, and the green speeds are as good as we've had in that time. We are delighted where the golf course is right now, and we think it's perfectly prepared to test the greatest players in the world.'

Congressional was ready to take the best that was thrown at it, thereby maintaining the dog-tough standard of play demanded at the US Open more than at any other golf competition in the world.

Too often, the Open made magnificent golfers look quite foolish.

In 2006, and again in 2007, five over par was the winning score. In 2010, Northern Ireland's Graeme McDowell won with an even-par 284 over the four days at Pebble Beach.

By Saturday evening, at the close of the third round of the 2011 Open, however, Congressional was having serious questions being asked of it. 'I'm a little disappointed with the golf course the last couple of days,' volunteered McDowell. 'It wasn't as firm and fast as I would like to have seen it, so it's not a true US Open test out there, to be honest.' McDowell had shot a two-under-par 69 in his third round, and would do so again the next day, but he had players on low numbers on all sides of him. Lee Westwood and Australia's Jason Day both shot 65 in their third rounds.

Such scoring totally eclipsed the performance of the field in 1997, when the championship had last arrived in Bethesda. Then, Ernie Els worked for four days to get to a winning total of four under, one shot better than Colin Montgomerie, and two better than the former US Ryder Cup captain, Tom Lehman. Those three were the only players to dip below par for the whole tournament.

With 18 holes still to be played in 2011, a total of 20 players were in the red numbers, and another six were at even par for the championship. All of them had their games hotting up, and they were in quite a clustered grouping.

The only thing awry, and it was of a giant-like quality, was the preposterously low scoring of Rory McIlroy. He was out of sight of everybody else. At Congressional, as he teed up his ball on the Sunday afternoon, at 3.20 p.m., he had twice as big a lead as he had enjoyed, and then allowed to suffocate his entire golf game, at Augusta National two months before.

In the earliest hours of Sunday morning, while the golfers had slept as soundly as they might, there had been some more rain in Bethesda. Late on the Friday afternoon, the course had already received a right drenching, and there had been that light drizzling rain during the first two rounds as well, so it was little wonder that every golfer left standing in the championship by Saturday night was firmly of a mind to attack the flag on every single green the following day.

'I don't think we're going to try to trick Mother Nature,' said Tom O'Toole, the day before the final round. 'This is what we got in 2011. You come to the US Open in the District of Columbia or in Maryland in June, that's the dice you roll. That's what we've got... we ended up with a soft golf course.'

Ken Venturi was two strokes off the lead with 18 holes still to be played. Out in front, still, was Tommy Jacobs, who had hit an historic low of 64 the previous day, and in his third round he had completed a new Open record of 206 shots for 54 holes, thereby bettering Ben Hogan's 207, which had been set 16 years earlier.

Venturi was still on his feet. 'I couldn't stop,' Venturi would recall nearly half a century later, when he revisited Congressional Country Club for the 2011 US Open Championship. 'I was making a comeback. I had to keep playing.'

The next day, *The Washington Post* would report that Ken Venturi was among a total of 398 people, mostly spectators, who needed medical assistance for heat-related problems during the three days of championship play. During the course of the last day, Venturi would lose just over eight pounds in weight, starting his third round at 172lb and finishing his fourth round weighing in at 164lb.

Conni Venturi was waiting anxiously outside the locker room, but remained unaware of her husband's collapsed state. She was found by Ray Floyd, who told her that Ken was 'sick', but Conni still didn't understand. She thought that Floyd was telling her that Ken was simply sick in the stomach at having bogeyed the last two holes of his third round.

'Yes, I know,' Conni replied. 'I am, too.'

'I mean he's really physically sick,' Floyd continued. 'He's lying down in the locker room and has just about passed out. There's a doctor with him.'

Floyd told Conni that the people looking after Ken did not believe that he would be able to play a fourth round of golf. When the time came for him to leave the locker room, Ken found Conni close to tears.

'Honey, how do you feel?' she rapidly asked.

'I'm just fine, hon,' he told her.

He then ordered Conni to go back inside the clubhouse, and wait for him there. It was dangerously hot, too hot for her out on the course. Conni watched Ken amble off gingerly in the direction of the first tee, with his small army of helpers and watchers spewed out around him, and more following close behind.

Rory McIlroy took the first swish of his favoured three-wood, and then bounced down the first fairway after his ball, which had been dispatched 290 yards down on the right-hand side. He was one shot closer to becoming the youngest winner of the US Open Championship since Bobby Jones, 88 years of golfing history earlier.

It was humid in the mid-afternoon sun in Bethesda. The place had certainly heated up, but McIlroy appeared impervious to the playing conditions, or the folk who shouted 'Go Irish!' and 'Rory Go Bragh!'

He had enjoyed his breakfast that morning. There had been a nice foursome at the table. His father Gerry, his manager Chubby and his ISM handler Stuart Cage, or 'Cagey', himself a former European Tour player who was now, aged 37, caring full-time for one player and one player only. They talked about the Formula One motor racing championship for the most part. McLaren's English driver, Jenson Button, had won the Canadian Grand Prix in Montreal the previous Sunday, and was leading the crack German behind the wheel of the Red Bull car, Sebastian Vettel, in the F1 drivers' standings. Nobody at the McIlroy table mentioned the final round of the US Open Championship.

The previous evening, he had sat down for dinner with his ISM stablemate, Lee Westwood, but he was not in the mood for any form of advice. The only revelation from either man was that they'd both ordered steak.

'I've gotta take care of my business, and take care of myself,' McIlroy had replied when questioned about their conversation.

However, once he took his first steps out on to Congressional's Blue Course for his final round, everybody looking at McIlroy, those standing five and six deep on the course, and the tens of millions watching the televisions in their own homes, wondered aloud about the whereabouts of Rory's demons.

The course had already welcomed the earliest golfers of the day. It had rolled over, and was having its belly tickled. Robert Karlsson was on six under par for his day's work, but the Swede would bogey six of the holes on the back nine and finish with a disappointing one-over-par 72. Gregory Havret, from France, had gone out all guns blazing, too, birdieing the sixth, seventh, eighth and ninth holes, but he, too, would be halted in his stride over the back nine, with three bogeys. Congressional might roll over all right, but it was never going to play dead.

Where were those little monsters of McIlroy's, and when would they make a nuisance of themselves? When they did appear, everybody knew that they would immediately whisper panicky notions in McIlroy's ear. Or the same demons, looking to trip a golfer up, would definitely advise McIlroy to start thinking harder, and longer, about his next shot.

McIlroy's drive off the first tee at Augusta National in April had also been one of perfection. It was his second shot to the green that had the tiniest little bit of a kink in it. That was the shot that had started McIlroy thinking about not just that slightly dodgy shot, but pretty much his entire golf game before the round was halfway through.

No doubt about it, McIlroy's demons were going to remain close enough at hand for the next nine holes, at least. They were not going to head off anywhere else. They would still be hanging around for a few more holes on the back nine at Congressional Country Club. Not until the 14th hole, perhaps the 15th if everything was still in fine mechanical working order and a healthy championship lead was strongly intact, would the first demon say cheerio for the day.

The first hole, with bunkers on either side of the landing area but especially the large step marks down the right side of the fairway, had been birdied by McIlroy in his first round, when he had played it as his 10th hole. On Friday and Saturday, as his first port of call for each day, he had parred it without too much bother. The relatively flat green on the first also is inviting, as are the two yawning bunkers at the front, right and left, to the wayward.

On CBS, Northern Ireland's punchy commentator, David Feherty, had earlier put on record that Tiger Woods, had he been in the field, would have had 'his arse served to him' by McIlroy in the form he was showing. Feherty might not have been too far wrong. Before McIlroy had even teed off, Phil Mickelson had completed his final round with a disastrous double bogey. The second biggest brand in US golf, after Tiger Woods, Mickelson had played his first two rounds with McIlroy and had been 12 shots behind the 22-year-old by the 36-hole mark. Mickelson then crashed to a 77 the next day, and by Sunday evening was seven over par for the championship and not in the top 50 finishers.

With neither Woods nor McIlroy watching the championship on TV, nobody had taken offence at Feherty's declaration. It certainly was not a prediction that would have done McIlroy any good whatsoever, if those words had been rolling around in his head.

In the second to last group on the final day, with Jason Day, was Westwood, who applied the slightest pressure on the leader by generating an approving roar with a clinical birdie. He moved to within eight shots of the leader. Day parred the first.

McIlroy's ball on the first fairway had stopped on the edge of a divot. It was a mildly distracting sight, but that's all it was.

He was 177 yards from the pin, pretty much the same yardage he had faced on the opening hole at Augusta National two months earlier. This time, his second shot to the first green was pitched to within six feet of the hole, leaving him with a testing putt to check if his eye was good for the final 17 greens.

He holed out and was nine clear of Westwood and everybody else. He had moved to 15 under par for the championship, another record for the officials of the United States Golf Association to digest.

Worried that Venturi might go into convulsions at any time, Dr Everett carried a hypodermic needle with him down the fairway of the first hole. Somehow, Venturi had whacked his ball down the middle. He knew of the needle in the doc's pocket, but he had warned Dr Everett that it could not be used unless he first gave the word or nod of approval. If he was in a position to nod, of course.

'All right, it's a deal, Ken,' he vowed.

Conni had been taken to the press tent, where she was able to watch the progress of the play for the next few hours more closely. There, journalists shot questions in her direction, too many questions, from all corners.

'If he doesn't win,' Conni stumbled in reply, still struggling to hold back the tears, 'he'll die trying.'

As he walked after his ball, down the first fairway, the words written down on the yellow lined paper by Father Francis Murray suddenly enlarged themselves in Venturi's head. Father Murray had told him to think of one shot at a time.

That's all I can now do, thought Venturi. *Fairways and greens... one shot at a time.*

Then he reminded himself that that was all he had ever needed to do – whether he was experiencing boundless energy as he chased down Tommy Jacobs' two-shot lead, or whether he felt as he did, almost baked to a standstill.

He parred the first hole. The next few holes seemed to come at him quite fast, but he remained focused on every single shot. He would remember little about any of them by the end of his final round. The par-three second hole was critical, with Venturi recovering from a bunker for his par. On the same hole, Jacobs would struggle for his five. Venturi continued through the first eight holes of his final round in one over par, missing only one short putt, which had died on the edge of the long par-four sixth hole.

The par-five ninth, the Ravine Hole, the longest on the course at 599 yards, looked like a mountain to climb. He drove solidly, but walked extra slowly. His second shot was an excellent one-iron. He approached the hole with a subtle nine-iron, pitching his ball to within 15 feet of the pin. It was a tough putt. Venturi imagined a serious break. It was a tricky downhill putt, definitely breaking right to left. The ball made its way slowly towards the hole, breaking a good 18 inches, before catching the low side and dropping in for a birdie four. He half-lifted his left arm in celebration, but did not have the energy to punch the air above his head, and quickly his arm dropped back to his side.

Venturi had gone out in an even-par 35, but not one single hole was lodged in his memory. He was still two under for the championship. More importantly, he was playing in a place, within his head, which recognised no dangers. There were no fears whatsoever.

'That makes him the leader!' he heard someone say. The words had floated past Venturi's left ear. Jacobs took six at the ninth hole, for 39 shots on the front nine, and he was now standing at level par for the championship. Palmer was two over for the title. Ken Venturi was leading the 64th US Open Championship by two shots.

McIlroy took it safely through the second and third holes. A long two-putt at the second was necessary, but the third hole showed rock-solid temperament. He pushed his drive slightly right into the rough, but he then sensibly ignored the flag tucked behind the greenside bunker on the right and played to the heart of the green. His caddie, J. P. Fitzgerald, took the stars and stripes cover off his man's putter and McIlroy simply two-putted for his par. Westwood and Yang remained at six under par, nine shots behind.

On the long, demanding fourth hole, a 470-yard dog-leg right with trees coverging on both sides of the landing area, another three-wood left the leader ideally placed to attack the pin on the smallish green. He knocked a wedge shot to four feet. The birdie was so easily assembled and executed that McIlroy's nerves did not appear to be at work in any portion of his body.

He was 16 under par, and he saved par on the fifth hole, with its dog-leg left and sloped fairway. From too far out, McIlroy's first putt looked edgy, but he drained his second without any doubt about his putting stroke, and with the unwavering intention to take the shot without the three practice swings that had been part and parcel of his game at Augusta National two months earlier, but had now been dispensed with altogether thanks to the sound advice of his putting doctor, Dave Stockton.

Beside him, Yang was holding his ground, rooted in his solid game and not really going anywhere. Westwood, meanwhile, was in the water half-guarding the front right of the sixth green.

With his approach to the same green, 15 minutes later, McIlroy also was too close to the pond for comfort, but he reached the putting surface. He walked off the green with his par five.

Yang birdied the same hole to close the gap between leader and second place. The difference was back to eight shots. McIlroy parred the remaining three holes as well to finish two under for the day on the front nine.

Rory McIlroy had gone out in 34 shots.

Ken had remained at the point of collapse for well over two hours, and Dr Everett had continued to interrupt his concentration to provide him with fluid, as well as salt tablets. In fact, before his round was completed, Ken would have received 18 salt tablets from the doc. But he wasn't counting the number of tablets, which on their own had been far too many and a great danger to his already troubled system. He had not been counting tablets, or scores. He had only ever looked for his ball, and thought of making the next shot.

The expanse of water in front of the 10th green presents itself as a place where demons could have an infinite amount of fun in so many ways.

The 218-yard par-three also has two large bunkers guarding the back of the green. The green itself has a spine dividing it, with the right front a natural collection area for golf balls, and the rest of the frontage ensuring that any ball that comes up short is reclaimed by the water. All in all, quite a delight in trickery.

But McIlroy's six-iron to the heart of the green paid absolutely no attention to any of these distractions and dangers, and his ball finally rested itself inches from the cup. His third birdie of the day moved him up to 17 under par.

Between the ninth green and the 10th tee, it formally registered with Ken Venturi that he was now in the lead of the United States Open. He held that thought, and he wondered how many people all around him, and watching on their television sets, were now waiting for him to crumble under the pressure.

But, when that thought landed in his head, it did not land with a bang or a thud. It landed softly. He remained unworried.

Venturi was *un-chokeable*. The writers and neuroscientists who, over all the years of professional golf, had sought to understand the act and manner of an elite professional choking under the most intense pressure, would have found Ken Venturi safely insulated, and incapable of a mental collapse, in the main owing to the extreme levels of distress and exhaustion that his body was experiencing. As Matthew Syed had written in *Bounce*, the best-selling book explaining performance and non-performance, Venturi was playing the most important 18 holes he would ever play in his life, entirely from his 'implicit' memory. 'Many hours of practice have enabled [the elite sportsman] to code the stroke in implicit rather than explicit memory,' Syed had written. '[This migration] enables the expert player to integrate the various parts of a complex skill into one fluent whole, something that would be impossible at a conscious level because there are too many inter-connecting variables for the conscious mind to handle.'

Venturi was not playing the game at a conscious level as he turned for home, leading the US Open Championship by two shots at Congressional Country Club on the afternoon of June 20, 1964. He was far, far away from a state of mind that can bring such peril to a man leading a championship with the whole world watching. As Sian Beilock, a psychologist at the University of Chicago, had also explained, 'It is not the pressure in a pressure situation that distracts us into performing poorly.

'The pressure makes us worry and want to control our actions too much. And you cannot think your way through a routine, practiced action, like making a three-foot putt. That's what happens when people choke. They try to think their way through the action.'

Venturi was bedded as deeply in his subconscious as any leader of any championship in golf had ever been. His game was indeed untouchable. As long as he could remain on his feet; as long as he did not, finally, collapse on those few closing holes.

'My mind was too vacant to wander to the wrong places, to the old demons,' Venturi would admit. 'I played strictly on instinct.'

On the par-four 10th hole, standing at 459 yards and with the green tightly guarded, Venturi had some good fortune in saving his par. His second shot struck a spectator's foot. He managed to get as close to the pin as he could, and seeing the line to the hole magnificently, his putt from 18 feet astonished those who had walked with him for almost three hours.

He could barely move at any sort of pace. His body was still shutting down, it appeared, and without the constant interruptions from Dr Everett, it surely would have done so, but Venturi could still see every shot that he needed to play.

There was a great roar from the gallery enveloping the 10th green, supported by rounds of whistling, and lengthy hand-clapping, as Venturi courageously grappled for his par.

People want me to win this thing, he told himself.

Rory's three-wood, more than any other club in his bag, was directing him home, to the sumptuous clubhouse high up on the hill at Congressional Country Club. That three-wood, which his caddie, J. P. Fitzgerald, had hauled out of his bag and handed to him on the first tee box, was the primary instrument that was bringing him the US Open title. It's an old three-wood, from times past, but a favourite, and possessing a lovable scratch on its head. It was a club as affectionately handled and held as a father holds a young child. There were so many nice things about that three-wood.

Like, for instance, back on the fourth hole, when his ball that had been hit with that club pitched into the primary rough but, rather than dig itself deep into the grass, it jumped out into the secondary cut, and then bounced back on to the fairway.

The little things that happen with a lovable club.

Whenever Venturi asked his caddie for a yardage, he was offered the same reply every time. 'You don't need the yardage, Mr Ken,' William Ward repeatedly responded. 'You're at the same exact yardage you were at this morning.'

Only after he had finished his round would Ward and others tell him that he used the same club on 14 occasions seeking to reach the green. But, in meeting the extraordinary demands of Congressional's Blue Course during Saturday's final two rounds of the US Open Championship, Venturi would use each of the 14 clubs in his bag at least once. This included his two woods: a driver and his home-made three-and-a-half-wood, which he had built up from a four-wood, his favourite wood.

When Venturi rolled in his putt from 20 feet on the 13th hole, the tough 448-yard par four, for a superb birdie, the crowd now swollen all around him roared their approval once more.

'YOU'VE GOT A FIVE-SHOT LEAD,' someone shouted in his direction.

Venturi was amazed. He had no idea that he had broken away from the rest of the field in such a manner over the preceding five holes. He had started his round two strokes back from Tommy Jacobs. If he actually had a five-shot lead, then there had been a seven-shot swing over the preceding 13 holes. But Ken knew little, if anything at all, about how that just happened.

Venturi was three under par for the championship. Jacobs was two over par. Palmer was three over.

A menacing gang of trees have guarded the left side of the fairway on the 12th hole at Congressional for quite some time. They make the severe dog-leg left a bit of a handful. The fairway slopes from right to left. The second shot plays slightly downhill to a green guarded left and right by sand.

A 471-yard par-four, it can be troublesome, and McIlroy and Yang both found trouble. Yang bogeyed. McIlroy opting for his driver might have been his first mistake on the hole. His second was a putt that slid by the cup when, the way McIlroy was playing, it looked just as easy to hole the thing.

He still led by eight shots walking to the 13th tee.

On the 14th tee, Dr Everett handed another bunch of salt tablets to Ken. He made him sip some more iced tea, and once again, as he had continually been doing for hours, he dipped a towel into a bucket of ice-cold water, wrung it out as hard as he could, and draped the cloth over Ken's head and shoulders.

On the 14th, Venturi hit one of his best drives of the entire day. When he stood over his ball, and took a few moments to try to somehow catch his breath, he decided that he needed a six-iron to hit the green, to be exactly where he wanted to be.

'No, it's a five-iron, Mr Ken,' William Ward insisted.

It was one of those very few occasions on the back nine when William Ward had spoken up and corrected Venturi.

Venturi stuck with his six-iron. He ended up short of the green by just a single foot, and in a trap. He had to blast out of the sand, using up more energy than he could afford. Too many bunker shots would be the undoing of his round. *They might actually finish me off*, thought Venturi. He had to settle for his bogey on the 14th, which brought him back to even par for his round. His lead was reduced to four shots.

He still knew he was hitting the ball solidly. 'On the hilly lies, I somehow knew the position I had to take and what I had to do,' he explained. 'I had done it a million times… relying on muscle memory… playing by feel.'

'There's a young, curly-haired kid out there going crazy on us,' McDowell told reporters when he finished his stubborn defence of his US Open title with a score of two under par for the championship. In any other year that might have been enough. Not in 2011, however.

McDowell was back home in Florida, and was seated with a friend in his local bar, The Tap Room at Lake Nona, back at the end of the first week of April, as Rory McIlroy was wretchedly making his way through the last 18 holes at Augusta National.

'I was a few pints deep,' McDowell would admit.

'There are very few golf tournaments that I will miss the cut in, and switch the TV on at the weekend. But Augusta is one of them.'

Two months later, even though he had already stated that the US Open at Congressional Country Club was not the stuff of a real US Open, he was thrilled to be at hand to see a fellow Northern Irishman succeed him as America's champion. A few hundred yards from where McDowell remained standing, doing his long round of post-tournament interviews with the world's media, McIlroy parred the 13th, 14th and 15th to remain in a perfect place; on the course and in that curly-haired head.

All available demons had gone home.

The 15th hole had Venturi close to home, but still seeming to be many, many miles from the safety of the clubhouse. It had all the appearances of a killer hole to all of those who had walked with Venturi for so long, and who now had faith in him making it the whole way to the 18th green, but who still found themselves being hit by waves of scurrilous doubts.

On the green, Venturi still had much work to do. He was 60 feet from the pin. Three putts would have been acceptable, even if a man had all of his senses fully at work. It was anyone's guess how Venturi would make it down, but he managed, somehow, to save his par with just two putts from so far away.

As he walked to the 16th hole, Venturi could not recognise anybody. He could not reply to anybody. He thought he had only minutes left. 'Venturi's gait was slow, and so was his swing, principally because he was so weak and tired that he couldn't possibly have overswung,' stated *The Washington Post* the next day.

On the 16th, he struck what most of those present felt was his greatest shot of the day, a one-iron to the heart of the green. His ball missed hitting the pin by two inches, and rolled 12 feet past. Utterly fatigued, Venturi stood over his ball. All he cared about was making his par. He stood there, trying somehow to get some air into his body, when he noticed the eyes of Joe Dey, the executive director of the United States Golf Association, who had walked with him unnoticed all through the afternoon, watching him. He made the par.

'Joe, you can penalise me two shots for slow play,' Venturi called over to him, 'but I've just got to walk slowly!'

Dey chuckled. He shook his head in Venturi's direction.

'Ken, it's downhill all the way to the 18th,' said Dey, who told Ken to keep his chin up and, no matter how slowly he was walking, to make sure that he had his head held high, as a champion's should be.

Venturi replied that he would do so. 'My head will be so high, they won't recognise me,' promised Venturi.

McIlroy's approach to the par-five 16th, with four small bunkers to the front right of the green, and one large monster of a sand-trap balancing the left side, was hit stone dead. The 579 yards had been gobbled up in two shots before that expert third. He made no mistake with his putt to go back to three under for his final round, and 17 under for the championship. Surprisingly, on the par-four 17th, he immediately gave the shot back to the course when, for the first time during his most glorious week, he took three putts on one green.

Buoyed by the support of the men from the USGA, Venturi felt stronger as he took on the 17th hole. But his drive caught the rough. He knew exactly what to do next, and that was to keep everything as simple, and tidy, as it had been for the preceding few hours. He deliberately played short of the bunker guarding the green, chipped to within 18 inches of the hole, and made his par.

Rory McIlroy posted his final round of 69. He had won the US Open by eight shots. He was 16 under par for the championship. He had built rounds of 65, 66, 68, and 69 to arrive at 268 shots.

It didn't matter who was second, but that totally forgotten position was Jason Day's on 276. Westwood and Yang shared third place, on 278, with the American pairing of Robert Garrigus and Kevin Chappell.

America lapped it up. 'Authenticity speaks for itself or not at all,' The Washington Post *would boldly state the following morning. 'Rory McIlroy seems to have it, both in his golf swing and in his face. From his understated gestures to his cocky-modest smile, from his twirl of the club as a perfect shot hangs in mid-flight to the image Sunday evening of his huge hug with his father beside the 18th green at Congressional Country Club, he makes us think,* There's the real thing.'

On the 18th tee box, Venturi took one last deep breath as he looked down at his ball. The official programme for the 1964 US Open described the final hole as, *One of the most spectacular and testing finishing holes in championship golf. Drive has to be threaded through an avenue of pine trees to descending fairway. Pear-shaped green juts dramatically out at an angle into a lake below the clubhouse. A trap short right, and a fringe of rough in front, dictate a bold second shot.*

It was just after 6.15 p.m., and the longest, hottest day in the history of golf was almost at an end. Venturi let it fly down the middle of the fairway. He had to walk 125 yards from the tee box down the fairway before he could take in a good view of the green. When he reached his ball, he also took in everything that lay in front of him – the magnificence of the clubhouse, the packed galleries that were six-deep on either side of him, and all of that water to the left of the green. 'That pond at the left, at that point, looked as big as the Pacific Ocean,' he would later reveal.

With his five-iron in his hands, he promptly knocked his ball into a right-hand bunker. 'I hit an iron to run up on the green,' he would recall, 'but instead of pulling left, the ball jumped right and went into the bunker. It shouldn't have, but it did.'

As he walked to the green, Venturi saw Joe Dey once again in the distance. He remembered to put his shoulders back, and tried as best he could to do just that, but without actually bringing much change at all to his physical appearance. His cap was soaked. He took it off his head as he reached closer to the putting surface.

There were more than 25,000 people waiting for him and, almost every man, woman and child in Congressional Country Club appeared to be cheering as heartily as any crowd had ever cheered in the long history of the proud home of golf in Bethesda.

Twice already, Venturi had earlier exploded out of bunkers. He confidently took his sand wedge from the hand of William Ward. His lie was clean, and the bunker had very little lip to it. Once more, he blasted out of the sand. His ball landed 12 feet from the hole.

A giant hush silenced the whole place. Venturi walked to his ball. The break was from left to right.

'But I pushed it! How it rolled up the incline and still found the hole is beyond me,' said Venturi, '...honest!'

There had not been a sound as Ken Venturi brought his putter back and struck his ball. The ball dropped into the hole and he dropped his putter to the ground.

'My God,' he cried out, 'I've won the Open!'

With the jam-packed galleries raised on their tippy-toes and roaring approval, Rory McIlroy walked off the 18th green where he met his father, Gerry.

'Happy Father's Day,' said the US Open champion.

McIlroy was surrounded by cheering supporters, and as he made his way off the green somebody in the crowd threw a Tricolour, the flag of the Republic of Ireland, in his direction. After so many of their great triumphs on the world stage, Irish golfers have traditionally wrapped themselves in the flag, and in its colours of green, white and orange, with the green representing the Gaelic or Catholic tradition, and the orange present to equally acknowledge the country's Protestant community and the followers of William of Orange, the Dutch king who fought and won the Battle of the Boyne in 1690, just north of Dublin, against the Catholic King James. The white of the flag divides the two colours, as a welcoming truce between the two warring populations in Ireland down through the centuries.

Any time Irish footballers or athletes have achieved on the world stage in modern times, the Tricolour has been paraded by the winners. And, especially after victories on golf courses and, in particular, Ryder Cup triumphs with Europe, Irish golfers have accepted the flag in celebration, most notably after the Ryder Cup victory over the United States in 2004 at Oakland in Michigan, when Ulster's Darren Clarke had the orange portion of the flag wrapped around his giant frame, while Padraig Harrington and Paul McGinley were left with the green end.

The flag landed against McIlroy's midriff. Moments later it was gone, out of sight completely. Nobody seemed to know what had become of it. For Rory McIlroy, pictures of whom can still be found on the internet as a big kid, sitting in a formal pose wearing a green jacket, with a gold three-leaf shamrock adorning his blazer pocket, before representing a 32-county Ireland in an amateur competition, that was probably a good thing.

McIlroy had risen to become one of the greatest golfers on the planet, without carrying with him even the slightest mark of any political or religious beliefs or preferences. Very few people who watched him at work would know that his mother's and father's families and their forefathers were Catholic, or that late one night in 1972 his great-uncle had been mercilessly gunned down in the kitchen of his own East Belfast home by an Ulster Volunteer Force hit squad, while his four young daughters, Rory McIlroy's aunts, slept in their bedrooms upstairs.

Gerry and Rosie McIlroy are Catholics, married in the church where their only son was baptised, and the same church in which Rory's great-uncle Joe, a completely innocent man not involved in any form of sectarianism, was mourned after his cold-blooded murder at just 32 years of age.

A few days after his victory at Congressional Country Club, McIlroy would fly into Belfast Airport by private jet. 'With a private security firm by his side,' wrote Suzanne Breen in the Daily Mail *newspaper, 'he returned home to the worst rioting in the city in years.' With images of hooded young men throwing petrol bombs on the streets of East Belfast, graphic TV footage that had appeared to have been a thing of the awful past for the people of the city, it was impossible for McIlroy not to comment on what was happening just a few miles from his parents' home the same week as he was being crowned US Open champion.*

Bricks and Molotov cocktails flew threw the air for two nights. The Police Service of Northern Ireland cited Loyalist paramilitaries, masked members of the UVF who were supposed to be observing a ceasefire, as the organisers of the rioting and for attacking Catholic homes in

Short Strand, a small Catholic community in the predominantly Protestant East Belfast part of the city.

Six shots were reportedly fired from the Catholic area, with Loyalists returning fire. Two men on the Loyalist side suffered gunshot wounds to their legs, but bullet marks on police vehicles were blamed on the UVF. These shots were treated as attempted murder of officers. The rioting continued, with police numbering the people involved at somewhere between 400 and 500, as nearby Holywood Golf Club, with its happily mixed membership of mostly Protestants, but with a decent number of Catholics as members also, was preparing a serious welcome home for their special boy.

'I know that 99.9 per cent of the population don't want to see that,' stated McIlroy. 'Everybody just wants to live in peaceful times. I am aware that I am going to be portrayed as a role model.

'I have to be careful in what I say... and do.'

Ken Venturi was on the point of collapse as the surge of emotion from winning the United States Open poured out of the wreckage of his body. Somehow, he had completed his final 18 holes and finished his four rounds of 72, 70, 66 and 70, for a two-under-par total of 278. He was only the second player in 64 stagings of the US Open Championship to break the magical 280 barrier, two shots off Ben Hogan's immovable total of 276 in 1948.

'The 66 in the morning was great and all that,' Venturi would remember by the year's end, 'but the 70 in the afternoon overshadowed it a thousand times. I really never knew where I was. Like a robot, I just kept going, going, going. The pin at the end of each hole looked like a telephone pole.

'All I could see was that pin. I would just keep moving from the tee to the ball to the green. The ball kept on going straight, and I would follow it.'

A 76 left Tommy Jacobs on two over par and in second place all on his own. The New Zealander, and reigning British Open champion, the left-handed Bob Charles, had played Saturday's double round sensationally in 71, 68 and was one shot further back in third place on 283. The former Open champion Billy Casper had also held strong on the Saturday for rounds of 69, 71 for fourth place. Meanwhile, Arnold Palmer finished in a tie for fifth place after his final round of 74 left him at six over par, on 286, and all of eight shots back from the new Open champion. Jack Nicklaus was among the also-rans. Defending champion Julius Boros, who had claimed the championship in the Country Club at Brookline after shooting nine over and then beating Palmer and Jacky Cupit in an 18-hole play-off, had perished faster than most in the severe heat. He did not make the cut.

The Blue Course at Congressional had won, hands-down, though, over almost all of the field during those three shocking days. Of the 410 rounds played in the championship, only nine were under par and 10 were even par.

Venturi felt too weak to bend down and actually take his winning ball from the cup on the 18th green. That act was completed by his partner, Ray Floyd, who handed Venturi his ball. As he did so, Venturi noticed that the young man's eyes were filled with tears. Venturi would also be handed a winning cheque after the 64th staging of the US Open that totalled $17,500. It was his first tournament win in four punishing years.

The last win had come in August 1960, when everything had seemed just so fine with his life and what lay in front of him. That was the year he was the second biggest money-winner on the tournament circuit. He had won the the Crosby in January, and in April he was sitting in the clubhouse at Augusta National, the Masters title apparently all his, before Arnold Palmer birdied the last two holes to snatch it away from him. By August of 1960, when he won the Milwaukee Open, he had notched up the 10th tournament victory of his young career, and had totalled $41,230 in winnings.

Then the four-year descent commenced, in which time he had dropped from No.14 on the PGA Tour money list in 1961, to 94th in 1963, when he had a pittance of $3,848 to show for his full year's work.

TIGER WHO? *asked the headline on the back page of the* New York Daily News. MOVE OVER TIGER! *ordered the* New York Post, *which did not impress the newspaper's golf columnist, Mark Cannizzaro, who argued that 'to suggest at this early stage of McIlroy's career that he's on his way to overtaking what Tiger Woods has done in the game is preposterous.' The* Chicago Daily Herald *was not taking any chances, and above a photo of McIlroy on its front page was the word* FLAWLESS.

USA Today *decided that the best thing to do was to poll its readers with the question, 'Do you expect McIlroy to chase down Tiger and Jack?' The question made people rein in their emotions somewhat.*

36%: 'No. Let us not get stupid over one victory'

35%: 'No. But he'll pass a lot of others'

17%: 'Yes. That US Open was a major announcement'

12%: 'Yes. What good is life if we can't dream'

The three-times major champion, Padraig Harrington, stuck to some maths. 'If you are going to talk about somebody challenging Jack's record [of 18 majors], there's your man,' stated the Dubliner. 'Winning majors at 22 with his talent… he'd have 20 more years or so… probably 100 more majors in him where he could be competitive. It would give him a great chance.'

Jack Nicklaus and Gary Player were in McIlroy's corner, Nicklaus especially. 'He's humble when he needs to be humble, and confident when he needs to be confident,' said the Golden One. 'I like his moxie – he's cocksure, and you've got to have that.'

Others brought golfing folk back a generation before Nicklaus and Player and Arnold Palmer. The longevity and general busyness of modern golfers was compared with the natural inclination of golfers in the 1920s, '30s and '40s to retire early. Former US Open champion Tony Jacklin reminded people that Byron Nelson had retired at 34 years of age to become a rancher, and that before him Bobby Jones had finished up at the foolishly young age of 28. Jacklin had no doubt that McIlroy had the right people around him to see him survive and prosper as a champion golfer. Jacklin labelled the money on offer to young men like Rory McIlroy as 'obscene', but advised McIlroy, 'You've still got to have a life, and have a good time.'

Rory McIlroy's cheque for winning the 2011 US Open Championship was €978,362. He had moved to No.3 in the world rankings, with only the shaky English pairing of Luke Donald and Lee Westwood standing between him and the No.1 position, but it was the late Seve Ballesteros whom most writers and broadcasters were twinning, in every second sentence, with the name of Rory McIlroy.

And it was not just journalists who were thinking of the former king of European golf. So, too, were some of the game's greatest players. Greg Norman had seen fit to text NBC's Jimmy Roberts, who read the Aussie's tribute on air. 'Europe lost a genius [Seve] this year, but has found his replacement.'

Chubby Chandler was leading that charge. 'I think he is going to be world-wide in popularity,' said the ISM boss. 'Seve was Spanish, but he was everybody's. Rory's Irish but everybody takes to him.'

The round figure of $1 billion in potential career earnings and endorsements was blurted out by one British sports marketing executive, and another, Steve Martin, the chief executive of MC Saatchi Sport Entertainment, said McIlroy could reach 'scary numbers' very quickly. 'Over the next 10 years, he is going to be the 100 million man. Not dollars, pounds!' stated Martin.

McIlroy's starting point upon officially being labelled a world superstar was already built upon blue-chip names, including EA Sports (he featured on the Tiger Woods PGA Tour PlayStation and X-Box games), Titleist (golf clubs and balls), Oakley (sunglasses and clothing), Audemars Piguet (watches), Jumeirah Group (Middle East luxury hospitality), Footjoy (shoes), Skins (compressed sport clothing), Sunseeker (speed boats) and Trion:Z (ionic bracelets).

'A lot of sponsors paid for the potential for what he had [in their original deals]. They have not come cheap,' added Chandler, happily, mentioning that four of the contracts had bonus clauses built in that would be triggered if Rory McIlroy happened to win a major during the contractual period.

One hefty clothing manufacturer, also, was making noises about moving in and 'cleaning up the logos' on McIlroy's person by buying out all existing contracts. Though that was not going to be a straight-forward conversation, as everybody liked what they had with McIlroy, in particular Audemars Piguet, the luxury watch maker, who had the immediate joy of having McIlroy fulfil a corporate engagement for them at Cape Cod on the Monday after his victory at Congressional Country Club, and who had their contract with him running until 2014.

'It's nice to play for a lot of money, week in and week out,' commented McIlroy. 'We're very fortunate we can do that. But the thing about these major championships is the history, the prestige. And just to be able to add your name to a list like Ben Hogan, Jack Nicklaus, Arnold Palmer... That's the most satisfying thing about it.'

When it came time to exchange scorecards with his playing partner, Ken Venturi realised that he was handing Ray Floyd a blank card. He had been too weak and ravaged with exhaustion to write down any scores over the preceding five hours. Venturi sat in the scorers' tent and didn't know what to say, or do. But a scorekeeper in his large entourage had kept a careful record of the day's scoring. The numbers were duly inserted into the blanks. Everyone knew that signing an incorrect card would mean disqualification. The numbers were double-checked, and then checked one final time.

'If you offered me a million dollars, I couldn't tell you one shot Ray hit,' Venturi admitted. He was unable to sign his own card either. He put the pencil that was in his hand back down on the table in front of him. He was too scared to move. He remembered nothing, not a thing. He sat there frozen, trying to think. 'Sign the card, Ken,' assured Joe Dey, 'it's correct.' Ray Floyd's final round had left him tied for 14th place.

So close to the power centre of the entire planet, just 10 miles from the White House and the US Capitol, the Supreme Court and the Pentagon, Rory McIlroy sat centre-stage in a golfing world that, post-Tiger Woods, was now patiently awaiting its new leader.

He sat in front of a preposterously large collection of media personnel in one single room, and awaited the questioning. When it came it was mostly reverential. Nobody was there to spoil the notion of a future coronation, even though in the days following some would mention a few small home truths, such as the receptive nature of the greens at Congressional Country Club that week. Colin Byrne, the popular caddie and best-selling author, said in his column in The Irish Times: *'Despite the sub-air system working overtime throughout the weekend in an effort to dry out the greens, the fact was that there was a soft "thud" as most players' approach shots landed on the greens rather than the hollow "thonk" that we expect at the event.'*

Byrne noted, especially, that the massive length of the Blue Course at Congressional, its soft greens and its non-penal rough, had all conspired to eliminate half of the field, and leave the US Open the preserve of the really long hitters. For men like McIlroy. The intense heat the week before the championship, and the thunderstorms during the week of the event, had left the organisers helpless in offering their course up in any other condition.

Byrne, though, like everybody else, remained in awe of the manner in which McIlroy and his caddie, J. P. Fitzgerald, had remained 'in full control of their faculties' for the four remarkable days, never once flinching like they had at Augusta National, and ensuring that right through the final round their aggressive strategy was maintained, with practically every shot finishing pin high.

At his press conference, McIlroy was quick to address his complete self-destruction over the final nine holes at Augusta National two months earlier. He knew it was demanded of him, and he did not falter. 'I felt like I got over the Masters pretty quickly. I kept telling you guys that, and I don't know if you believed me,' he stated matter-of-factly.

'But, here you go [pointing to the US Open trophy]… nice to prove some people wrong. I was very honest with myself, and I knew what I needed to do differently. And that was the thing. I had a clear picture in my mind of what I needed to do, and where my focus needed to be when I got myself in that position again.'

McIlroy knew that he had learnt more about himself in the two months after his loss in the Masters than many golfers discover within themselves in their entire careers. He had no doubt.

'If you'd asked me, when I turned pro when I was 18, do you think you'd win a major by the time you're 22? I'd have said, "No." But to contend in the majors, how I have so early, I don't really know what I can put it down to, if it's just hard work and practice, or if I feel I just have a little bit more focus or intensity for major weeks. I'm not too sure.

'All I wanted to do was to play golf when I was growing up. I wanted to become the best that I could be. I probably said back then, I want to try to become the best in the world! In some ways, I'm on my way to trying to do that.'

Though the hard work had started so far back. 'A lot of those early days was fundamentals,' he explained about his work with Michael Bannon over 15 years. 'Getting a good grip, good set-up, good alignment, everything like that, building the base of the swing.' He explained what happened after that.

How, at an early age, he used to be very upright, how his left arm used to be very, very high at the top. Then he remembered, at about 13 or 14, he began to develop a very flat swing. Bannon and he worked, daily, to get that swing just right. By 16, that swing was *pretty much where the coach and pupil wanted it to be, and that was where it still remained.*

He reminisced about the science that Hurrion brought to his putting game, and the simplicity that Stockton had recently added to those technical necessities. 'People often said to me, We think you're too quick on the greens! *But he [Stockton] thought the opposite.* You're taking too much time. Why are you taking three practice strokes? Don't take any practice strokes any more! *I see the target, where I want to hit it, and just go with it. If I have any sort of technical thing in my thought, in my stroke, it would just be to keep the back of my left hand going towards the target, and that's all we really worked on.'*

Fifteen years of such hard work with Michael Bannon, finished off by two months of relaxed tutoring with Dave Stockton, and Rory McIlroy had become a golfer capable of ruling both of the world's greatest tours, in the United States and Europe.

In the Congressional clubhouse, Ken Venturi took a call from San Francisco, from his parents. Ethyl Venturi could barely speak between sobs of absolute joy for her son. Fred Venturi didn't gush.

Venturi Sr didn't need to. Neither did his son need to hear Fred say too much. Both men remembered one of their great, though short, conversations, which came at the end of a year in which Ken had won the San Francisco Amateur and the Californian Amateur titles, and some other assorted championships. Ken had begun to tell Fred how good he might be as a golfer, but his father stopped him in his tracks, early.

'Son, if you're as good as you say you are, you can tell anybody, but when you get really good, they'll tell you!'

Ken and Conni hugged long and hard. But the press were waiting, that large group of golf writers and broadcasters who had once loved young Ken Venturi, but had grown tired of him in the preceding four years. Suddenly, they would have a lot to chat about. But, first, to a man, they all rose and offered the professional golfer they had considered broken and best forgotten not too long before, a sustained and standing ovation. That surprised Ken. But his audience was equally surprised when the newly crowned US Open champion had more to say about a priest, a Father Francis Kevin Murray, assistant pastor at the St Vincent de Paul Church in the Marina district of San Francisco, than anybody else.

'I am happy and grateful, and thankful,' stated the champ, 'because eight or nine months ago, I thought that such days as this were over. I don't know what was wrong with me for certain, but one man told me many things that helped me, a man from San Francisco called Father Francis Murray.' Ken explained where he had been in his life when he met Father Murray, how he was ready to give up on golf, and was ready to go back to selling cars. And how his life had been changed through their meeting. 'Through Father Murray, and my wife Conni, I have been able to make this day possible. Now I am lost for words. This is the happiest day of my life.'

Before the press briefing was completed, there was one last question.

'Out there, Ken,' came the question, 'did you think at all about the last round when you blew the Masters in '56?'

Ken thought long and hard before answering. He then threw out some thoughts, before gathering himself again. It was a question he wanted to answer emphatically. 'It was a windy day [at Augusta in 1956] but I didn't play too badly,' he finally commenced, seeking to nail his answer to the clubhouse door in Congressional Country Club.

'Sure, I hit 42 on the back nine, but I still insist that I didn't play that badly. I tell you this, if I had to do it all over again, I wouldn't change one thing that has happened to me in my whole life, because I've found out a lot about myself, a lot about my friends, a lot about life and, even if I never win again, it's proved to me that I could do something I hoped and prayed for all my life.'

Before finishing, Ken was the person to bring up Augusta National one last time. 'The last time I talked to some of you fellows was at Augusta in 1960 when Palmer made those two birdies on the final two holes. Somebody walked in and yelled "PLAGUE", and you all ran out. I was sitting there twiddling my thumbs and drinking a soft drink.' With that, the talking soon ended.

Ken Venturi had to find someone else fast. William Ward, when they came eye to eye, was controlling his excitement and complete satisfaction at a job expertly done. When Ken handed him a cheque for $1,000 and told him it was his, Ward finally broke down, but just a little.

'Mr Ken,' he said, 'you're the damndest golfer I ever saw in my life.' For the rest of their lives, their friendship would endure.

Any time Ken arrived back at Congressional Country Club he would seek out his old caddie. That was usually after Ken's career as a pro golfer had ended, and he was turning up with the CBS team to cover the Kemper tournament in Bethesda. Ken liked to hit chip shots and putts for half an hour on such visits, and always William Ward would be back at his side, 'shagging' balls for his favourite golfer.

And, always, when the pair hugged at the end of each of those meetings, Ken Venturi clasped two $100 bills into Ward's rugged hands.

Rory McIlroy was honest enough to admit that he had not spoken often enough to his caddie, J. P. Fitzgerald, before and during their final round at Augusta National. 'That was another thing I learnt,' he had informed the media. 'I feel like, even if it's not about golf, having a conversation about something completely different is probably the best thing for me because it takes my mind off it, and it stops me getting too involved in what I'm doing.'

During the final round at Congressional, McIlroy had chatted to J. P., on every fairway, conversation after conversation, about everything and anything, trying not to think about the very next shot until the time came for the two of them to size up what that shot demanded of them. It had worked brilliantly.

'We sat down after Augusta and realised where we both went wrong. We didn't communicate like we usually do. Everything had gone very quiet; everything went way too serious. Okay, you're leading the Masters, so of course it's serious. But it [Sunday] was different from the way I'd treated the Thursday at the Masters. I'd warm up, I'd chat, I'd just be loose, then go out and shoot 65. There is no reason why it shouldn't be exactly like that on the Sunday afternoon. You're just going out to play 18 holes of golf.'

Conni and Ken Venturi stayed at Congressional Country Club for many more hours. There was the lovable fussiness of the official presentation, and lots more grand speech-making. There was, also, the peacefulness of cleaning out his locker. When they finally got back to the Governor's Motel, where there was champagne and hors d'oeuvres awaiting them, Venturi did something that he had not done all year. He had a drink.

He poured himself a glass of white wine, and privately thanked Dave Marcelli, the bartender in San Francisco who had told him, nine months earlier, that it was time for Ken Venturi to get his life back on the right track. There were dozens of messages of congratulations awaiting Ken and Conni, and there were important calls to return, among them one to Byron Nelson. When Nelson got to speak with his best-loved pupil, quietly, there was 'Grade A' pride welling up inside the old master, who had won his own US Open, one of five major triumphs in his glorious career, exactly 25 years earlier.

Bing Crosby also needed to talk to the young man he had taken care of on so many occasions during his fledgling career. Bing cried, and cried the tears of a happy man, on the other end of the line. The famous TV chat-show host, Ed Sullivan, also called personally. He wanted to book Venturi on the most watched show in the country, which had welcomed The Beatles to America for the first time just four months before, for the following night.

Venturi was told that the White House had just issued a special invitation from President Johnson to lunch, so that the President could personally congratulate the new US Open champion on his splendid win. That telephone call especially tickled Venturi and his wife more than any other. At the beginning of the week, Ken Venturi was considered not made of right enough stuff to attend the pre-tournament function at the White House with the favourites and past champions. Now, the President wanted to meet him one on one.

Ken felt enormously honoured and excited, but he knew that he must turn down the most powerful man in the Western world. He had to rush to New York on Sunday afternoon for *The Ed Sullivan Show* on CBS and then, the following day, he had an important lunch at Toots Shor's restaurant in the city, which he would not miss for the whole world.

'With no disrespect to the President, please give him my regrets,' said Ken. 'But I have an appointment with Toots Shor.'

Three weeks earlier, when Venturi had eaten in Toots's place and knew he had barely enough money in his pocket to pay for his plate of food, he had been told that Toots had offered a drink to everyone in his establishment, courtesy of Mr Ken Venturi himself! Toots loved athletes of every persuasion. He had a soft spot for Ken Venturi as well. And, when Ken quickly told Toots that he was barely able to pay his own way, never mind pay for drinks for everyone packing the place out, Toots had patted him on the back, and told him not to worry about paying for anything at all in his restaurant.

'Who's worrying, pally?' Toots had said. 'Forget it.'

Ken assured him he'd be back. 'Toots, I'll come back when I win one,' he replied. 'I will be back!'

'I know you will, you crum bum!' laughed Toots, showering Venturi in the sort of affectionate language that he normally reserved for footballers and all other ball players.

Now Toots had invited him back to his place, and Ken would show up and receive a standing ovation. He tried his best to wrap his arms around Toots, who was delivering a crushing bear hug in return, and he told Toots that this time, he was the champ of the United States, and he could pay his way.

'I've been in the restaurant business a lot of years and this is the first time everybody in the joint acted like yokels,' said Toots.

'What'd ya do… ya win something, ya bum?'

Holly Sweeney stood at the back of the room in Holywood Golf Club, as Rory McIlroy talked excitedly to the mostly Irish and British journalists packing out the place. There were not only golf writers and sports journalists in the room. There were journalists of all natures and descriptions, and a good number of female news reporters who had been dispatched by their editors, to the homecoming of the US Open champion in Belfast, to find out a great deal more about the exact state of Holly and Rory's loving relationship.

His parents, Gerry and Rosie, his uncles and aunts and all of his cousins were at their local golf club, where Gerry had once tended the bar when he was trebling up on his jobs to pay Rory's way from boyhood to manhood on the golf course. There was pandemonium outside the modest brick building, with hundreds and hundreds of people milling about the place, and so many cars, TV trucks, friends and inoffensive busybodies turning up. It was an overcast day but still some members of the Holywood club stuck to tradition and headed out on to the course, overlooking a glum Belfast Lough on a showery day. But in the car park and inside the clubhouse, with its threadbare carpet and that stuffy, soiled air that is so common to every busy little golf club, there was an overwhelming mood of great joy.

Knowing the layout of his club inside-out, it had been no problem for McIlroy, wearing a black T-shirt with sponsors' names, jeans and with his white baseball cap featuring the word 'Jumeirah' *loudly across the front, to slip into the clubhouse through a rear door. Deep inside the little building, he quickly had to run through the order of his life for the next few weeks, officially getting his comings and goings down on record.*

Rory informed everyone that he had decided to take the next several weeks off in order to fully savour his first major triumph. The Open Championship, at Royal St George's in Sandwich, on the south-east coast of England the following month, was named as his next scheduled date on a golf course. He was then going to take another week off, before lining up in the Irish Open in Kerry, and the WGC-Bridgestone Invitational at the Firestone Country Club in Akron, Ohio, before heading south to Atlanta for the US PGA Championship.

He'd had messages of congratulations from everyone, he said, from Jack Nicklaus to Arnold Palmer. 'Anything from Manchester United team boss, Alex Ferguson?' he was asked. 'Uh... I'm sure there is,' he hesitated slightly, 'but there have been so many!'

'Anything from Tiger Woods?'

Again, McIlroy faltered for a second or two. 'Err, no,' he replied, before remembering after a second pause that he had seen a congratulatory note.

There was one big question, however, in among all of the golf talk. 'What about Holly and Rory?'

'Last week was fabulous,' McIlroy told everyone who was packed into the function room at his home club. 'The golf I played... I've never played before in my life. I always wanted to believe I could win a major but... until you do, you never know.' Holly Sweeney remained at the back of the room as he spoke.

The talking inside lasted for two hours, and a large crowd had gathered outside the tiny clubhouse balcony to properly cheer their man when he did appear with his trophy held tightly with both hands.

'One for the ladies, Rory,' suggested a female reporter. 'You're one of the most wanted men in sport right now. Could you put all of the ladies out of their misery and tell us are you single, or have you a lady friend?'

Rory smiled, and waited a moment, and then proudly made Holly's presence known to everyone who had not already noticed her within the tightly compressed room. 'She's waving at you from the back of the room,' Rory replied breezily to the question. Holly looked so happy and so young, and she beamed, gently acknowledging the TV cameras and the many heads twisting around to look at her.

'So you're both back on track then?' came a second question.

'Uh... yeah!' Rory replied.

The entire room seemed to share one prolonged giggle of happiness for the 22-year-old US Open champion and his 20-year-old partner.

Rory, finally, was told that it was time to make his way out on to the small clubhouse balcony and say hello to his fans waiting patiently for him. He clutched his US Open trophy and walked outside.

Bottles of champagne were opened, and sprayed at the champion. He laughed and waved, and thanked everyone for coming out to see him. Holly didn't join him on the balcony.

Holly remained inside, while Rory got through the celebration alone.

A couple of weeks after his US Open win, it was time for Ken Venturi to head back home to San Francisco, where he was to be honoured with a welcoming parade in his native city. On the flight, he was delighted to find himself sitting next to Joe DiMaggio, someone he had idolised all his life. Baseball, after all, had been Ken's first love, and it was also the first game he found that he could play damn well, and leave his faltering confidence and stammering well to one side.

He was happy out there, manning centre field, alone, not having to talk to anybody. He had been good enough to catch the eye of the famous scout for the New York Yankees, Lefty O'Doul, and he had a try-out with them, but quickly Venturi chose the minor luxuries of being a golfer to the smelly, shuttling buses that had baseball players crammed inside of them.

Ken and DiMaggio had been friends for some years. They had played golf together quite often, though usually in private, as the great legend of the ballpark didn't like galleries. He had never managed to beat his handicap to lower than a 16. 'You're Joe DiMaggio,' Ken had always told him. 'Who cares what you shoot?'

But Joe always cared.

Now, on a plane headed west, Ken and Joe talked like two of the greatest sportsmen in the world might talk together. Conni left them alone and moved back down to the rear of the plane to read.

When they neared San Francisco, Ken asked the living legend if he would do him the great honour of walking off the plane with him and his wife?

'Nothing doing,' replied DiMaggio. 'This is your day, Ken.'

When the doors of the plane finally opened, Ken could not see DiMaggio anywhere. He stood there with Conni, waiting to leave the plane last, but he had not seen Joe leave. Hours later, he would discover that Joe DiMaggio had asked the stewards to allow him to exit the plane on the hoist truck that removes the empty food containers.

Neither did Ken Venturi see Joe DiMaggio for the rest of the day, in the home town they both shared. The most famous sportsman in all of America simply disappeared, leaving Ken Venturi alone on the greatest stage he had ever dared imagine in his life. He received the key to the city that afternoon, and Ken and Conni were then carried in the front car of a thronged parade down Market Street, San Francisco's very own Fifth Avenue, on an amazing three-mile ride from the Embarcadero on the waterfront to the hills of Twin Peaks.

CHAPTER THIRTEEN

Ken ... after journeying from Augusta to Bethesda

In October 1964, Ken Venturi flew to England with Conni to play in the Piccadilly World Match Play Championship at Wentworth. In his first match he was drawn against Gary Player. It was a severely cold afternoon, with the bitterest of north-east winds blowing over the whole country, and constant rain showers didn't help to warm anybody up either. At the end of 31 holes, Venturi and Player were all-square. Strangely, on that 31st hole, Venturi had half-topped his shot to the green.

On the next hole, he topped another iron shot. He blamed each effort on the biting cold, and the numbness that was setting in along his fingers. Venturi lost the match 2 and 1, but on those last four holes he noticed that his fingers were blistered, and that the skin had begun to peel. He put the condition of his hands down to the cold, or some allergy or other.

The next month, he was playing in the Mexican Open. It was more of a family holiday for the Venturis, and Ken was not too bothered that he was playing poorly once again, but in the chill of the hotel swimming pool, he again noticed that his fingers were whitened. They looked withered even. There was, on occasion, no feeling in the tips of them at all.

In December, in Palm Springs, it snowed of all things! Venturi was playing a match with Big Mike Souchak as his partner, and the course had to be closed because of the gathering whiteness. But midway through the round Venturi lost all feeling in the middle finger of his right hand. It was also starting to hurt intensely.

Over the course of the final three months of 1964 he had been to several doctors. Nobody could explain to him what the problem was, but for Ken Venturi there was also so much *not* to worry about. By the year end, he was named PGA Player of the Year. He was elected to *Golf Magazine*'s All-American team, and *Sports Illustrated* named him on the front cover as its Sportsman of the Year, after he had out-polled baseball's Ken Boyer, swimmer Don Schollander, who had won four gold medals at the Olympic Games in Tokyo that summer, and the Baltimore Colts' quarterback Johnny Unitas.

He had ended 1963 with winnings of $3,848. By the close of 1964, he had earned himself $62,466 in official tournament money, and when added to endorsements, appearances and other bits and pieces, his grand total for the 12 months was very close to $200,000.

The pain in Venturi's hands continued, however. Lee Walls, an outfielder with the Los Angeles Dodgers, told him it looked like a problem he'd seen before with one of his team-mates, and mentioned a doc he should go to. The doctor duly told Venturi his problem was a circulatory disease, known as Reynaud's phenomenon. Under further questioning the doctor explained that the problem could go away or, worst case, the circulation could be choked off in his fingers and gangrene could set in. The fingers in that instance might have to be amputated, the doc concluded. Venturi was put on heavy doses of cortisone.

By the time he played in the Crosby at the start of 1965, Venturi was showing his hands to Arnold Palmer and Bob Goalby, who would win the Masters tournament the next year, and they were observing, Venturi remembered, the 'hands of a corpse'. There was little feeling left in either hand. He had trouble trying to wrap his fingers around a club. Golf tournaments came and went and Venturi tried to play, but he had little hope of doing anything out on the course when he had trouble enough handling his knife and fork over the dinner table in his home. Others were out-driving him by 100 yards. Instead of a five-iron approach, he was reduced to taking a full three-wood to reach some greens. His fingers were swollen by the cortisone injections, and he had to file off his wedding ring before it dug completely into his flesh.

At Augusta National, in April of 1965, Ken Venturi failed to make the cut, hitting 77 and 80 in his two opening rounds. At the dinner table, in the clubhouse on the Friday night of the tournament, Souchak insisted that Ken get an appointment with Dr James Roos at the Mayo Clinic in Minnesota. It was decided that he needed to go immediately. But Venturi was unable to fly out from Augusta the next morning. He needed a plane. The words were hardly out of his mouth when Arnold Palmer, the man who had haunted Venturi more than any other, insisted on Ken taking his.

'Take it any place you have to go,' Palmer told him, 'and keep it as long as you need it.'

At the Mayo Clinic, tests began afresh and, after several days, Dr Roos said he was fairly certain that Venturi had carpal tunnel syndrome. The doc explained that the nerves, tendons, ligaments and veins in his hands were being strangled by the band of tendons encircling his wrists, 'much like subcutaneous handcuffs'. He was told that surgery was required. Venturi wanted to defend his US Open title first. The doc warned him that he did not have time to wait. Gangrene would set in, soon enough, he was told. Venturi, nevertheless, decided to defend his Open title in St Louis, in June, and the preparations began. But his hands were a mess and the withdrawal symptoms from the lack of cortisone had him turning from a state of normality to a raging tantrum in seconds.

He would shout and scream, and cry uncontrollably at home with Conni. He picked up chairs and pictures and smashed them against walls. Several windows in the house were broken. One night, in a town named Banning, a 90-minute drive from Palm Springs, he was in a restaurant having a coffee at two o'clock in the morning.

He had no idea where he was.

He asked the staff to help him find his way back home. It was 5.30 a.m. before he got into his bed, and back to a state of some calmness.

But Ken still wanted to defend his US Open title at the Bellerive Country Club in St Louis, and had begun to paint the palms of his hands with Benzoin, a sticky balsamic resin, so that the club would not move in his hands when he struck the ball.

In the hours before the first round in Bellerive, Conni helped her husband get dressed. She then massaged his hands for almost an hour, in order to get the circulation going, and to enable him to open and close his fingers. In the first round he hit an 81. In his second round, he nailed an 18-foot birdie putt on the last for a 79. The tournament was over for him by Friday evening. Conni and Ken left the next morning for the Mayo Clinic.

The surgeon explained, before the procedure began, that once the carpal bands were cut, the blood should start flowing freely into his hands once more. Incisions were made at the bottom of each palm, and the wrists were sliced open. The left hand took 16 minutes; the right hand took 18 minutes.

A trace of gangrene was found in only one finger. By the time he was wheeled back into recovery, Venturi could feel the blood flowing back into his hands. There were 10 more days in hospital.

Venturi's hands were swathed in bandages, and back home on the West Coast Ken relied on Conni to bathe and dress him daily. Nevertheless, he felt the luckiest man in the world. He had a golf career awaiting his return.

That career recommenced in September, at the Ryder Cup at Royal Birkdale in north-west England, when the United States team, led by Venturi's loving mentor, Byron Nelson, took on Great Britain and Ireland. In the morning's foursomes on the opening Thursday, Venturi and Don January, from Texas, were paired against Peter Alliss, the famed BBC golf commentator from later years, and Ireland's untouchable Christy O'Connor Sr, a match the US would lose 5 and 4.

And Venturi would also lose to Alliss, 3 and 1, in their singles match on the closing Saturday. But the United States would win the cup 19½ to 12½. Ken Venturi thought he was back.

****

Ken Venturi would not come back. His hands would never fully recover. Too much damage had been done. And too little knowledge, in the mid-60s, about treating carpal tunnel syndrome would be the undoing of his career as a professional golfer. A decade or more later, doctors would be quite comfortable treating people with carpal tunnel as outpatients, stabilising the affected area with a splint and offering every chance of total recovery.

Many months into 1966, however, the pain in Venturi's hands remained. The whiteness would return at his fingertips, and any hope of playing the game as faultlessly as he once had, or any chance of swinging the club so fluently that even his fellow professionals shook their heads in admiration, was fading fast.

Venturi's last win as a professional, his 14th on the US Tour, would be in his own home town of San Francisco.

The Lucky International Open was played, in the spring of 1966, on the Harding Park public course on which Venturi had grown up, and where his father, Fred, was manager. It was a place that Venturi knew inch by inch. He was familiar with almost every blade of grass, though the deteriorating condition of the course and the antiquated facilities would mean that, by the end of the decade, the PGA would leave Harding Park for good. In 1966, however, the narrow and always demanding course had been left unplayed for almost two months in preparation for the big pro tournament. It was as perfect as it possibly could ever have been, and among the world-class field that flew into San Francisco to compete was Arnold Palmer. Venturi's last win as a professional golfer would come against the man who had stood in his way, more than any other golfer, and the man who had twice denied him at Augusta National Golf Club. The win over Arnie would be enacted in front of his mother and father, in front of Conni and all of his friends and neighbours.

On the first day, Venturi scored a 68, three under par, after hitting all 18 greens in regulation, but missing with putts eight times from within 10 feet. He was close to the leaders.

The Friday was colder on the West Coast. Venturi felt the old pains and general discomfort return to his hands. His old friend, Bill Varni, from the Owl and Turtle restaurant, who had once offered Venturi $50,000 in return for his year's winnings in the tough times of the past, carried four powered hand-warmers to help Ken. A photograph in the newspapers the next day would show Venturi, strangely, with his hand in Varni's pocket. At the halfway stage, Venturi was still in good shape, on 136.

The rain on the Saturday was an icy downpour. Venturi was in such trouble with his hands that he considered withdrawing from the tournament. His friends told him to give it one more hole, and one more after that. With his hands aching, Venturi tried, but knew it was impossible. He was saved by the cancellation of the day's play owing to the weather. When the third round recommenced on Sunday morning, Venturi felt better and finished with a 71. He was four behind the leader, Frank Beard. Souchak and Ray Floyd were tied for second. Venturi was neck-and-neck with Palmer. The final round was played on the Monday.

Venturi birdied the first hole of his final round, and reached the turn in 33 shots. He and Palmer were now tied for second place, but Beard was still four in front of them. Venturi decided to forget about Beard altogether, and think only about beating Palmer, the hot pre-tournament favourite. When he came off the 16th green, he heard that Beard had suffered a streak of bogeys.

Venturi was leading at Harding Park by one shot from Arnold Palmer, who would not birdie another hole. Venturi completed the back nine in another 33 shots, to finish with a 66, and an 11-under-par 273.

He had won. Palmer was two shots back. If he had been told, that evening, that he would never win another golf tournament as a professional, Ken Venturi would hardly have cared. But his last hurrah had, indeed, been played out at Harding Park.

****

Ken Venturi would never again show up at Augusta National with any real intent. His final visit to East Georgia was in 1969, when he missed the cut. The US Open Championship was also, very quickly, a competition that he needed to forget all about and he missed the cut there, also, when he played it one final time at Winged Foot in New York in 1974.

But, back in the summer of 1968, when he arrived in Grand Blanc, Michigan, for the Buick Open Invitational, Venturi had been told that Frank Chirkinian, the producer of golf coverage for CBS, wanted to have a word with him. The man from CBS wanted to know if Venturi was interested in doing 'some television'. *Didn't he know I was the guy who stammered?* Venturi thought to himself.

Venturi turned down the offer the first time he was asked. By then, he was spending more and more time in Palm Springs with a new friend in his life, Frank Sinatra. The pair would end up sharing a house together. Sinatra called Venturi, Kenneth, and

Venturi returned the compliment, calling the legendary entertainer Francis. During that time, Venturi noticed a side to Sinatra that was never disclosed in the media. He'd find Sinatra scouring the newspapers most mornings, looking for people who might need some help. He witnessed him hand Toots Shor $50,000, when Toots was down on his luck in the restaurant business.

****

Venturi always insisted that he and Sinatra never chased women together. But, while in Palm Springs with Sinatra in 1967, Ken Venturi met 'the first woman I ever really loved', as he stated in his second autobiography, *Getting Up and Down*, which was published in 2004, 38 years after his first autobiography, *Comeback.*

He was meeting Sinatra at Ruby's Dunes for dinner, but the first person he saw that evening was a woman in an orange dress, standing no more than five foot tall, called Beau. She worked as a hostess in the place. Venturi claims they fell in love with each other instantly. However, with Beau and himself both married, they knew there could be no relationship. One year later, Venturi would return to the same restaurant in order to see Beau one more time. He knew that both of their lives had to change.

Ken had dedicated his first autobiography, published in 1966, *To my wife Conni, and all the others who kept their belief in me through the darkest hours.* He had met Conni MacLean in 1952, when they were both at San Jose State, and throughout that 184-page autobiography he professed how much he always loved her, and how much he also owed her for being there for him through the 'darkest hours', which consumed long passages of his young life.

'I had Conni's fully restored love and understanding wrapped close around me,' he wrote in his first book, describing how she stood by him when the triumph of his US Open victory was suddenly stopped in its tracks by his own crippled hands. He had

Conni 'providing a warmth and sympathy'.

But, in his second life story, Ken painted a very different picture of his life with Conni. In this book, he made it quite clear that in his mind their marriage was not the real thing. He wrote that he had been 'masquerading' as a happy husband in love with a beautiful wife, and that both he and Conni were deserving of 'Oscars' for their performances.

'But, if you look closer, much closer, at some of those same pictures,' wrote Ken in that second autobiography, 'it is easy to see that I was not a happy husband. I was always gazing into the distance, not at Conni.'

In the second writing of his life's story, Ken was unequivocal about Conni MacLean's role in the great triumph of his golfing career. 'The Open was my triumph, not hers.'

He cited Conni for being loyal only when he was doing well on the golf course. He revealed that he might have loved her at a time in his life when he really knew nothing about love or real commitment. In putting his life down on paper, at the second attempt, Venturi did not spare his first wife.

****

In 1970, with his right hand developing atrophy once again, Ken Venturi went back under the surgeon's knife. He was told that there was every chance that he might lose parts of three fingers on his right hand. The operation lasted for four hours. At the end of it, Ken was told that his fingers had been saved, but that his career as any kind of competitive professional golfer was, finally, at an end.

The contract from CBS, however, was still on the table. Venturi signed it, and began a long and honourable career that, eventually, would see him become the No.1 voice of golf in the United States.

By that time, he and Conni had been separated for many months. Soon they divorced. Fourteen-year-old Matt Venturi chose to live with his father. Eleven-year-old Tim, by court order, stayed with his mother, but a few months later Tim Venturi also decided to live with his father and brother. After several appearances in court, alimony payments to Conni Venturi were terminated.

Ken and Beau married in Palm Springs in November, 1972. There, they lived happily together. And, most Monday nights, Frank Sinatra would call in to the Venturis for *Monday Night Football*. Beau cooked the pasta, Sinatra brought over the wine. Life was looking good for Ken Venturi, perhaps as good as it had ever looked. In 1976, Ken and Beau decided to move to Florida, to be closer to the places and tournaments on the CBS golf schedule. The close relationship with Frank Sinatra petered out over time, with both men living on opposite coasts, but Venturi was ready to start his life afresh on Florida's Marco Island.

Ken Venturi remained with CBS, an exalted figure in the 18th tower, until his retirement in 2002. For 35 years, he called it as he saw it out on the course, working his way into a formidable broadcasting threesome, completed by Pat Summerall and Jim Nantz. The players loved him, and he loved them, especially when he took up his special position at Augusta National, overlooking the 13th hole.

The Masters tournament and Ken Venturi would, after all, develop a special friendship as he worked the venerable course, as a player and commentator, for just short of 50 years. He had played the Masters 16 times, and he had visited Augusta National as part of the CBS team on twice that number of occasions.

In 1983, Venturi had the opportunity of tackling the course one more time with the new breed of modern golfer. He was asked to fill in for Byron Nelson as an honorary starter, and played the front nine with Gene Sarazen and Sam Snead.

Venturi was hot for an old boy, and with four birdies and one bogey he actually reached the turn in 33 shots. Ken wanted to keep on playing at that point. 'I can lead this tournament,' he chuckled to Sarazen.

The threesome were on their way to the 10th tee box, when Sarazen stopped in his tracks. 'To hell with it, you can't lead anything, Venturi,' laughed Sarazen. 'Let's get some lunch!'

All three players thought that a wise decision.

In one of his visits to Augusta National as a television analyst, in the mid-70s, Venturi was playing the par-three course when he noticed Cliff Roberts staring at him. Eventually, the boss of the golf club, and the Masters tournament, approached. He put out his hand. 'I hope that you can find it in your heart to forgive me for what I have done,' stated Roberts. 'It was wrong.'

It was a private conversation but it was the first time that the chairman of Augusta National had ever admitted that his ruling, in favour of Arnold Palmer in 1958, should never have been made.

'Mr Roberts,' replied Ken, 'you've soothed a lot of wounds.'

Five months later, Clifford Roberts blew his brains out, close to where he stood that afternoon with Ken.

****

Ken Venturi lost Beau in 1997. Beau Venturi died in her husband's arms in their home in Florida, after having cancer diagnosed, for the third time in her life, only months earlier.

Beau had among her special causes the plight of abused women and children. After her death, Ken began fund-raising, with the aim of building a shelter for abuse victims in her memory. The golf community marched forward in support of raising the $6.5 million needed for Venturi's project, and in 2002 the Beau Venturi Home: The Wings of Hope officially opened.

Ken also joined the board of the Stuttering Foundation of America, and would travel the country to speak about the needs of individuals so afflicted, and to remind people that he himself, and they, are among a band of huge names down through history who suffered in making themselves heard, including Winston Churchill, Marilyn Monroe and Bruce Willis.

This celebrated list also included King George VI of England, the monarch whose fight to overcome his own accursed stammer became the heroic storyline of the multiple Oscar-winning movie, *The King's Speech*, in 2010. Venturi watched the movie twice. The manner of the King's conquest of his affliction did not come as a surprise to Ken, however, as he, too, found unusual ways and means to train his own efforts of putting words together, smoothly and triumphantly, and building full sentences. Ken's methods included the finely tuned, rhythmical swinging of his golf clubs. It was something he had picked up as a solution himself. 'It was the rhythm of swinging the club and talking with it,' explained Venturi. It just seemed to work better than anything else.

His voluntary work also embraced Guiding Eyes for the Blind, a cause that became close to his heart when, at the fateful Masters tournament in 1956, he first met Charlie Boswell, a captain in the Second World War who lost his sight saving three young soldiers from a burning tank.

Venturi would also help golfers, any golfer, who called him and asked for help. He never charged a player for his services, but would always tell them, 'I've got good news and bad news. The bad news is that it's really going to cost you. The good news is that you can write the cheque to the charity of my choosing.'

****

In January, 2001, Venturi was back in Palm Springs. He was undergoing treatment for prostate cancer at the Loma Linda Proton Treatment Center, and one evening a friend persuaded him to go out for dinner. When he walked into the restaurant he 'found a second miracle'. A beautiful woman in a pink dress was serving as the hostess. Her name was Kathleen and she was helping out a friend of hers, who owned the place. The owner offered to introduce Ken. The next night Ken and Kathleen had dinner together at the same restaurant, and in March 2003 they were married in Las Vegas, in the company of a few close friends.

****

In June 2011, Ken Venturi returned, with Kathleen, to Congressional Country Club in Bethesda during the third staging of the US Open Championship there. He had decided to donate some items he had used during his victory there in 1964, along with his trophy.

After an emotional dedication ceremony, the precious gifts from Ken Venturi were put on display for good in the clubhouse, in a wood-panelled corridor leading to the men's locker room. In a glass case were placed Ken's cap, and his four scorecards from June '64, including the card of the final round, with Ken's 3s, 4s and 5s lightly written into each appropriate box. Also placed in the case was a letter Ken received from President Eisenhower, and a personal note from Bobby Jones. Included also were the set of irons he used that week, a set he built himself – shafted, weighted and gripped, just to his own needs.

In the same magnificent Mediterranean-style clubhouse, set back from River Road, Ken and Kathleen stayed as special guests for the week in one of the beautiful suites.

Ken had arrived at Bethesda at the end of a cruel week of blistering heat, but he looked unworried.

'I really won't care,' he told anyone who asked. 'I'll be in the clubhouse.' When he did wish to venture out on to the course, Congressional had kindly placed their golf cart No.58 in his hands for the week. It bore the name 'Venturi' on the front.

From there, Ken watched Rory McIlroy complete *his* journey from Augusta to Bethesda, not after eight suffering years and some months like Ken Venturi had, but, incredibly, in just 70 days.

Eleven days after being inducted into the World Golf Hall of Fame, Ken Venturi died on May 17, 2013. He had been hospitalised for two months for a spinal infection, pneumonia and other complications, before passing at Rancho Mirage, in California on a Friday afternoon. He was 82 years old.

He was survived by his wife, Kathleen, his two sons, Matt and Tim, and his four grandchildren, Peter, Andrew, Sara, and Gianna.

He is greatly missed by two generations of golf fans.

There had been no chance of him being able to attend his induction on May 6, when Matt and Tim accepted on his behalf after a hugely emotional tribute from Ken's old television colleague, Jim Nantz. 'When Dad did receive the election into the Hall of Fame, he had a twinkle in his eye,' stated Tim. 'And that twinkle is there every day.'

Nantz knew Ken Venturi better than anybody as a friend and work colleague. 'He was a deeply principled man with a dynamic presence,' remembered Nantz. 'He just exuded class.

'Through his competitive days and unequalled broadcasting career, Kenny became a human bridge connecting everyone from Sarazen, Nelson and Hogan, to the greatest players of today's generation. Kenny faced many adversities in his life, and always found a way to win.'

One of his former pupils, John Cook from Ohio, who won 11 times on the PGA Tour and was a member of the 1993 Ryder Cup team, remarked that there was nobody in the Hall of Fame who had done as much for golf as Ken Venturi.

'Maybe some have better records,' stated Cook, 'or they may have more tournament wins, but the whole thing? None. He transformed television. He's been the biggest philanthropist in golf history of the things he's been involved in that people don't even know about.

'Lifetime achievement?

'That barely covers it,' informed Cook.

Jack Nicklaus led the field of mourners with fond words of his own. 'We all knew what a wonderful player Ken Venturi was, and how he fashioned a second successful career as an announcer,' stated the Golden Bear. 'But far more important than how good he was at playing the game or covering it, Ken was my friend.

'Ken was fortunate that the game of golf gave him so much, but without question Ken gave back far more to the game he loved than he ever gained from it.

'If there is some sense of fairness, it is that Ken was inducted into the Hall of Fame that he very much deserved to be in and, in fact, should have been in for many years,' Nicklaus concluded. 'I am certain that there was an overwhelming sense of pride and peace that embraced Ken. It was a dream of Ken Venturi's that became a reality before he sadly left us.'

Days before he passed away, Ken had agreed with Nicklaus, perhaps the greatest natural golfer there has ever been.

'The greatest reward in life is to be remembered,' said Ken Venturi in a shaken, quiet voice.

CHAPTER FOURTEEN

Rory ... after journeying from Augusta to Bethesda

Rory McIlroy spent the last few days of his three-week break after winning the US Open Championship at Bethesda visiting the All England Club in south-west London to watch the tennis at Wimbledon.

Tennis, after all, had been his first love once upon a time. At the Aorangi practice courts at Wimbledon, he was introduced to the British No.1, Andy Murray from Scotland. They had a good chat and McIlroy also got to bump into the legendary John McEnroe, whose battles with Lendl, Borg and Connors, among others, and those further raging battles with his own demons on the court, were a little before McIlroy's time. McIlroy's hero had been Britain's Tim Henman, who broke more hearts at his near-triumphs than tennis rackets like McEnroe. 'I grew up watching him,' McIlroy revealed, 'cheering him on every summer. And now that's passed over to Andy. We're all behind him.'

As it happened, McIlroy's favourite women's tennis player, Denmark's Caroline Wozniacki, had been knocked out of the tournament the previous week by the Slovak Dominka Cibulkova. But despite the usual and painfully annoying interruptions from lengthy rain showers at Wimbledon, when workers had to repeatedly race out and wrench covers over the lawns, McIlroy enjoyed his last few days of R'n'R, twice being invited into the Royal Box at SW19, where he was seated to observe his friend Rafa Nadal lose the men's final to Novak Djokovic.

On the Saturday night, he had also flown quickly in and out of Germany as well, when he decided to look in on the world heavyweight boxing contest in Hamburg, where Britain's David Haye was unsuccessful in trying to unify the division and was beaten on points by fellow world champion, Wladimir Klitschko. But, while he was there, McIlroy got to meet Caroline Wozniacki and they had a few drinks together.

So all in all, everything looked good and all appeared to be perfectly set up, both physically and mentally, for the longest and most satisfying summer of Rory McIlroy's golfing life.

****

At the end of June, 2011, there was no indication that the second six months of the year would be a near hallucinatory roller-coaster ride for Rory McIlroy, and for many of his closest friends and business colleagues. On that ride would be Holly Sweeney, his soul mate and loving partner. Also in for a bumpy time would be Chubby Chandler, the boss at International Sports Management, who much like Holly Sweeney was preparing himself for a lifetime with the most thrilling and the highest earning young sportsman in the world.

****

The ups and downs, and general clatter, which characterised the second half of Rory McIlroy's year would formally announce themselves during the Open Championship at the Royal St George's Golf Club, in Kent. That came in July 2011.

Created to be England's great rival to Scotland's untouchable St Andrews, St George's, or Sandwich as it is known after the Kent seaside town in which it resides, has always been a severe test. Until 2011, only three Open winners there, Bill Rogers in 1981, Greg Norman in 1993 and Ben Curtis in 2003, had managed to be under par after 72 holes in the 13 previous occasions that the Open had visited.

That number was increased to four in the summer of 2011 when the 42-year-old Darren Clarke, Rory McIlroy's hero as a boy and mentor as a young man, closed with an even-par 70, in downpours and unrelenting wind, to claim the winning Claret Jug with a five-under-par total of 275 in 2011. It meant that three Ulstermen, born less than an hour's drive from one another, had won three of the previous six major titles.

In all, the awakening experience of visiting Haiti in June, and the triumphant act of removing the monstrous expectation and always hefty pressures from his own shoulders by winning the US Open at Congressional Country Club in the same month, should have left McIlroy supremely contented, or very definitely strong and calm within himself. Those two events in his life, and then Clarke's emotion-laden comeback after the death of his young wife, Heather, from cancer, and the resurrection of his dwindling career, might have left McIlroy without any immediate worry of his own.

But McIlroy found himself left in a bit of a heap in the month of July. There had been considerable talk, coming into the Open, of McIlroy's future trajectory as a championship-winning golfer, and lots of talk of him and Tiger Woods. Tiger, who would pull out of the Open owing to his continuing injuries, was in on it as well, admitting that McIlroy's swing looked better than his had at the same age. It was at 23 years of age, Tiger Woods explained, that he had further tweaked his own swing, and got it into a far more solid working order so that he claimed an unprecedented clean sweep of all four majors in 2000 and 2001.

'What Rory did was cool to watch,' said Woods. 'He had softer conditions and he was able to go slow, but he was able to continue pushing it… and that's fun.' Woods, though, did ominously add that McIlroy needed to work on his game if he was to experience a supreme level of consistency.

Jack Nicklaus was even more cautious in his view of McIlroy, asking golf fans not to anoint him as their 'crown prince' just yet. Nicklaus, like Woods, wanted to give the young man time for further growth. 'He has won one major,' summed up the Golden Bear. 'When he starts to win two, three, four, then you can say he's the guy to watch… period.'

McIlroy had been down to Royal St George's on the Tuesday and Wednesday of the week before the Open, for his traditional two days of quiet, uninterrupted practice. He said he loved the course. He'd played there in the 2005 Home Internationals, and also the following year in the British Amateur Championship. It was his type of golf course. 'Some people think it's a bit quirky in places, but I believe it's a good test of golf,' he proclaimed.

McIlroy was the pre-tournament favourite in the 156-strong field for the 140th Open Championship, despite the wise words from Woods and Nicklaus. It had all the makings of a tournament to remember, not least because iconic images of Seve Ballesteros were stencilled into the hoardings in front of the grandstand around the 18th green. Forecasters warned of 30 miles per hour wind for the early starters on Thursday morning, and Royal & Ancient officials were prepared to bring the tees forward if the wind did not die down during the week. They especially had an eye on the 564-yard par-five seventh hole. In practice, some players had had difficulty in reaching the fairway.

McIlroy teed off at 9.02 a.m., beside the young American Rickie Fowler and the 1992 Open champ, Ernie Els. He had already received a helping hand from Els the previous Monday morning when he flew into Kent with his parents, Gerry and Rosie, and discovered that there was no car to pick them up. He had to call Chubby Chandler, and then he had to sit and wait as Chubby reallocated one of the two cars that had already been sent to the airport to cater for Els and his entourage.

At the end of the first round, the Open Championship was led by Denmark's gritty veteran Thomas Bjorn and the 20-year-old British amateur, Tom Lewis. Both shot 65s. Darren Clarke and Graeme McDowell both hit 68s. McIlroy had scrappy bogeys on the first and third holes, but a birdie at the eighth helped him to the turn in 36 shots. He finished with a 71 after struggling the whole day with the speed of the greens more than anything else.

Hitting an 80 in his second round at St Andrews 12 months earlier, in such similar conditions, had taught him so much, McIlroy insisted. The next day McIlroy ground out a 69 to sit in the clubhouse tied for 19th place after 36 holes. But, in his third round, he fell nine shots behind the leader, Clarke, who at his 20th attempt would win the tournament by three shots and become the oldest winner of the Open since 1963.

McIlroy had a three-over-par 73 for his final round, finishing the tournament 12 shots back from the winner, whom he had joined for dinner in one of the ISM houses in Kent the evening before. McIlroy was delighted for Clarke. He was more sincere in his congratulations than any other golfer in Sandwich, telling everyone how often Clarke texted him, between tournaments, during tournaments, and how the big man had 'always been on the other end of a phone for me'.

But then McIlroy, inexplicably, did a seriously good job of reducing in size Darren Clarke's magnificent triumph. 'I'm not a fan of golf tournaments where the outcome is predicted so much by the weather,' he commented, quite ridiculously for a young man who was born and raised on some of the most brilliant and weather-buffeted golf courses in Ireland, but who looked, still, to be unsettled by his bogey-bogey finish to the final 18 holes.

'It's not my sort of golf. My game is suited for basically every golf course... and most conditions, but these conditions I didn't enjoy playing in really. I'd rather play when it's 80 degrees, sunny and not much wind.'

Meanwhile, Chubby Chandler was heartily celebrating *his* third major victory in a row, with Clarke joining Charl Schwartzel and McIlroy to form three parts of the 'Chubby Slam', as it was already being called. It looked as though ISM, pretty much, had it all.

****

His outpouring of random thoughts during the finest hour of Darren Clarke's career had not been Rory McIlroy's smartest moment of 2011. But a far greater public relations debacle was just around the corner, one in which McIlroy incorrectly portrayed himself as an irritable, brattish young champion who did not care for anyone saying boo to him.

McIlroy was back home in Ireland, and had completed his opening round of 70 in the Irish Open in Killarney, when the BBC radio commentator and former European Tour pro, Jay Townsend, tweeted, 'McIlroy's course management was shocking,' before adding, for good measure, 'some of the worst course management I have ever seen beyond under-10 boys' golf competition.' Townsend also suggested that it might be a good idea for McIlroy to think of employing the services of Tiger Woods' former caddie, Steve Williams.

McIlroy instantly fumed. 'Shut up... you're a commentator and a failed golfer, your opinion means nothing,' he tweeted in reply.

'I stand by my comments,' tweeted Townsend.

'I stand by my caddie,' tweeted McIlroy.

'As you should, I respect that,' replied Townsend.

It sounded a childish and awfully unnecessary exchange on such a public social networking stage. McIlroy, more than the double bogey he had just suffered on the 18th hole when he went from the fairway bunker into the pond in front of the green, had to defend his tweeting, as soon as he had the world's media assembled in front of him. 'He's been having a go at J. P. [Fitzgerald] every now and again since [the Masters] and this was the first time I've responded. It was the straw that broke the camel's back... now, I've blocked him on Twitter so I won't be reading anything more.'

****

The week before the Irish Open, McIlroy had publicly announced that his six-year relationship with Holly Sweeney was over. A statement from ISM left no room for any doubts. 'Rory McIlroy's long-time relationship with Holly Sweeney came to an amicable end before the Open Championship.'

Holly had been to Augusta to be there for McIlroy after his huge disappointment, but she had not turned up in Bethesda at all. However, she had been as close to his side as anybody could be on Twitter.

'My fabulous boyfriend has played flawlessly all week!' she had proudly told everybody and anybody, continuing, 'Drink up Northern Ireland, he's done us proud. Champagne flowing.?.?. Sooo happy for the curly one! 1st major down, millions to go!'

McIlroy would reveal, a couple of weeks later, that he also had had a change of heart about playing in America. He said that he was going to take up his PGA Tour membership again, and that he was going to look for a new base for himself in Florida as soon as possible. So much had changed after his US Open triumph. For starters, he'd had to employ security guards on his $2.3 million, 14-acre home, to keep cars and unknown persons off his driveway. 'It's tough, and definitely a lot tougher than it was three months ago,' he explained. 'It's something I am just going to have to deal with.'

After winning the US Open, McIlroy had admitted that, after their temporary break-up six months earlier, he had had to work extra hard to talk Holly into giving him a second chance in her life. A few weeks after this admission, ISM made the formal announcement about their break-up.

When asked if the changes in his personal life were a factor in his decision to live in Florida, McIlroy replied, 'Maybe a little bit.'

The thought of leaving his lovely new residence in Moneyreagh, outside Belfast, left him with a heavy heart. Abandoning his state-of-the-art practice facility, and leaving his dogs, Gus and Theo, behind, was all going to be tough, he realised.

'When you grow up and dream of being a professional golfer and dream of winning majors, all you really think about is the golf and playing in front of great crowds and on unbelievable golf courses and winning trophies,' he stated, with an honest face. 'You never think about the other side of it and that is the side that takes a bit of getting used to. It is also something that you don't really expect.

'It doesn't really affect me when I am playing golf. The five hours I am on the course is my own time... it's lovely as a bit of tranquillity, if you like.'

The same week as McIlroy made it known that he had parted from Holly, there were reports that he had already grown close to the world's No.1 ranked tennis star, Caroline Wozniacki.

****

In his first round at the 2011 US PGA Championship, at the Atlanta Athletic Club, McIlroy attempted a seven-iron recovery shot from next to the exposed root of a tree. He damaged his wrist, after connecting with the ball and the root, which necessitated an MRI scan to determine if he was fit to carry on playing in the tournament. He had continued his first round at the time, with the help of an ice pack, some on-course physiotherapy and hasty strapping. He had, somehow, shot a level-par 70. The next day he signed for a three-over-par total of 143, and admitted, 'Even with a broken wrist, I should be putting better than this.'

His wrist was not broken, but the incident heaped more pressure on himself and his caddie, and shot back up in the air the question of how good the pair of them were in making the correct decisions out on the course. When asked if J. P. Fitzgerald should have talked him out of attempting the shot in the first round, McIlroy snapped, 'He's my caddie, not my father!'

However, he did admit to fully discussing that foolish shot with the man on his bag. 'We talked about chipping it, and in hindsight it was probably the better option. But he said to me, *If you're comfortable doing it, go ahead... and if that's the shot you see, just go ahead and do it.* In the back of our minds it was a case of, you know, if it comes off, it comes off.'

He finished the PGA Championship tied for 64th position, on 291, with only six players below him on the leaderboard on the Sunday evening, and 19 shots between him and the winner, 25-year-old Keegan Bradley, from Vermont. On the ninth hole, McIlroy had ended up shooting his ball into one of the hospitality tents, when his fairway bunker shot flew over the green and entered one of the dining units. It had been a distracting week all through. He had talked of going house-hunting in Florida for the following few days, but informed the media that he was instead heading to Cincinnati. 'I hear it's nice this time of year,' he added.

****

Twenty-one-year-old Caroline Wozniacki's tour schedule had her in the same city, for the Cincinnati Open, the following week when she would suffer a shock second-round loss to the 76th-ranked Christina McHale. McIlroy watched as the Dane fell to a miserable

6-4, 7-5 defeat, the first time she had lost to an opponent outside the world's top 75 in more than two years.

McIlroy now had no obvious concern about disclosing to the world's media that their relationship was nicely up and running, and was for real. For the rest of 2011, he would remain unashamedly forthright about the world's No.1 women's tennis star, and their deepening relationship. Holly Sweeney was not spared in any of his affectionate utterances about how Caroline held a unique place in his life.

'I think she's been a great influence on my career already. She understands the lifestyle, so that definitely helps,' stated McIlroy. 'And it's nice to go out with someone who shares your sense of ambition. She definitely works harder than I do and that's rubbing off on me as well.' He did stress that the pair did not spend too much time talking about their careers. Spending time together so infrequently, owing to their individual schedules, meant that such time needed to be of a quality nature. 'We've got to the stage where we talk about things that all couples talk about. I don't want to sound too soppy, but meeting Caroline was definitely the best thing that happened to me this year away from the course.' The pair, in the British and American tabloid newspapers, were being teamed up as 'Wozzilroy', as some form of demented new world brand.

In March 2011, when playing an exhibition match against Maria Sharapova in New York's Madison Square Garden, Caroline insisted on Rory joining her on court and playing shots on her behalf. By that time, Wozniacki was dropping from No.1 to No.4 in the world rankings, while McIlroy, twice in the first half of 2012, would jump over England's Luke Donald and command the world No.1 position in golf.

Holly Sweeney displayed no bitterness about the break-up of her relationship with McIlroy. The thought that their parting might just have been amicable, despite McIlroy's heavy-handed and amorous pronouncements about his Danish girlfriend, looked like it may have had substance to it after all. Holly concentrated on finishing her studies, and on a fledgling modelling career.

In April, however, when appearing on an Irish television show, TV3's *Come Dine With Me*, which features 'celebrities' cooking dinner for one another with prize money going to charities of their choosing, Holly themed her party as a tennis night, with her guests asked to wear their all-whites.

****

The overhaul of Rory McIlroy's professional life had been completed much earlier, in the autumn of 2011, when he bumped Chubby Chandler and ISM out of his golf career.

After Augusta National, McIlroy had taken advice from a number of people whom he knew and trusted. Among that number, obviously, was Chandler, who had visited McIlroy at his new home in Belfast 10 days after the Masters tournament. Rory was also in touch with Manchester United's legendary manager, Sir Alex Ferguson, who had guided his football team with an iron fist, and the ruthless streak of a reigning monarch from a bygone era, for more than 20 years. 'Obviously you are going to be disappointed and hurting,' Sir Alex had told him, 'but go and speak to people you trust... family and friends... people who are close to you. Those are the people who will tell you the truth.'

In mid-October 2011, McIlroy informed Chubby Chandler, who had been profiled in *Sports Illustrated* magazine as 'the hottest agent abroad' just a few months earlier, that he wished to leave International Sports Management. Chandler put a brave, business-like face on it for a few days, but eventually, when on holiday with his two children in Dubai, he told Derek Lawrenson of the *Daily Mail* newspaper that he had been shocked at losing the most talented golfer on the planet. 'I don't know whether it was his girlfriend

[Wozniacki] getting in his ear or someone else,' said Chandler, 'but I thought we were doing a pretty good job, and I think that's how the outside world saw it.'

Chandler explained that when they had sat down, McIlroy had told him that he was not satisfied with one or two things. 'I thought we were sorting things out to his liking. We'd just spent 10 days travelling around the world and had a fantastic time,' Chandler further explained. McIlroy had turned to Chandler, while taking a private flight bound for JFK Airport in New York and asked if they could have a few minutes to talk alone. There, at a great height, he dropped the bombshell on his manager.

Chandler mentioned that Darren Clarke might also be disappointed with McIlroy's decision. 'I've a feeling there's a big man who has known Rory for a long time who is going to feel a little let down.' Chandler also wondered publicly if McIlroy had concerns about his manager's larger-than-life image. During the course of the previous few months McIlroy had referred to Chubby Chandler as a 'celebrity manager' on a few occasions. 'Which I thought was an odd thing to say,' said Chandler.

McIlroy had decided to join up with the Irish-based Horizon Sports Management, which also represented Graeme McDowell. While Chandler came to terms with ISM's loss, McIlroy was on holiday in Istanbul with Caroline Wozniacki.

'Life goes on,' admitted Chandler, 'and while there's hurt, I certainly don't bear any bitterness towards Rory. We all know how good he is for our sport, and I'd rather reflect on the four good years we had together.' Despite moving management stables, the massive sponsorship deals that ISM had contracted on McIlroy's behalf remained in place, some of them running up to 2015.

Between the loss at Augusta and the win in Bethesda, Chandler had taken time out to give his honest appreciation of Rory McIlroy's career. His principal worry was not burning out his young star.

'It's a massive responsibility, massive,' he had revealed. 'Never mind the money side of it and maximising his earnings, you don't want to burn him out. Rory's the first guy I've ever looked after whom I've thought, *You could actually kill him [as a player], you could actually have him hating the game by the age of 25*.'

McIlroy, quite clinically for a 22-year-old, somewhere between 20,000 and 30,000 feet, had absolved Chubby Chandler of all future responsibility.

****

Rory McIlroy closed out 2011 by winning the UBS Hong Kong Open in December, and back on the US Tour in March of 2012, just before he claimed the world's No.1 ranking, he fended off the challenge of Tiger Woods to take the Honda Classic in Palm Beach Gardens in Florida. He was playing the best golf of his young life. He had the management company he wanted and, by his side, he had the woman whom he had admired on a tennis court for several years.

Ahead of him lay Augusta National. It held no fears for McIlroy. He said he had grown up in the previous 12 months, thanks in no small part to the Masters tournament. He felt he needed to be aggressive at Augusta National in 2012.

In his opening round of the tournament he felt relaxed as he waited on the first tee to be announced to the large gallery. He remembered what had occurred on the same hole, 12 months previously, when he led the tournament by four shots and seemed destined to take one of the club's green jackets all for himself. But that memory did not disturb him.

In April 2011, he had parred the first hole in each of his opening three rounds, and he had struck his opening drive of the final round sweetly down the middle of the fairway. It had been his second shot, a simple enough wedge, which overshot the green and which had ever so slightly distracted him.

Something strange, something different, had coursed through his body as he struck that wedge to the opening green in his final round in 2011. He had felt it. And he had subsequently bogeyed that opening hole as step one of that awful day at Augusta National.

But, that was now history. McIlroy walked after his ball down the first fairway in April 2012. He was over that memory of bogeying the first hole in his final round the previous April and, with his US Open triumph two months later, he felt he had also buried the unsightly 80 that had filled his scorecard at the end of that round.

He had no intention of allowing Augusta National to trick him, or torment him. But McIlroy, incredibly, in his first round in 2012, would get into a bit of a fluster by the time he holed out for a double-bogey six on that par-four first hole. He would shoot an opening round of 71.

The next day he parred the first hole and shot a more finely-tuned 69, which left him alongside Sergio Garcia and Lee Westwood on four under par for the tournament, in a group of six players trailing leaders Jason Dufner and Freddie Couples by a single shot. His strategy of aggressively taking on the greens at Augusta National was still in place after 36 holes of the tournament.

In his third round, McIlroy, amazingly, got it all wrong again and double-bogeyed the first hole for a second time. With the demons on his back for the remainder of his round, he finished with a wickedly manufactured 77.

In his final round at Augusta National, the first hole once again grabbed him by the ankles as he began his day. This time he bogeyed the hole, shot a 76 on the Sunday, and was left slumped but wearing a peculiarly accepting smile long before the finish of his round, that left him way down in 40th position.

Augusta National had ridiculed the most naturally talented golfer in the world, and it had done so on its opening hole, making him take 21 shots over the four days, a downright ugly total of five over par on one simple enough 445-yard par-four hole.

McIlroy ended 2012 with his second major, dominating and finally decimating the richest collection of the world's greatest golfers for a second time, but he started into 2013 like a mini-tornado – and that was not a good thing for Rory McIlroy.

In May of 2013, as Ken Venturi was inducted into the World Golf Hall of Fame and received the fondest and most permanent of farewells from almost everyone in the game, Rory McIlroy could still find no calming or lingering peace with his own golf game.

When he walked the fairways, his admirers and his growing number of critics parted to make way on either side of him. Meanwhile, McIlroy was leaving his fellow golfers, and some of his closest of friends, quite confused by his actions and his temperament with each passing week.

In August of 2012, at Kiawah Island in South Carolina, he walked away with the 94th US PGA Championship when, for good measure, he also decided to wear red for the final round, taking a leaf from the book of Tiger Woods, who always declared war on every course he played by wearing the same signature colour every Sunday. McIlroy birdied the 72nd hole, and grabbed the championship with an eight-stroke victory margin, a US PGA record. At 23 years of age he was the fourth youngest PGA champion of all time.

It was only the sixth professional win of his career, and his second victory in 17 major appearances, but he was still younger, if only by a handful of months, than Woods was when becoming a double major winner.

It was time for McIlroy's career to enter cruise control. Instead, something else happened.

McIlroy announced in January of 2013 that he had signed a 'multi-year' sponsorship agreement with Nike which was valued by most commentators at somewhere in the region of $250 million. In March, when defending his Honda Classic in Florida, just a few miles down the road from his new home in Jupiter, he walked off the course during his second round after recording a triple bogey and a double bogey. The next month, back in Augusta National, he tied for 25th place after rounds of 72, 70, 79 and 69, when his scorecard on the Saturday was entirely ruined by three bogeys, one double bogey and a triple bogey. Then, worse followed, and at the US Open in Merion Golf Club in Philadelphia, in June of 2013, McIlroy ended the championship on 14-over par and with only 13 working clubs in his bag.

On the 11th hole at Merion, his first tee shot splashed into the water. He took a drop and then sent another ball into the same creek. As he walked in the direction of his second errant shot, McIlroy bad-temperedly jammed his Nike iron into the ground and completely buckled the club.

He finished the US Open in 41st position.

Still, back in the press room after shooting a six-over 76 in his final round – and halfway through a fast-moving 2013 – he utterly refused to lay the blame for the appalling state of his game on his new set of Nikes. 'I sort of needed to play a little bit more,' he stated, gingerly. 'It's definitely a different feeling. The thing about new equipment is that you can stand on the range all you want and hit balls, but you really need to test it on the course.'

On Twitter he wrote, 'A lot of comments about my bent nine-iron. Moment of frustration and silly thing to do. That's what Merion can do to you!'

Most watchers disagreed.

It seemed that McIlroy was doing most of the damage to himself by not affording his golf career the time and ease it needed.

Amongst those watching and tweeting was former US Ryder Cup captain and ESPN golf analyst, Paul Azinger. He had witnessed McIlroy miss the cut in his first tournament of the 2013 season in Abu Dhabi, lose in the first round of the WGC-Accenture Match Play Championship, and then high-tail it out of the Honda Classic before the tournament was even halfway through. 'The worst thing a pro golfer can do to his GOLF GAME is change clubs for the money,' tweeted Azinger. 'Loving the clubs you play is priceless!'

By the end of the first half of 2013, Tiger Woods was sitting comfortably enough as world No.1 all over again, having overcome the personal turmoil in his life and taking back his coveted ranking by winning the Arnold Palmer Invitational and a string of tournaments before that.

Rory McIlroy appeared to have other things on his mind.

Golf fans and writers were wondering about his relationship with his Danish girlfriend, Caroline Wozniacki. Were they breaking up? Or were they getting engaged and talking marriage? Fans and writers were also looking for answers to questions about the management of McIlroy's career.

McIlroy's relationship with Horizon Sports Management appeared to be in some doubt as well – 18 months after he had hurriedly completed his time with Chubby Chandler's ISM Group – before it had ever been afforded time to gather the momentum it deserved. Horizon refused to comment. McIlroy had nothing to say publicly. But, there was speculation that McIlroy was looking set to start up his own management company, with his father, Gerry, in pole position with Rory to make crucial decisions about the future.

McIlroy's desire was to be his own man.

Like two of the greatest sportsmen in two other fields, Roger Federer and Lionel Messi, who are their own men, and who have family and the closest of friends on the shoulders of their tennis and football careers. While watching Wozniacki play in a tournament in Brazil at the very end of 2012, McIlroy had sat down for dinner with Federer, a 17-times Grand Slam winner, and talked about life, and talked about the business of sport.

'He's a role model, someone I can pattern myself after,' McIlroy informed *The New York Times*.

At 24 years of age, and with time running out too fast for his liking, and majors too far out of his reach far too often, Rory McIlroy wanted it all, and he wanted it all done his way. He was wrong.

Ken Venturi could have explained exactly why Rory was wrong.

Ken might have told him about the comings and goings of golfers he knew. Men like Byron Nelson and Ben Hogan, and Arnold Palmer and Jack Nicklaus. Ken might have told Rory about his own life experience.

He might have told Rory to seek calm, to begin with, and then reach out and seek true greatness on the golf course.

They had only ever spoken once, and that was fleetingly on the final evening of the 2011 US Open in Congressional Country Club in Bethesda, Maryland.

A second conversation in 2013, as Ken Venturi had only weeks and days to live, and Rory McIlroy had a rich and wonderful life as a professional golfer still stretched out in front of him, would have been very helpful.

Author's Note

A great many people took the long journey, between 1956 and 1964, from Augusta to Bethesda with Ken Venturi. In the summer of 2011 a far greater number of people were with Rory McIlroy as he made the same journey in double quick time.

I would like to thank all of those golfers, caddies, and journalists for their thoughts and observations which have been documented in many hundreds of publications.

Most especially, I found the following books, and newspapers and websites, to be extremely helpful in guiding me along that same journey, which, in my case, took just under two years before this story was completed.

Books:

The Masters: Golf, Money and Power in Augusta, Georgia, Curt Sampson; Villard Books

Comeback: The Ken Venturi Story, Ken Venturi and Oscar Fraley; Duell, Sloan and Pearce, New York

Getting Up and Down: My 60 Years in Golf, Ken Venturi with Michael Arkush; Triumph Books

Men on the Bag: The Caddies of Augusta National, Ward Clayton; Sports Media Group

Shark: The Biography of Greg Norman, Lauren St John; Rutledge Hill Press

The Match: Hogan, Nelson, Venturi, Ward, and the Day Golf Changed Forever, Mark Frost; Sphere

Bounce: The Myth of Talent and the Power of Practice, Matthew Syed; Fourth Estate, London

Newspapers/Websites:

Highest standards applied even as Roberts took his own life, Mark Hodgkinson, telegraph.co.uk, April 2004

Roberts Rules, Steve Eubanks, sportsillustrated.cnn.com, April 1997

George Cobb designed golf courses, Joe Passov, golf.com, December 2006

Stop the presses, Michael Bamberger, sportsillustrated.cnn.com, April 1999

Golf great Bobby Jones baptized just before death, georgiabulletin.org, January 1972

Bobby Jones: brief life of a golf legend, Craig Lambert, harvardmagazine.com, Mar-April 2002

Bobby Jones was golf's fast study, Larry Schwartz, espn.go.com

Sports and recreation, georgiaencyclopedia.org

Cities and counties, georgiaencyclopedia.org

History and archaeology, georgiaencyclopedia.org

Land and resources, georgiaencyclopedia.org

Membership has its privileges, Ron Sirak, portfolio.com, April 2009

And then Jackie Burke took charge, Herbert Warren Wind, augustagolf.com, Sports Illustrated Masters Recap, 1956

When Amen Corner was born, Thomas Bonk, masters.com

50 greatest golfers of all time, Ken Venturi, Golf Digest

A man of the game, Jim Langley, sportsillustrated.cnn.com, June 2010

The many Masters of Ken Venturi, Stephen Goodwin, theaposition.com

With a growing stable of stars, Chubby Chandler is the hottest agent abroad, Michael Bamberger, golf.com, March 2011

How the Jerry Maguire of golf became a major player, James Corrigan, independent.co.uk, June 2011

My shot, Guy Yocom, golfdigest.com, October 2011

How is Masters leader Rory McIlroy spending his night?, Steve Politi, nj.com, April 2011

Family and friends keep teenage prodigy's feet firmly on the ground, Paul Gallagher, irishtimes.com, October 2005

Northern Ireland's McIlroy transcends boundaries, Niall Stanage, nytimes.com, July 2011

Revealed: PSNI reinvestigating murder of Rory McIlroy's great uncle Joe by gang of UVF killers, Mick Browne, dailymail.co.uk, June 2011

And the real winner is... peace, Suzanne Breen, dailymail.co.uk, June 2011

What makes McIlroy tick: look to his roots, John Leicester, AP, usatoday.com, September 2011

Holywood star taking it all in his stride, Philip Reid, irishtimes.com, February 2009

Claims are rife that Rory McIlroy 'Bunkergate' inquiry was a whitewash, Mark Reason, telegraph.co.uk, April 2009

Honey, we're backing the kids, Paul Gallagher, irishtimes.com, May 2009

Northern soul, Keith Duggan, irishtimes.com, November 2010

Jack Burke Jr, the hero of '56, renews Augusta National ties, John Garrity, contributing writer Sports Illustrated, golf.com, April 2009

Norman falters in the end, Andy Johnston, Augusta Chronicle, April 1996
Shark smells blood, David Westin, Augusta Chronicle, April 1996
Room offers champions quiet time, John Boyette, Augusta Chronicle
When disaster strikes, Joe Posnanski, sportsillustrated.cnn.com, April 2011
Rory McIlroy's tactics were misguided, but he has time on his side, Colin Montgomerie, Daily Telegraph, April 2011
Two frenzied hours, Alan Shipnuck, sportsillustrated.cnn.com, April 2011
Humbling Haiti trip is making of Rory McIlroy, Karl MacGinty, Irish Independent, June 2011
Rory McIlroy puts US Open prep on hold for inspiring trip to earthquake ravaged Haiti, Barry Svrluga, washingtonpost.com, June 2011
Tears that turned me into Glory McIlroy, Derek Lawrenson, Daily Mail, December 2011
Putting it bluntly, Denis Walsh, The Sunday Times, April 2011
For McIlroy, a collapse he never saw coming, Bill Pennington, nytimes.com, April 2011
Holed in one, Harry Mount, dailymail.co.uk, April 2011
Educating Rory lays foundations for a Holywood blockbuster, Paul Gallagher, irishtimes.com, June 2011
Breaking up is hard to do, Karl MacGinty, belfasttelegraph.co.uk, January 2011
Holly is still Rory's driving force, Catherine Fegan and Patrice Harrington, dailymail.co.uk, April 2011
Politics as usual: the remarkable history of Congressional Country Club, Michael K Bohn, McClatchy-Tribune News Service, June 2011
Congressional secrets, Jason Horowitz, grantland.com
The history of Bethesda, Mark Walston, bethesdamagazine.com, Nov-Dec 2009

Congressional has undergone many changes over the years, Barry Svrluga, washingtonpost.com, June 2011
Faith, hope and Venturi, Joseph C Dey Jr, usgamuseum.com
Sportsman of the year: Ken Venturi, Alfred Wright, sportsillustrated.cnn.com, December 1964
The longest day, Kathy Chenault, bethesdamagazine.com, June 2011
Why me – a tale of 1964, Ken Venturi with Roger Ganem, usgamuseum.com
Victory in the heat of battle: The 1964 US Open, Shirley Povich, washingtonpost.com, June 1997
Ken Venturi's 1964 victory was a scorching one, Brendan Prunty, Star Ledger, nj.com, June 2011
Dealt a bad hand, Rick Reilly, sportsillustrated.cnn.com, May 1994
Golfers take advantage of vulnerable Congressional, Gene Wang, washingtonpost.com, June 2011
I was crying my eyes out: Rory said it's only a game of golf Mum, Lawrence Donegan, guardian.co.uk, April 2012
Potential to make scary numbers, Philip Reid, irishtimes.com, June 2011
Rory has all the attributes to be new king of the majors, Colin Byrne, irishtimes.com, June 2011
I was shocked: Chandler reveals the truth behind McIlroy split, Derek Lawrenson, dailymail.co.uk, October 2011
Rory McIlroy worth £10m to axed Chubby Chandler, Oliver Brown, dailytelegraph.co.uk, October 2011
So long Kenny, Michael Bamberger, sportsillustrated.cnn.com, June 2002

Worldgolfhalloffame.org
Augusta.com